vol. XIX, no. 33, Fall 2019

CINÉMA&CIE

INTERNATIONAL FILM STUDIES JOURNAL

**Avant-garde and Popular Forms Between Music and Visual Media.
Transhistorical and Intermedial Investigations**

Edited by
Simone Dotto, François Mouillot and Maria Teresa Soldani

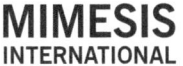

MIMESIS
INTERNATIONAL

Cinéma & Cie is promoted by
Dipartimento di Lettere, Lingue, Arti. Italianistica e Culture Comparate,
Università degli Studi di Bari 'Aldo Moro'; Dipartimento di Lettere, Filosofia,
Comunicazione, Università degli Studi di Bergamo; Dipartimento delle Arti —
Visive Performative Mediali, Università di Bologna — Alma Mater Studiorum;
Dipartimento di Scienze della Comunicazione e dello Spettacolo, Università
Cattolica del Sacro Cuore; Università degli Studi eCampus (Novedrate, Italy);
Dipartimento di Comunicazione, arti e media "Giampaolo Fabris", Università
IULM, Milano; Dipartimento di Civiltà e Forme del Sapere, Università di Pisa;
Università degli Studi Link Campus University, Roma; Dipartimento di Studi
Umanistici e del Patrimonio Culturale, Università degli Studi di Udine.

International Ph.D. Program 'Studi Storico Artistici e Audiovisivi'/'Art History
and Audiovisual Studies' (Università degli Studi di Udine, Université Sorbonne
Nouvelle — Paris 3).

Subscription to *Cinéma & Cie* (2 issues)

Single issue: 16 € / 12 £ / 18 $
Double issue: 20 € / 15 £ / 22 $
Yearly subscription: 30 € / 22 £ / 34 $

No shipping cost for Italy
Shipping cost for each issue:
EU: 10 € / 8 £ / 11 $
Rest of the world: 18 € / 13 £ / 20 $

Send orders to
commerciale@mimesisedizioni.it

Journal website
www.cinemaetcie.net

© 2020 – Mimesis International (Milan – Udine)
www.mimesisinternational.com
e-mail: info@mimesisinternational.com

isbn 9788869772962
issn 2035-5270

© MIM Edizioni Srl
P.I. C.F. 02419370305

Cover image: Matias Guerra, *Nekrotzar. Following the rainbow* (2016-2017)

Contents / Table des matières

Avant into Pop, Pop into Avant:
Interplays between Music and Visual Media[1]

Simone Dotto, Università degli Studi di Udine
François Mouillot, Hong Kong Baptist University
Maria Teresa Soldani, Centro per l'Arte Contemporanea
"Luigi Pecci" / Università di Pisa

Advancing through Time. Avant-garde and Mass Culture.

When considered separately from any reference to specific art work or movements, the notion of "avant-garde" calls for a trans-historical, or at least trans-temporal, perspective. Derived from the French warfare lexicon in use since the Middle Ages and originally indicating a contingent of forerunners leading a military formation, the word took a more figurative nuance as early as the mid-sixteenth century, when literary historian Etienne Pasquier described Renaissance poets as "the avant-garde" in "a war against ignorance".[2] Such a use of the term foreshadowed the romantic meaning it would eventually took up three centuries later among Saint Simon's disciples, for whom it outlined the role of the artists as forerunners, paving the way of the future society by promoting revolutionary changes.[3] In transposing its military semantic field in which it functioned as a spatial concept to a temporal metaphor, the notion posits an understanding of time as a linear and evolutionary progress (an "unexorable march", so to speak) which has deep roots in modern thinking. On a broader level, the very idea of an avant-garde is in fact 'directly indebted to the broader consciousness of modernity – a sharp sense of militancy, praise of nonconformism, courageous precursory exploration, and, on a more general plane, confidence in the final victory of *time* and immanence over traditions'[4] to the point where it can also be read as a dramatization and radicalization of modernity's main tenets. To simply state that an art-work is

---

[1] This introductory essay was conceived and developed by the three authors in close collaboration. However as regards the draft of the single sections, Simone Dotto wrote the first paragraph 'Advancing through Time. Avant-garde and Mass Culture', François Mouillot wrote the second paragraph 'Moving in Between. Intermedial Art and Networks', and Maria Teresa Soldani wrote the third paragraph 'At the Criss Cross between Music, Art and Visual Media'.

[2] Etienne Pasquier, *Oeuvres choisies*, ed. by Léon Feugère (Paris: Firmin Didot, 1849), vol. 2, p. 21 (our translation).

[3] The first acknowledged use of the word in this sense is dated back to Olinde Rodrigues's 'L'artiste, le savant et l'industriel: Dialogue' in *Opinions littéraires, philosophiques et industrielles* (Paris: Galerie de Bossange Père, 1895).

[4] Matias Calinescu, *Five Faces of Modernity: Modernism, Avant-garde, Decadence, Kitsch, Postmodernism* (Durham: Duke University Press, 1987), p. 93.

"ahead of its time" already implies awareness of historicity, an unshakable faith in progress and ultimately, the very possibility to predict the course of action. As Hans Enzensberger noticed, according to this logic:

> The arts are regarded not as historically unvarying activities of mankind or as an arsenal of timelessly extant 'cultural goods' but as continually advancing progress, as a work in progress, in which every single production participates [...]. The forward march of the arts through history is conceived of as a linear, perspicuous and surveyable movement in which everyone can himself determine his place at the forefront or with the hangers-on[5]

It is precisely this conception of time that underlies the controversial relationship with what we may broadly define as "the cultural values of mainstream society". While acting in view of a popularization of their ground-breaking ideas which will eventually occur in the future, exponents of art and literary movements in the early twentieth century took the duty to fight against the *status quo* constituted both by the present they lived in and by past traditions. Avant-garde art-making is thus often conceived as socially/politically *oppositional* and *elitist* on an aesthetic level. This adversarial attitude mostly depended on the urge for a radical change in social life and took the bourgeois class and at the institutionalization of art as its main targets – an aim partially shared with concurrent political revolutionary movements. According to Peter Bürger, radicalness served as 'the self-critique of art in a bourgeois society', since 'the unification of art and life intended by the avant-garde can only be achieved if it succeeds in liberating the aesthetic potentials from institutional constraints which blocks its social effectiveness'.[6] What we have named "aesthetic elitism" is less a deliberate objective than a natural consequence of such a radical agenda: in spite of the fact that giving up the well-respected social status of the artist was one of the commitments imposed by the aforementioned unification of art and life, the concurrent rejection of any accepted convention or formal tradition was necessarily doomed to infringe on the expectations of the general public. Exploring a totally new creative and social horizon which could be properly appreciated only by the future audiences equated to throw down a challenge against not only the social and institutional powers but also the understanding of the ordinary receiver. However aesthetic elitism was also invested with an increasingly "political" meaning as soon as it was discursively put in opposition with mass culture. Art theoreticians and critics of the first half of the twentieth century championed different artistic expressions as the ideal counterpart of the industrialization of society and culture. To name but the most representative examples of this tendency, it suffices to recall Clement Greenberg's praise of "absolute", "pure" art in opposition to

---

[5] Hans Enzensberger, *The Aporias of Avant-garde* (1964), trans. by John Simon in *Modern Occasions*, ed. by Philip Rahv (New York: Noonday Press, 1965), vol. 2, 74-100 (pp. 81-85).
[6] Peter Bürger, 'Avant-garde and Neo-Avant-garde: An Attempt to Answer Certain Critics of Theory of the Avant-garde', *New Literary History*, XL, 4 (November 2010), 695-715 (p. 696).

mechanically produced "kitsch [...] destined for those who, insensible to the values of genuine culture, are hungry nevertheless for the diversion that only culture of some sort can provide";[7] in a similar fashion, Adorno conceived the non-reproducible and autonomous characters of avant-garde art as signals of criticism and resistance to the instrumental logics of the culture industry and its production of interchangeable commodities.[8] However, as the critical reception of their works later clarified, both theorists used the word "avant-garde" as a synonym for "modernism", a related but distinct trend which emphasized "purity" as the ultimate goal of differentiation between and specialization of artistic disciplines. This emphasis on aesthetic autonomy constituted the main difference between modernist painting and literature analysed by Adorno and Greenberg and the art movements now commonly referred to as "early avant-gardes". According to Bürger, this is demonstrated by their 'divergent attitudes towards the culture industry and popular literature.' He further contends that: 'Whereas modernism is anxious to preserve the aesthetic sphere and to reject popular literature as a whole, the avant-garde finds many starting points in it'.[9] It took post-modernist critical revisionism to definitely dismantle the modernist misconception of aesthetic elitism and unearth the 'hidden dialectics' occurring between art movements and one of the constitutive feature of mass society: mass media. Rediscussing the 'great divide' between high and low culture in modernity, Andreas Huyssen saw the role of media technologies 'a crucial, if not *the* crucial, role in the avant-garde's attempt to overcome the art/life dichotomy and make art productive in the everyday life'.[10] More recent scholarship in film and media studies has variously elaborated on this idea, addressing Dada's and Futurism's subversive aesthetics as "parasitic" attempts to irritate the emerging means of communications[11] or addressing the mutual dependence between European avant-garde film-makers on the one hand and film-industry on the other.[12] As in a self-fulfilling prophecy, a wider look on the entanglement of avant-garde with the structures of mass society and beyond their supposedly aesthetic self-sufficency became only possible retrospectively, that is to say not only when they had already exhausted their historical function but also when their linear-progressive conception of time was itself historicized.

[7] Clement Greenberg, 'Avant-garde and Kitsch' (1939) repr. in Id., *Art and Culture: Critical Essays* (Boston: Beacon Press, 1961), 3-33 (p. 16).
[8] See, for instance, Theodor Adorno, *Aesthetic Theory* (1970), trans. and ed. by R.H. Kentor (London and New York: Continuum, 2002), pp. 33-36.
[9] Peter Bürger, 'Adorno's Anti-avantgardism', *Telos*, 86 (December 1990), 49-60 (p. 53).
[10] Andreas Huyssen, *After the Great Divide. Modernism, Mass Culture, Postmodernism* (Bloomington and Indianapolis: Indiana University Press, 1986), p. 9.
[11] Arndt Niebitsch, *Media Parasites in the Early Avant-garde. On the Abuse of Technology and Communication* (New York: Palgrave Macmillan, 2010).
[12] Malte Hagener, *Moving Forward, Looking Back. The European Avant-garde and the Invention of Film Culture, 1919-1939* (Amsterdam: Amsterdam University Press, 2007).

Moving in Between. Intermedial Art and Networks.

By the mid-twentieth century avant-garde had been pronounced dead several times in the wake of its sudden popularization in the American art circuits and museums and by the art criticism after the end of WWII. In one of the eulogies written for avant-garde in the 1960s, literary critic Irving Howe noted that 'the middle class has discovered that the fiercest attacks upon its values can be transported into pleasing entertainments, and the avant-garde writer or artist must confront the one challenge for which he has not been prepared: the challenge of success'.[13] Similar positions were later transported in the field of arts by Bürger who saw this success of the avant-garde aesthetics as a co-optation of its once disruptive techniques by its former enemy, the art institution.[14]

It is precisely against this institutionalization process that the other key notion outlined in the title of this special issue, "intermediality", emerged and gained some theoretical consistency in the arts. Dating back to the scientific discourse of the eighteenth century, the term "intermedia" was re-signified by Dick Higgins in 1965 as what 'falls between the media", "an uncharted land that lies between collage, music and the theater. It is not governed by rules; each work determines its own medium and form according to its needs'.[15] In Higgins' own words, intermediality served as a way to 'demystify [...] what was then known as "avant-garde: for specialists only"'[16] and, on a broader level to finally get rid of the compartmentalized approach inherited from the bourgeois ideology and a response to the problems of the then dawning "classless society". While openly addressing the modernist notion of "medium-specificity" — which had been strongly advocated by Clement Greenberg among others[17] — Higgins acknowledged the role of Futurists, Dadaists and Surrealists as ancestors of an aesthetics of contamination between different disciplines.

Although in this context the word "medium" indicates the material means for making art, the concept as a whole cannot be fully understood if not placed against the backdrop of mass communications. Higgins himself addressed this issue in his later writings, pondering how 'due to the spread of mass literacy, to television and the transistor radio, our sensitivities have changed'[18] and calling

---

[13] Irving Howe, 'The Culture of Modernism', *Commentary*, XL, 5 (November 1967), [repr. as 'Introduction' in Id., *The Idea of the Modern in Literature and the Arts* (New York: Horizon Press, 1968)] p. 24.

[14] Peter Bürger, *Theory of the Avant-garde* (1974), trans. by Michael Shaw (Minneapolis: University of Minnesota Press, 1989), pp. XLIX – LV.

[15] Ivi, p. 53.

[16] Dick Higgins, 'Intermedia' (1965-1980), repr. in *Leonardo*, XXXIV, 1, 2000, 49-54, (p. 50).

[17] See Noël Carroll, 'Medium Specificity Arguments and the Self-Consciously Invented Arts: Film, Video, and Photography', in Id., *Theorizing the Moving Image* (Cambridge: University of Cambridge Press, 1996), 3-24.

[18] Dick Higgins, 'Statement on Intermedia', *Dè-coll/age*, 6 (July 1967) repr. in *Theories and Documents of Contemporary Art. A Sourcebook of Artists' Writings*, ed. by Kristine Stiles and Peter Selz (Berkeley: University of California Press, 1996), 728-729 (p. 728).

for a use of intermedia as a new way of communicating capable to respond both to the social issues and the technological challenges of the time. The same ambivalence became even stronger as Gene Youngblood borrowed the term for his column on the *Los Angeles Free Press* in 1967 and later featured it in his major work *Expanded Cinema*: in his writings, the "intermedial" adjective applies both to a range of artistic practices and to a system of global communication. In a fashion reminiscent of Marshall McLuhan, Youngblood compares the contemporary artist to an ecologist within an "environment" much more influenced by the presence of technological media than by nature. Within this context, intermedia art is presented as a progressive counteraction to the pervasiveness of the intermedia networks and an invitation to re-invent mass cultural means for higher purposes.[19] Whereas mass information and commercial entertainment are "redundant" (they give the audience what they already know) and "popular" by definition (as they speak a common, standardized language), what we call art must 'go on from there', providing 'new instruments to think with and new areas to explore in our thinking'.[20] These instruments are supposed to be materially carved out of the already existing media: thanks to the artists, cinema, television and computers will be freed from their prescribed place within society, and their unexpressed creative potentials finally redeemed with the ultimate aim to create a new global consciousness.

Given how quickly and complexly the notion had developed across different fields of knowledge, it would be misleading to suggest that intermediality is the exclusive domain of the arts or a distinctive hallmark of those post-war art movements later formalized as "neo-avant-gardes". Nevertheless, in Higgins' and Youngblood's theoretical accounts, the notion does meet some of the conceptual tensions which were already crucial in the early twentieth century avant-garde movements: a thrust to overcome the hierarchical separation between the different art sectors, the aim to crush the barriers between the aesthetic and the mundane, and an explicit will to 'invent the future in the present'.[21] In addition, intermediality also offers a new shade of meaning perhaps more closely tied to the specificity of the arts between the 1950s and the 1970s. The concept of intermedia is in fact more spatial than temporal, one that indicates the possibility of an "in-betweeness" or, in other words, the chance to look for a synesthetic and syncretic outcome by seamlessly *moving* from a discipline to another and, by extension, from the everyday routine of an highly technologized society to artistic creation and exhibition — the intermedia network has made us all artists by proxy.[22] In this sense, intermedium theories show some conceptual continuity with the emphasis put on the concept of 'flow' by the Fluxus founders and, to

---

[19] Gene Youngblood, *Expanded Cinema* (New York: P. Dutton & Co., 1970), p. 374.
[20] Ivi, p. 87.
[21] Ivi, p. 69.
[22] Ivi, p. 58.

a wider extent, with the extemporaneous character of their happening and the aleatory nature of John Cage's works: all of these manifestations, in fact, share an implicit understanding of what Leonard Meyers called the "anti-teleological"[23] drive of post-war experimentalism. To put it simply, Youngblood's idea of the artist as an ecologist in a networked environment diverges quite significantly from the metaphor of the military vanguard that is looking forward for new directions. In Youngblood's terms, artistic innovation may not necessarily have a destination to be reached. The chance for artistic and social innovation does not lie ahead of us, as in an unknown future, but is instead to be found in-between what is already existing, as a possibility which still has to be disclosed. Conceiving the arts no more as a 'continually advancing progress'[24] but rather as a 'dynamic steady-state'[25] which allows for the 'simultaneity of the radically disparate'[26] led intermedia artists and theoreticians in the second half of the twentieth century to a more open consideration of the pervasiveness of mass media in order to exploit their creative potentials and turning it against them.

At the Criss-cross between Music, Art and Visual Media.

If we were to follow one consistent line of thinking of post-modern criticism, it would be tempting to conclude our brief historical outline with a striking paradox: when all of the barriers and boundaries separating the aesthetic from the mundane and "high" from "low" culture finally collapsed, it was neither due to some subversive revolution nor to a sudden awakening of (artistic) consciousness. Instead, it was only thanks to the market's rapid taking over of art both in its institutional and disruptive forms. This seems to be implied in Huyssen's statements on the advent of late modernity as the 'dead-end of the avant-garde'[27] as well as in Fredric Jameson's oft-cited passage according to which 'aesthetic production today has become integrated into commodity production generally: the frantic economic urgency of producing fresh waves of ever more novel-seeming goods (from clothing to airplanes), at ever greater rates of turnover, now assigns an increasingly structural function and position to aesthetic innovation and experimentation'.[28]

That art-making today is supported and conditioned in a quite different way than it was in the early-century bourgeois society is a sure fact. Nonetheless, conceiving mass media and culture in strictly economic/productive terms

[23] Leonard B. Meyer, *Music, the Arts and Ideas. Patterns and Predictions in Twentieth Century Culture* (Chicago: University of Chicago Press, 1967), p. 72.
[24] Enzensberger, *Aporias*, p. 81.
[25] Meyer, p. 96.
[26] Bürger, *Theory*, p. 63.
[27] Huyssen, pp. 160-178.
[28] Fredric Jameson, *Postmodernism: or, the Cultural Logic of Late Capitalism* (Durham: Duke University Press, 1991), p. 5.

fails to address several important social and cultural issues at stake. These issues become all the more apparent when analysed against the backdrop of the experimental art forms whose very existence is inherently tied to mass media technologies. In recent times, film scholars and historians have taken a more nuanced view on the relation between artistic avant-gardes and mass consumerism. On the one hand, as mentioned above, they critically re-assessed historical avant-garde film-makers' experimental aesthetics by considering the active role they also played in the field of advertising and sponsored films.[29] On the other hand, when looking at the current mass marketed situation, they do acknowledge the existence of an avant-gardist/experimental "persistence" in film-making by variously addressing it for its distinguishing aesthetic features,[30] as 'a cultural formation' whose members share a 'conscious association as group identification'[31] or as 'a mesh of institutional frameworks and practices and [...] a set of exigencies or modes of production'.[32] The boundaries become even more blurred when it comes to the medium of video: welcomed at first for its technological specificity (i.e. for allowing a synchronic recording and a synesthetic rendition of image and sound altogether)[33] it has been progressively considered less in an essentialist fashion and more in terms of contextual relationships. In other words, video cannot be fully understood if not at the intersection of a plurality of forms (from video-art to home video), cultural and social contexts (from the tv broadcast schedule to the art gallery) which can be considered separately but are never totally independent from each other.[34] The fluidity between those apparently autonomous realms comes to the fore while dealing with some peculiar cases, such as that of the music video: not only did several video artists and experimenters directed music videos to be broadcast on a regular schedule, but music video itself eventually became an institutionally acknowledged art-form outside the context of television. As Arnold et al. have suggested, 'taken together these tendencies constitute

[29] See Hagener, *Moving*; Michael Cowan, *Walter Ruttmann and the Cinema of Multiplicity: Avant-garde, Advertising, Modernity* (Amsterdam: Amsterdam University Press, 2014).
[30] According to Michael Pray, from the 1970s onwards avant-garde film-making witnessed "a shift from ascepticism to aestheticism. In an Oedipal reaction, the young film-makers what had been anathema to their elders: subject matter". *Avant-garde Film: Forms, Themes and Passions* (London and New York: Wallflowers, 2008), p. 108.
[31] Joan Hawkins, 'Downtown Cinema Revisited' in *Downtown Film and Tv Culture 1977-2001*, ed. by Joan Hawkins (Chicago and London: Intellect, 2015) xi-xxx (p. xii). The term 'cultural formation' is quoted from Raymond Williams, *The Sociology of Culture* (New York: Schocken Books, 1982), p. 68.
[32] Paul Arthur quoted in Malcom Turvey, Ken Jacobs et al., 'Obsolescence and the American Avant-garde Film', *October*, 100, 2002, 115-132 (p. 116).
[33] See Holly Rogers, 'The Unification of the Senses. Intermediality in Video-Art Music', *Journal of the Royal Music Association*, CXXXVI, 2, 2011, 399-428.
[34] Sean Cubitt, *Videography. Video Media as Art and Culture* (New York: Palgrave Macmillan, 1993), pp. xiv-xv.

part of a complex "video culture" [...] ranging from the most commercialized culture to avant-garde aesthetics'. [35]

Either retracing the long-standing relationship between artistic and industrial discourses across the history of the moving image or undertaking an exhaustive analysis of the ambivalence of film, video and their successors as means of artistic expression and mass communication would be a task far beyond the scope of this special issue. Our intention here is rather to further complicate the matters at stake by looking at several media and artistic domains at once: by keeping in mind the shifting boundaries and relationships between the avant-garde and the popular in the area of (audio)visual media, we also intend to take in full account another set of tensions that underlies music as an art and an industry. Scholarship on popular music, in particular, will provide us with a parallel and equally viable entry point to question the understanding of mass-culture as a flat and one-dimensional concept in strict opposition with avant-garde art instances. As pioneers of the then-emerging academic field of popular music studies, Howard Horne and Simon Frith adopted a sociological angle to investigate in further detail how stances coming from the world of arts were gradually assimilated from the record industry. In *Art into Pop,* the authors proposed a double focus: on the one hand, they foregrounded the role played by Art Schools as a social subject crossing class and ideological divisions between high and low culture to educate 'petit-bourgeois professionals who, as pop musicians, apply 'high art' skills and identities to a mass cultural form'[36]. On the other hand, they acknowledge the importance of musicians as artists by putting them at the core of the pop production process, thus dismissing the 'assumption that while high art meaning is derived from the artists themselves — from their intentions, experience and genius — mass cultural meaning lies in its function (to make money, to reproduce social order).'[37] Other than providing a methodological guidance for the study of popular music in general, Horne's and Frith's groundbreaking study contributed in establishing a canon of bands and performers between the 1960s and the 1970s which were later variously labelled as "art", "avant" or "experimental rock". More recent scholarship has followed *Art into Pop's* lead by singling out significant periods, scenes and figures on both sides of the Atlantic. Doye Greene's *Rock, Counterculture and Avant-garde* considered the Beatles, Frank Zappa's Mothers of Invention and the Velvet Underground as case studies to investigate the period between 1966 and 1970 as years during which avant-garde art significantly interweaved with popular aesthetics and practices;[38] cultural

---

[35] Gina Arnold, Daniel Cookney at al., 'The Persistence of the Music Video Form from MTV to Twenty-First Century Social Media', in *Music/Video:Histories, Aesthetics, Media,* ed. by Gina Arnold, Daniel Cookney at al. (New York, London: Bloomsbury, 207), pp. 1-14 (p. 10).

[36] Simon Frith and Howard Horne, *Art into Pop* (London and New York: Methuen, 1987), p. 2.

[37] Ibidem.

[38] Doyle Green, *Rock, Counterculture and the Avant-Garde. How the Beatles, Frank Zappa and the Velvet Underground Defined an Era* (Jefferson: McFarland & Co, 2014)

theorist and music critic Simon Reynolds focused instead on some key-figures of the New York scene of the 1960s and 1970s such as Yoko Ono, Brian Eno and Arto Lindsay, presenting them as the first (non-)musicians to apply art-ideas not solely on the "packaging" of pop music but directly on its practices, thus transposing the aleatory compositional and performative techniques of post-war experimentalism in the context of popular culture and establishing a point of reference for the art school trained generations who would later give way to post-punk.[39] As an art college graduate himself and one of the most eminent exponents of the post-punk scene, David Byrne was at the core of philosopher Sytze Seenzstra's *Song and Circumstances*, an extended essay devoted to dissect the composer/writer/director's "intermedial" work as well as to shed light on his inspiration in conceptual arts.[40] Additionally, Benjamin Piekut's book *Experimentalism Otherwise: The New York Avant-Garde and Its Limits* has traced the myriad ways in which an avant-garde musical network was shaped around 1964 in New York by various people, their encounters (i.e. Leonard Bernstein's New York Philharmonic Orchestra's encounter with John Cage's composition *Atlas Eclipticalis*), specific events (i.e. Charlotte Moorman's premiere of John Cage's *26' 1.1499" for a String Player* and further controversial performances of the piece), structures (i.e. Bill Dixon the Jazz Composers Guild) and the achievements, failures and conflicts they generated. Although he ultimately argues for the exclusion of specific popular music-oriented artists like James Osterberg (Iggy Pop) and the Stooges from the particular world of experimental/avant-garde music that he seeks to reconstruct, Piekut's analysis points to the variety of ways in which these popular music artists were connected – notably through John Cale's working history with La Monte Young and the ONCE Festival in Ann Arbor, Michigan – with avant-garde music practices and aesthetics of the time. Significantly, Piekut's account 'offers a way of understanding the complexities of attachment – how the Stooges can be both *associated* with a particular formation and *absent* from [the New York avant-garde music's] canonical history'[41].

These scholarly studies have in common a concern with musicians who were well aware of the aesthetics of the twentieth century avant-garde, either for having studied in art schools or for having personally taken part in art movements and collectives. After all, most of the musical figures and scenes analysed in these works occurred between the 1950s and the 1970s, at a time when the historical avant-gardes' heritage became increasingly "popularized" and accepted by institutions and when the so called American neo-avant-gardes were about to emerge. In this

[39] Simon Reynolds, 'Eno, Ono, Arto. Non-musicians and the Emergence of Concept-Rock', in Id., *Totally Wired. Postpunk Interviews and Overviews,* (London: Faber and Faber, 2009), 367-380.
[40] Sytze Seenzstra, *Songs and Circumstances. The Work of David Byrne from Talking Heads to the Present,* (New York: Continuum International Publishing, 2010).
[41] Benjamin Piekut, *Experimentalism otherwise. The New York Avant-Garde and its Limits,* (Berkeley, Los Angeles and London: University of California Press, 2011), p. 196.

context, the existence of a dialogue between art and popular culture was, if not self-evident, at least easily provable. Other authors had looked instead for a less explicit "avant-pop connection", one grounded more on transhistorical linkages than on social-cultural proximities. American music critic Greil Marcus' *Lipstick Traces* proposes an imaginative narrative of the cultural roots of English punk music, taking the Sex Pistols' *Anarchy in the UK* as an entry point in the 'secret history of the twentieth century'. Whenever taken seriously, the comparison of punk with the Dada movement or the Letterist International collective leads to 'something that was less a matter of cultural genealogy, of tracing a line between pieces of a found story, than of making the story up. [...] a story seemingly endemic to the century, a story that repeatedly speaks and repeatedly loses its voice; it was, it seemed, a voice that only had to speak to lose itself'.[42] Similarly, albeit through a less impressionistic approach than Marcus's, philosopher Bernard Gendron took a wide look at the twentieth century as a whole in the attempt to 'connect the dots' and discern a 'meaningful historical trajectory' from the Montmartre's cabarets in the late nineteenth century Paris to the New York new wave of the 1970s, including the post-WWI and post-WWII jazz scenes and the cultural accreditation of the Beatles. Observed through this *longue-durée* perspective between avant-garde and popular culture looks like an ongoing negotiation in which the former is interested in the entertainment industry's economic capital, while the latter strives for emancipation from its "mass-marketed" condition and for subsequent cultural recognition.[43] By conceiving of the historical development of avant-garde and popular cultures as "parallel convergences", these and other scholars assumed that breaking down the hierarchies between high and low culture was not exclusive of late modernity and, more importantly, that the disruptive practices and stances brought forward by some exponents of popular music could not be read so much as mere appropriations as they constituted (more or less aware) *applications* of avant-garde practices in a different context.[44]

Being in some ways indebted to both of these lines of inquiry, this *Cinéma&Cie* special issue aims at pushing the discussion on the "avant-pop connection" further by embracing a wider angle of observation. Other than acknowledging the central position of (cultured and popular) music for its long-standing entanglement with both the art and mass cultural discourses, we saw no reason to impose further restrictions narrowing the focus on a specific time period or on a single artistic discipline. Instead, our call for transhistorical and intermedial investigations aims precisely at re-framing the general topic as a matter of contamination and

---

[42] Greil Marcus, *Lipstick Traces. A Secret History of the Twentieth Century* (New York: Harvard University Press, 1989), p. 13.
[43] Bernard Gendron, *Between Montmartre and the Mudd Club. Popular Music and the Avant-Garde* (Chicago: University of Chicago Press, 2002).
[44] See also Scott MacKenzie, 'De Do Do Do, De Da Da Dadaism. Popular culture and the Avant-Garde', in *The Routledge Companion to Global Popular Culture*, ed. by Toby Miller (New York: Routledge, 2015), 175-186.

continuities between apparently distinct moments and "sectors" of cultural history.

The following essays share what we may consider a global perspective on cultural history that represents the background to discuss all the operating terms ("avant-garde", "popular", "intermedial", "transhistorical"). By stressing the concept of cultural history more than the specificity of film history, media history, and music history, the authors will provide some analytical and theoretical tools that go beyond the traditional scholarship on the topic that has been mainly centered on UK/US and Europe/USA contexts. Their aim is to suggest original concepts and methodologies to explore such intermedial *exempla* between avant and pop in transhistorical terms and not only in the postmodern one-way move from pop to avant.

Beckmann's essay starts from a key reference to the avant-pop connection in the field of popular music studies,[45] as well as a paradigm of such a relation between music and visual media:[46] the U.S. punk scene and New York underground film culture at the beginning of the 1980s. Spampinato switches from punk and DIY films to post-punk and DIY videos, including between the two of them the national television: keeping in mind the international framework on the topic, he investigates it from the more peripheral angle of the Italian scene among the video self-production, the raise of the commercial TV, and the historic national broadcast. From video as television to video as game, Fullam offers a different reading of the avant-pop issue by adopting a strongly diachronical and transhistorical approach that inscribes Fred Turner's concept of 'democratic surround', stated for the 1960s countercultural productions, in the contemporary 'algoritmic culture'. From TV and videogame to video-art as an interdisciplinary experience, Lischi and Guerra present an in-depth investigation of the process of creating a media intercultural art-work, which is an ongoing art practice between the international history of the Western avant-garde and national heritage of music folklore in Azerbaijan. From contemporary video-art to experimental cinema, Nori still holds the reference to the popular as non-Western traditional music composition and consumption, analyzing the key role of it in the Indian broadcast mainstream media and clashing the notion of experimental and commercial in cinema. Lastly, Liu offers in return an interesting perspective on the supposedly oppositional stances of avant-rock music as well on its connections to the non-Western traditions, keeping the attention on the historical facts over the postmodern *pastiche*, completing the discourses on the English/American art-rock/post-punk.

The range of audiovisual productions explored in such essays is exemplar of different forms and media that have been analyzed in a national field or in a

---

[45] See Frith and Horne; Gendron; Reynolds, *Rip it Up and Start Again: Postpunk 1978-1984* (London: Faber & Faber, 2005).
[46] See Maria Teresa Soldani, 'Within the Ruins of New York City: No Wave as a Paradigm of American Independent Cinema', *Cinergie*, 13 (2018), 59-65.

inter-national panorama, with practices inspired by Dadaism and Fluxus: the independent Cinema of Transgression in New York, the experimental Indian cinema, the Italian post-punk as well as UK new wave videoclips, the intercultural video of Cahen and Guerra, and the global medial panorama of videogame. All these media interact with the chain of circulation of the cultural production: from the composition (*Imaginary Video Landscape*) and recording (Japan's *Tin Drum*) to the distribution (the DIY film festival in downtown New York; the Italian national broadcast and the TV-show *Mister Fantasy*; MTV as the main global/trans-cultural channel; the radio network in India). Moving across this wide range of subject matters, this issue also recollects vary methodologies: the theoretical essay (Fullam); the analytic study of a body of works clearly determined in time and space (Spampinato, Beckmann, Nori); the singular case study of an audiovisual production (Liu) and an art practice, investigated by a scholar with a practitioner (Lischi and Guerra).

The essays also exemplify different possible interplays between the concepts of "avant" and "popular" in music, without assuming any fixed observation-point, considering both the cases in which the latter takes in the practices and aesthetics previously experimented by the former, and vice versa. Whereas, as Fullam's essay demonstrates. the now historicized experience of the twentieth century avant-gardes can provide a "technological engine" or an aesthetic inspiration for popular audiovisual form to draw upon, popular music and culture can also be scrutinized for the "raw materials" it provided to avant-garde experimentalism. In this context, the popular components have been interpreted both in terms of "pop" (mass culture and consumption) and "traditional" (communities and folk heritage) culture, a pop-duality between videogame music and Japan's chart music on the one hand, as well as the traditional Mugam and Indian music on the other. The "avant move" is expressed by the underground US scene of 1980's bands such as the Butthole Surfers, composers such as John Zorn – informed by the practice of avant-garde musician such as John Cage and Pierre Schaeffer – and post-punk/new wave styles that move among UK, US, and Italy.

The medium itself becomes a critical methodological tool to analyze the interplay between avant and pop, between elite and mass culture: Beckmann suggests to adopt the concept of 'messiness' to explore the DIY productions made in downtown New York City during the 1980s analyzing the phenomenon by taking a festival as a medium conveying such intermedial and trans-historical stances; when dealing with the interplays between popular music and experimental film or with the ones among mass media, popular entertainment, and underground music, Spampinato and Nori respectively consider the radio and the TV medium as *tropes*. Nori and Liu also analyze the idea of an 'Avant/Pop Otherness' that goes in two seemingly "counter" moves (from Western pop music to Asian culture, from Asian popular music to Western classical music). Liu in particular proposes the concept of 'Avant-Orientalism' to generate critical discussion on the adoption of cultural stereotypes in avant-pop, discussing the cultural values and implications linked to the appropriation of perceived historical and folkloric elements of Chinese popular culture and their transposition into the realm of Western pop through the post/modernist practices.

In conclusion, even if contemporary global culture no longer allows for easy distinction between "high" and "low" or "back" and "forth", the conception of time and (media) spaces implied by the notions of avant-garde and intermediality can still perform a heuristic function, serving as "cartesian axes" from our observation deck and preventing us from flattening our ideas of mass society or cultural history in general. Focusing on the interplays between the art-avant-gardist and the pop-cultural discourses equates to questioning the very possibility of a critical and adversarial stance *within* mass culture, exploring the strategies and tactics by which, on the one hand, avant-garde re-affirms its otherness from the mainstream in order to preserve a relatively independent position and, on the other hand, popular culture renews itself by incorporating and drawing upon experimental practices. "Avant" and "pop" may also become tools to analyze art/film/music practices in order to recollect again any historical meaning that has been largely neglected by the postmodernist theory, as Liu suggests. Beyond the study of styles and techniques implicated in these artworks, this special issue foregrounds the notions of "avant", "pop", and "intermedial" as a movable 'axes' rather than as fixed concepts. It is our hope that, with this conceptual orientation, the notion of the "trans-historical" can be used not only as a method, but also as a matrix for the study of recurring topics in media history and of concepts that might emerge as scholars move along these axes in their analyses of various avant, pop and intermedial phenomena.

It wasn't…pristine: (Re-)visiting the New York Film Festival Downtown

Marie Sophie Beckmann, Goethe University Frankfurt

Abstract

The New York Film Festival Downtown (1984-1989) was, in the strict sense, not a film festival. But then again, it depends on how film is defined. On three nights, on the stage of a downtown night club, films were shown unfinished, as excerpts or slides, they alternated or shared a stage with performance, theater and dance pieces involving projections, or experimental live happenings. This essay articulates that the festival's messiness–that 'it wasn't pristine', as festival organizer Ela Troyano described it–should above all be considered as its most productive structural element: The New York Festival Downtown both reflected and encouraged the downtown scene's mixing of media, and its collaborative, experimental, and interdisciplinary practices. In doing so, it not only pushed the format of the film festival, but challenged the notion of film itself. And while remaining a local artist-curated initiative, the festival's program also traveled, thereby bringing downtown to Berlin, Bielefeld and Buffalo, and stretching the scene's local boundaries.

Going Down To See It

'New York Film Festival New York Film Festival New York Film Festival New York Film Festival New York Film Festival New York Film Festival'. The four black lettered words are repeated six times, shrinking from top to bottom on the neon pink paper, like an echo, until they make room for 'DOWN TOWN', in capital letters, as if the moniker of Manhattan's southernmost part was being shouted out loud. At the top, we read the declaration 'The Film Society of Limbo Center presents' and on the very bottom, wiggly letters form the name 'LIMBO' and seem to be dancing out of the lines of the triangle that surrounds them.

So it's a film festival in New York and you have to go down town to see it. But what does that actually mean? And what else do we learn from this flyer (fig. 1)? Let's flip it over. The back informs us about the dates ('21–23 October'); the presenters of the festival ('Ela Troyano and Tessa Hughes-Freeland in conjunction with LIMBO ARTS INC.'); where it takes place ('Limbo Lounge, 647 East Ninth

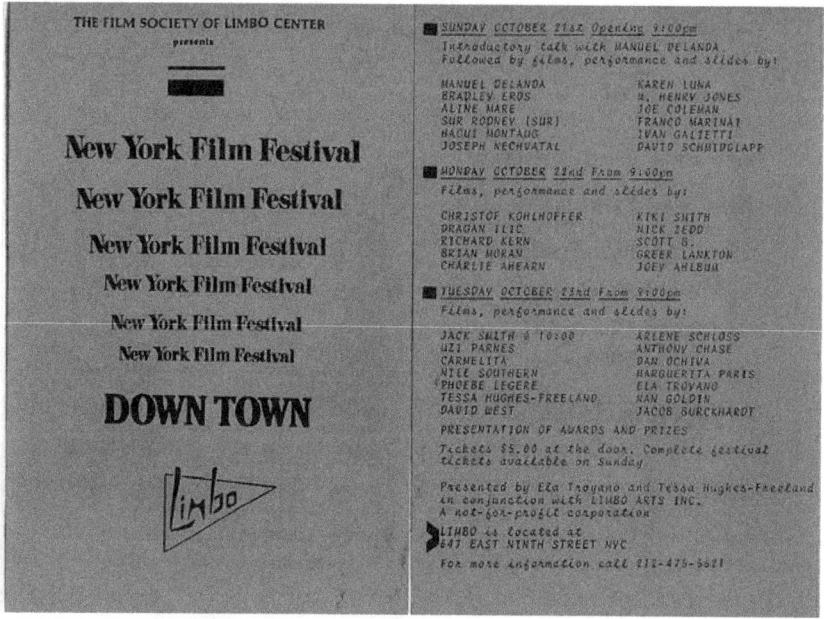

Fig. 1: Flyer for the New York Film Festival Downtown 1989
(Courtesy of Tessa Hughes-Freeland & Ela Troyano).

Street NYC'); a presentation of awards and prizes; and the ticket prices ('five USD at the door'). What first appears to be a regular film festival could actually turn out to be an event of a different kind: what we also learn — or rather, don't learn — is what exactly we would get to see at this festival. On Sunday, Monday, and Tuesday, from 9pm onwards, there will be 'Films, performances and slides by' a list of a total of 36 names that may or may not be familiar to you. There are no further specifications on titles, formats, lengths, or the running order, but you can call 212-457-5621 to ask for more information.

In 1984, these pink xeroxed flyers promoting the New York Film Festival Downtown (NYFFDT) were laid out in clubs, cafés, bars, copy shops, and film labs like Rafik Film & Video[1] in downtown Manhattan, or at the New York Film Festival in midtown, which closed that year on 14 October with *Paris, Texas* (Wim Wenders, 1984). For the New York Film Festival's regular visitors, our pink flyer must have evoked familiarity. Not only did it use the font of the midtown festival

---

[1] Rafik Film & Video was founded in 1974 by Rafic Azzouray. It's a post-production facility for video and audio duplication, transfer, conversions, and editing which also lent filming equipment to local filmmakers. Rafik sponsored the fourth and fifth edition of NYFFDT. The same location housed O-P Screen, a screening space that could be rented for a 15 USD rental fee to show 16mm films. In an advertisement published in the East Village Eye in 1979, it says 'O-P Screen will show anything, just contact Rafik a minimum of two weeks in advance'. This opportunity was used by many of the Downtown filmmakers.

and simply added 'DOWN TOWN', but it also mockingly assumed its air of institutional formality by exchanging 'Lincoln' with 'Limbo'. Founded in 1963, the New York Film Festival is, since 1969, presented and hosted by the Film Society of Lincoln Center. This institution supports various film festivals and theaters, publishes *Film Comment Magazine* and makes up one branch of the prestigious Lincoln Center for Performing Arts. The Limbo Lounge on the other hand was a small East Village gallery and performance space with no associated society whatsoever. Indeed, the very notion of 'society' would seem to belong more to 'Lincoln' than to 'Limbo' Center.

The NYFFDT was founded by the filmmakers Tessa Hughes-Freeland and Ela Troyano in 1984 and it was not by accident that its first edition immediately followed the midtown festival. Rather, there was the 'vain hope that someone from there would come down to see it',[2] that the NYFFDT could piggyback off the influx of visitors generated by the more established festival whose name they boldly appropriated, and to receive the attention of international critics or programmers. Until its last edition in 1989, the NYFFDT established itself as a recurring annual event. At least to a certain extent it took on the functions, structures, and rituals related to the long-established film festival format, ultimately aiming to bring local films into wider circulation.[3] However, the fact that the audience of the NYFFDT had to 'come down to see it' must also be understood in the sense that the festival grew out of the downtown scene, where film, performance, and music shared the stages and screens of night clubs.

Venues such as Max's Kansas City (1965–1981), CBGB (est. 1973) or the Mudd Club (1978–1983) had already encouraged the cross-fertilization of music and filmmaking in the fields of Post-Punk and No Wave.[4] The subsequent wave

---

[2] Tessa Hughes-Freeland, interviewed by Marie Sophie Beckmann, 13 September 2018.

[3] The film festival format has taken on various shapes and forms since its emergence in postwar Europe. The first festivals in Cannes, Locarno, Venice and Berlin, not unlike art biennials or large scale exhibitions like documenta, had political agendas, and they also account for the recognition of most national new waves and *auteur* directors. As Thomas Elsaesser argues in *European Cinema. Face to Face with Hollywood* (Amsterdam: Amsterdam University Press, 2005), these early festivals were crucial for the generation of these very categories. Further, attracting both tourists and local audiences, film festivals are historically linked to the strategic (re-)branding of a city as a cultural center. The 1960s saw the rising of festival sub-circuits for minor genres (such as events targeting a feminist, gay and lesbian, or Black/African American community), and in the 1980s, the format's proliferation shifted the traditional centers and turned the festival circuit into a global one. Borrowing from the vocabulary of modern system theories put forward by Latour or Luhmann, Elsaesser conceives the festival as a complex but also porous network 'with nodes and nerve endings.' Taken together, international festivals form yet a larger network, which amounts to a global platform that increasingly determines distribution, exhibition but also the production of films outside the Hollywood network, becoming more and more its powerful counterpart, or rather, interface. So when the NYFFDT was launched, film festivals already constituted a complex but ubiquitous reality, one that, with Bill Nichols, provides a 'continuous, international pattern of circulation and exchange for image-culture,' sustaining a certain 'traffic in cinema' which 'allows the local to circulate globally.' Bill Nichols, 'Global Image Consumption in the Age of Late Capitalism', *East-West Film Journal,* 8.1 (1994), 68–85 (p. 68).

[4] For a general account of the No Wave music and filmmaking scene, see Marc Masters, *No*

of clubs, including Danceteria (1979–1986), Club 57 (1980-1983), and Pyramid (est. 1981), as well as Limbo Lounge, Darinka, and 8BC, which all opened between 1983 and 1984, took an even more ambitious, or rather, liberal approach to programming: Scheduled or unscheduled concerts, film screenings, drag shows, readings, slide projections, and all kinds of dance parties deliberately or coincidentally blended into one another. And although '[i]t wasn't all happening at the same time, but on the same night and at the same place, […] it had this sense of continuity. You wouldn't be going to see this one thing, but the ongoing, the whole surrounding.'[5] The experience of a continuos flow of events was enhanced by the fact that most clubs were located within the same neighborhood, namely the East Village, making club-hopping easy. As crucial sites for 'socializing, for entertainment, for doing things',[6] these clubs operated 'as both a scene unto itself and also as a scene generator, or a place where it was possible to make connections and begin collaborations.'[7]

The NYFFDT began as precisely such a collaboration. Hughes-Freeland and Troyano met at the Pyramid, where Troyano worked as a projectionist. Between 1982 and 1984, together or each themselves, they organized irregular screening events featuring their own work along that of other Super 8 filmmakers and collaborated on doing multiple projections, which they later referred to as live expanded cinema performances. East Village clubs functioned as hosts for their screenings, such as Danceteria, Limbo Lounge, Club 57, or Chandelier Club, which Troyano ran together with photographer, filmmaker, and multimedia performance artist Uzi Parnes.[8] It was after their weekend film program Celluloid Cantina at the Limbo Lounge that they decided to found the NYFFDT. First, because dragging a projector and rolls of film from one place to the next for single events became tiring and second and more importantly, because they had the wish to adopt a format that would allow for a more dense and concentrated

Wave (London: Black Dog Publishing, 2007); Duncan Reekie, Subversion: The Definitive History of Underground (New York: Wallflower Press, 2007); Thurston Moore and Bryan Coley, No Wave: Post-Punk. Underground. New York. 1976–1980 (New York: Abrams Image, 2008); and Captured. A Film/Video History of the Lower East Side, ed. by Clayton Patterson (New York: Seven Stories Press, 2005), especially the essays by Harris Smith ('No New Cinema: Punk and No Wave Underground Film 1976–1984', 173–178) and Matthew Yokobosky ('No Wave Cinema, 1978–87. Not a part of Any Wave: No Wave', 179–183). For the historization of the No Wave scene, see Mark Benedetti, 'Canonization and No Wave Cinema History', in Downtown Film & TV Culture 1975–2001, ed. by Joan Hawkins (Bristol and Chicago: Intellect, 2015), 265–281.
[5] Ela Troyano, interviewed by Marie Sophie Beckmann, 7 September 2018.
[6] Tessa Hughes-Freeland, interviewed by Marie Sophie Beckmann, 13 September 2018.
[7] Tim Lawrence, Life and Death on the New York Dance Floor. 1980–1983 (Durham and London: Duke University Press, 2016), pp. 22–23.
[8] The reason for putting on screenings at clubs was mainly that their owners were considered to be more open to experimental formats and a cross-medial program than venues with a curated film focused program. Ela Troyano recalls that at the Pyramid there was blind trust, while, for instance at the Millennium, 'you had to explain what you were doing' (Troyano). Also, since the clubs made revenue at the bar and often charged a small entrance fee, filmmakers would get paid, which wasn't always the case in non-profit venues.

presentation of the East Village's filmmaking and its pairings and mixings with other media.

It is important to note that by the mid 1980s, 'East Village' and 'downtown' respectively had already come to denominate highly visible cultural genres, loosely defined 'by the production and consumption of the various forms of style concentrated below Fourteenth Street'.[9] Tim Lawrence notes that the downtown club culture of the early 1980s, in which 'everything seemed to be tied to everything and nothing really had a name',[10] was intriguing precisely because of what he aptly calls '*in*disciplinarity'. So rather than generic coherence, it was, with Joan Hawkins, 'the neighborhood itself that provided a sense of artistic cohesion'.[11] It is however crucial to note that the labeling with geographic epithets such as 'downtown' and 'East Village' resulted from an interplay of ascription (by local and international media) and self-ascription by the scenes themselves. And it was these labels' identification with cultural innovation which was then exploited by real estate developers who increasingly invested in the area. As Christopher Mele summarises this process, 'the downtown scene was transformed by media, spectators and participants from the marginal and rebellious to an urban genre well suited for urban revitalization.'[12] Moreover, these geographic prefixes can be misleading if they suggest that a scene is essentially local and formed by actual physical encounter. Will Straw reminds us that as 'default label for cultural unities whose precise boundaries are invisible and elastic', the term 'scene' may circumscribe 'local clusters of activity' but may also 'give unity to practices dispersed throughout the world.'[13] In the pre-digital age, zines, letters, or VHS mail order were just as crucial for the sharing of knowledge, the dispersion of tastes, and the circulation of, in our case, films. Equally, while the NYFFDT emerged as and within a local cluster of activity, it also repeatedly acted as a catalyst for new connections and joint activities that expanded and dispersed the scene beyond its local realm, as will be shown at a later point.

Nonetheless, we begin by looking at the NYFFDT in its local context. In downtown Manhattan, the festival was hosted by 'extra-theatre venues [that] lent themselves to the creation of layered texts.'[14] Its cross-medial program never started earlier than 8pm and downtown performance artists were employed as masters of ceremonies (MCs) to entertain the audience while the stage was prepared for the next act. Each festival ended with an award ceremony. And

---

[9] Christopher Mele, *Selling the Lower East Side. Culture, Real Estate, and Resistance in New York City* (Minneapolis: University of Minnesota Press, 2000), p. 217.

[10] Lawrence, p. ix.

[11] Joan Hawkins, 'Downtown Cinema Revisited', in *Downtown Film & TV Culture,* ed. by Hawkins, pp. xi-xxix (p. xii).

[12] Christopher Mele, 'Forging the Link between Culture and Real Estate: Urban Policy and Real Estate Development', in *The Gentrification Debates,* ed. by Japonica Brown-Saracino (London: Routledge, 2010), 127–132 (p. 129).

[13] Will Straw, 'Scenes and Sensibilities', *Public,* 22.23 (2001), 245–257 (p. 248).

[14] Hawkins, p. xix.

just as Hughes-Freeland and Troyano followed a decidedly open, experimental, inclusive, but however highly subjective agenda in terms of curation, their award ceremony had neither specific categories nor a jury.[15] Based on their own judgment, they awarded selected filmmakers with a cheap 'Oscar' candle figure, a tongue-in-cheek reference to the golden über-prestigious 'Academy Award of Merit'.[16] The festival nights themselves did not follow a rigidly scheduled program, but rather had the quality of an ongoing experience, where one performance or screening blended into the next. The two organisers stated that programming the NYFFDT's first edition implied making a long list of 'all these things that wouldn't fit into the more established art culture,' and putting them together 'in such an order that always kept it moving, in an environment which on every level wasn't pristine'.[17]

With the above described circumstances in mind, I want to propose that this messiness — that the festival 'wasn't pristine' — should above all be considered as its most productive structural element. But what does it mean to take 'messiness' as the defining structure of a film festival? As will be shown in the following, the NYFFDT both reflected and encouraged the downtown scene's mixing of media, and its collaborative, experimental, and interdisciplinary practices. The fact that the festival displayed film and performance in the context of a messy club night[18] also meant that film itself wasn't treated as a pristine object either. Rather, films alternated, shared a stage and were mixed with performance, theater and dance pieces involving projections, or experimental live happenings.[19] Films were shown as work-in-progress, as excerpts, or as slides. And if someone was

---

[15] 'We only said no to one entrance. I don't even know the name of it anymore…but it was flowers…for a long time.' Ela Troyano, interviewed by Marie Sophie Beckmann, 7 September 2018. However, being inclusive not only meant having a relaxed curatorial agenda, but also a political one. Female, queer, and non-white filmmakers and artists were explicitly invited to show or perform their work. Further, since the selection committee included only the two initiators, the programming of the festival was first and foremost based on personal taste and personal relations.
[16] '[W]e just decided on random reasons.' Tessa Hughes-Freeland in an E-Mail to Marie Sophie Beckmann, 7 December 2018.
[17] Ela Troyano, interviewed by Marie Sophie Beckmann, 7 September 2018.
[18] 'In instances where the films were projected behind bands, the story was not the point — and people rarely stopped dancing in order to gaze at the movie. When the film was shown in a backroom, people did watch the film in pretty much a traditional way — but there was more coming and going […] and the audience was vocal — yelling out opinions and questions, and cheering whenever someone they recognized came on-screen.' Hawkins, p. xix.
[19] Of course, the pairing of live music, dance, performance and film wasn't a novelty when the NYFFDT was launched, but rather an already common practice in the downtown scene which in turn had its roots in multimedia events and expanded cinema performances of the 1960s. What comes to mind are for instance Carolee Schneemann's multimedia/kinetic theater performance *Snows* (1967), where live performers and the on stage installation where covered by a projection of her anti-war film *Viet Flakes* (1965), or Andy Warhol's infamous multi-part expanded cinema production *Exploding Plastic Inevitable*, which was orchestrated from 1966 to 1967 and included a vast array of projections, recorded and live music, on stage dancing. The most comprehensive theorization of such works can be found in Gene Youngblood, *Expanded Cinema* (New York: Dutton, 1970).

working on a film and hadn't finished it in time, she or he would be encouraged to show it anyway.[20] In the 1986 program, the listing of David Schmidlapp's *a place to beware* comes with the following comment: 'This is a title I came up with last night. I don't really work towards a finished product. There could be a lot of excuses for this: but the truth of the matter is the more I work, the less I finish'. In the case of Andy Soma's film *White Rabbit* however, the film not being finished in time meant that no actual film was shown at all at the NYFFDT's third edition in 1986. Rather, by getting on stage and describing the images that should have appeared on the screen, Soma spontaneously turned the film into a performance *in situ*.[21] Collaboration, improvisation, and the welcoming of the unfinished were thus sometimes born of necessity, but often they were inherent elements of the film (as) performance as well. In the following, we will take a closer look at three cases of collaboration and cross-disciplinarity at the NYFFDT which led to film being merged with performance, dance and music and to film sometimes *happening* 'without ever making it onto celluloid'.[22]

Film happens

The following discussions must be preceded by a remark. The ways in which the films and live events happened at the NYFFDT were very specific to the festival's spatial and temporal context and were, in most cases, not documented via photograph or film. In fact, many of the performances that happened in the downtown clubs of the 1980 weren't documented at all.[23] I will not elaborate on this extensively here. However, if we follow Philip Auslander's thesis that performance documentation is performative in so far as it constitutes performance art (whether it had an initial live audience or not) as such,[24] then a reason for the lack of documentation in our case could be that these live events were in fact never meant to be embedded in a history of art and performance. In order

---

[20] Tessa Hughes-Freeland, interviewed by Marie Sophie Beckmann, 13 September 2018.

[21] This was apparently common practice for Soma. On the closing night of 8BC in October 1985, he presented one of his films in a similar manner. A journalist form the New York Times describes it as follows: 'A room full of 1980's Bohemians laughed knowingly at a movie screen that showed only white light. Sitting nearby, Andy Soma declaimed the 'script' of his 'film'. "Shot of the Jefferson Airplane on the cover of Life magazine," Mr. Soma intoned. "Pan across a shot of Frank Zappa. There he is. Face of Verushka holding a crystal ball. Timothy Leary cutting his lawn."' Michael Gross, 'The Party Seems to be Over For Lower Manhattan Clubs', *The New York Times*, 26 October 1985, p. 1.

[22] Cynthia Carr, *On Edge. Performance at the End of the Twentieth Century* (Middletown: Wesleyan University Press, 2008), p. 82.

[23] 'In the 80s I saw a lot of performances that nowadays would be recorded and should have been recorded. Back then, it just wasn't something which was automatically done'. Tessa Hughes-Freeland interviewed by Zora von Burden, in *Women of the underground: Art. Cultural Innovators Speak for Themselves*, ed. by Zora von Burden (San Francisco: Manic DPress, 2012). n.p.

[24] Cf. Philip Auslander, 'The Performativity of Performance Documentation', *PAJ: A Journal of Performance and Art*, 28.3 (2006), 1-10.

to discuss these contributions I therefore draw on impressions and memories of festival visitors, organizers and participants, and especially on interviews I conducted in Berlin and New York in 2018. Textual and oral documentation, festival ephemera, newspaper clippings are collected as fragmentary, sometimes conflicting documents of a scene that itself is constructed by ephemeral interaction. Structural 'messiness' therefore also pertains to the material and methodology, or rather, to the messiness of memory and history. Not attempting to (re-)construct historical order or coherence, this text is rather an offer to let different, often seldom heard voices speak with each other, cut each other short or finish each other's sentences.

Since the organizational effort for the festival took up a lot Hughes-Freeland's and Troyano's time, little was left to finish their own respective films. Instead of showing films, they often did performed their collaborative multimedia projections at the NYFFDT such as *Playboy Gold Noon Cult Digger,* which was announced as an 'expanded cinema experience' in the 1989 program. This practice had its roots in what Hughes-Freeland describes as an improvised jam session:

> [Ela Troyano] was doing projections at the Pyramid together with John [Zorn] and other musicians, and there was one night at Chandelier when we started jamming together and did it all night long, and then we decided that that was a fun thing to do, so we'd do it in lieu of finishing a film. [...] The projectors are like instruments. We play them like that.[25]

As for material, Troyano used three-dimensional everyday objects like color transparencies, homemade slides, and found images which she arranged on several projectors at once, manipulating the image by hand and oftentimes based on scores provided by musician and composer John Zorn. Hughes-Freeland, Troyano and Zorn collaborated on several films and live projections, such as *Playboy Voodoo* (1991) or *Elegy for Jean Genet* (1994–97), which involves multiple projections of Super 8 and 16mm film, 35mm slides, original and found imagery of 1970s gay, S&M porn, and pop culture. The visual score is improvised to the four tracks of Zorn's *Elegy* composition and footage manipulated by the artists through the use of colored gels, mirrors and other materials. A brief excursus into Zorn's practice will help to gain a better understanding of how notions of improvisation and collaboration from the field of music have informed the performance of moving images at the NYFFDT.

Zorn's work in composing is known to be eclectic, experimental, and genre-transgressing, with a vast output that oscillates between jazz, rock, hardcore punk, classical, extreme metal and klezmer music. Between the late 1970s and mid 1980s he developed a series of 'game pieces', one of which is *Cobra* from 1984. Borrowing its name from a 1977 World war II simulation game, *Cobra* is played, quite literally, like a game. Its score consists of a set of cues noted on cards,

---

[25] Tessa Hughes-Freeland, interviewed by Marie Sophie Beckmann, 13 September 2018.

which are held up to the players by a prompter and rules corresponding to the cues, which can signify body motions, a change in tempo, a pause, or a fading out. The players can react to these cues individually, or call for a change in actions themselves; pointing to one's nose while holding up one finger and making eye contact with another player means requesting a duo, for instance. One can also become a 'guerrilla player' at any point in the game by putting on a headband. If the prompter puts on a headband as well, the player has the freedom to do almost anything he or she wishes, ignore the cues, make any calls or order other players to stop playing. These are just examples for the many, often quite complex and abstruse rules. In any case, as the number of players, the instrumentation and length of the piece are indeterminate and the players always improvise, *Cobra* will not only sound but also look entirely different from performance to performance. John Brackett quotes Zorn in saying that his game pieces deal much rather with form and relationships than with content or sound. Indeed, it is a piece that is made to be watched, to observe the hectic gestures and excited facial expressions of the players, the interaction between them.[26] In this sense, *Cobra* emphasizes a performance-based understanding of music[27] and renders visible the social aspect of live music in general and improvisation in particular, where scores are offered not only as framework for artistic interpretation, but also for social interaction.[28] Zorn is not only a composer who collaborated with artists and filmmakers (such as Jack Smith, whose performances and slide shows Zorn often accompanied with music), but one whose 'poetics of composition'[29] is argued to derive from the structural and unifying possibilities associated with filmic montage.[30]

So while Zorn applies the filmic stylistic device of montage to compose music, Hughes-Freeland and Troyano choose terms from the field of music to describe the work on their multimedia projections, where projectors are being played like instruments and the multimedia projections come together via the logic of the indefinite 'jam session'. What emerges from this are 'unrepeatable movies made on spot',[31] that come together momentarily as a live event.

---

[26] New England Conservatory, *John Zorn: Cobra* [YouTube video], 21 January 2015 <https://www.youtube.com/watch?v=UdNdSJUf_8I > [accessed 4 December 2018].

[27] Nicholas Cook urges to shift from a text-based to a performance-based understanding of music, which means to acknowledge it first and foremost as a social phenomenon and to derive from the notion of a work that exists above its instantiations. Cf. Nicholas Cook, 'Music as Performance', in *The Cultural Study of Music. A Critical Introduction,* ed. by Martin Clayton, Trevor Herbert and Richard Middleton (New York: Routledge, 2003), 204–214.

[28] Nicholas Cook, 'Scripting Social Interaction: Improvisation, Performance, and Western "Art" Music', in *Improvisation and Social Aesthetics,* ed. by Georgina Born, Eric Lewis and Will Straw (Durham and London: Duke University Press, 2017), 59–77 (p. 67).

[29] Brackett mainly refers to Zorn's practice of adapting, modifying and incorporating music by other composers into his own work, his avoidance of features of development, and therefore the creation of a unity that is associative rather than seemingly organic. Cf. John Brackett, *John Zorn: tradition and transgression* (Bloomington: Indiana University Press, 2008), p. xvi.

[30] Cf. Ibidem.

[31] Carr, p. 82.

For the next two cases, I'd like to turn to an account by the writer and critic Cynthia Carr. Her text should not so much be considered as delivering historical evidence as be read as the 'documentary traces'[32] of the events that it conveys to us and through which we can establish a relationship to them. Carr reported regularly on experimental art and performance for the *Village Voice* and her impressions of the NYFFDT's second edition in 1985 begin as follows:

> I'd gone to the Downtown Film Festival at the now-defunct 8BC [...] and found the place to be packed to the bricks. [...] Took me ten minutes to squeeze within view of the stage. Jo Andres appeared midway through the evening's dozen films and slide shows for an "expanded cinema" performance. This is a dance for people who hate dance. [...] At the Film Fest, she worked with slide projections on four layers of tulle-like fabric, fat human outlines in red yellow green blue, stretching and playing with the figures, lifting the veils to show that only on color was visible on each layer of "alternative screen". [...] The piece ended with Andres, Steve Buscemi, and Cynthia Meyers squiggling over their black clothes with phosphorescent liquid as they danced, splattering phosphorescence over the stage and out into the audience, covering the first rows in glowing spots.[33]

It is noteworthy that Carr framed her visit to the NYFFDT as being essentially connected to the evident shift from what many still liked to describe as underground to a more and more tangible gentrification of the East Village. In the face of a waning club culture, Carr dedicated her text to 'Illegal Performances', namely those taking place in venues that were either already shut down or on the verge of losing their licenses. That the critic also took the visit as a very physical experience becomes noticeable not only when her body squeezes through the crowded space, but also when she describes the performance as a series of physically connoted acts of stretching, squiggling, splattering, as something that, quite literally, spilled over the stage.

Andres frequently performed her film/light/dance shows at the NYFFDT.[34] In her pieces, bodies dressed in black are swallowed by the darkness of the venue. Their movements only become visible once the bodies turn into surfaces for projections, setting the images in motion, distorting and twisting them. The dancers smear themselves with light and bathe in the eerie glow that emanates from a TV screen, as described in Sally Barnes's impression of *Liquid TV* at one of Tom Murrin's monthly 'Full Moon Shows:'[35]

---

[32] Amelia Jones, '"Presence" in Absentia: Experiencing Performance as Documentation', *Art Journal*, 56.4, (1997), 11-18 (p. 12).

[33] Carr, p. 74.

[34] Jo Andres is featured in the NYFFDT programs as follows: Jo Andres, *Devil's In The Dish* (Film/ Dance Performance) (1986); Film from performance piece *Lucid Possession* (with Jo Andres, Cynthia Meyers, Rebecca Moore) (1988); *Expanded Cinema Performance* by Jo Andres (1989).

[35] Tom Murrin performed his 'Full Moon Show' in honor of his moon goddess, Luna Macaroona. When he had a club date that fell on the full moon, he invited other performers to the stage of a.o. Performance Space 122 and La Mama Experimental Theatre Club for a variety show; when there

Andres, Lucy Sexton, and Anne Iobst look like Amazons in their short haircuts, black sleeveless T-shirts, black jeans, and black combat boots. They seem to stand six feet tall. They rock their hips as they advance in a kind of chorus line then drop their dancerly demeanor to walk back and begin again, in what struck me as a very tribal manner. Later they dance in front of TVs that face them, not us, so the effect is of an eerie, other worldly light bathing these other-worldly maiden-warriors. And, still later, one reason for their sinister costumes comes clear when the lights go out and slide projections of a human figure dance and multiply through layers of cloth borne and twisted by agents now made invisible in their black garb. They rip apart a glowing figurine and smear themselves with his light.[36]

Andres projected moving images onto 'alternative screens' such as moving bodies and flimsy fabrics, and blended the action of a film with live action onstage.[37] Her frequent collaborators Iobst and Sexton also performed together as the duo Dancenoise in downtown clubs, theaters, at Murrin's 'Full Moon Shows' as well as at the NYFFDT. Their frantic, music- and dance-based performances were usually short (often no longer than 10 minutes), featured an array of props and costumes, and while they could enter the stage with their bodies entirely covered in gift wrapping,[38] many written accounts of their shows mention that the finale would usually involve fake blood and nudity.[39] By giving the stage to such ephemeral, genre-transgressing happenings, the NYFFDT decisively presented itself as a platform for 'any kind of moving image,'[40] thereby not only pushing the conventional understanding of a film festival but also of film itself.

For the last case, we will squeeze again into 8BC's auditorium with Carr…:

The next night, that first row was in danger of more indelible spots, when a naked and shrieking Brian Moran poured a bucket of blood over his head. It was Cinema of Transgression night, a real droolfest of current underground gore, plus two performances. Filmmaker Nick Zedd, wearing a black dress, Cleopatra wig, and the

was no booked event he often performed his ritual on the street. Cf. <https://www.howlarts.org/event/the-full-moon-show-2016-11-16-2017-01-14-2017-03-14/> [accessed 15 December 2018].
[36] Sally Banes, 'Moon Over Loisaida (Revenge of the Full Moon Show)', in *Performance Art and Paratheater in New York, 1976–85,* ed. by Sally Banes (Ann Arbor: The University of Michigan Press, 1988), 254–255 (p. 255). Originally published in *Village Voice*, 7 August 1984.
[37] 'At times, the films were blended with action onstage. As patterns swirled across the screens, a figure in white emerged from the darkness, and some of the same patterns swirled across her robes. All three screens showed a woman dancing under el tracks. Suddenly, however, there was a live dancer moving in front of one screen while the el stretched away on film behind her'. Jack Anderson, 'Review/Dance; Movement, Live and Filmed', *The New York Times*, 22 October 1990, p. 18, <https://www.nytimes.com/1990/10/22/arts/review-dance-movement-live-and-filmed.html?module=inline> [accessed 01 March 2019].
[38] *"Dance Noise" Performance Art at The Pyramid Club's 7th Birthday Party* [YouTube video], 13 June 2011, <https://www.youtube.com/watch?v=4Fn6koxuaPU> [accessed 14 December 2018].
[39] Cf. John Kelly, 'they stripped with their boots on: REVENGE WITH REPRIEVE', *movement research performance journal,* 34 (2009), n.p.
[40] Tessa Hughes-Freeland, interviewed by Marie Sophie Beckmann, 13 September 2018.

gaze of a dying starlet, drifted across the stage, accompanied by a schmaltzy soundtrack that might ordinarily signal the entrance of a mutant B-movie crab. Richard Hell narrated.[41]

…who is noticeably unimpressed with the 'droolfest' featuring Richard Kern, Brian Moran and Nick Zedd. The first act, which seems to be inspired by the provocations of Viennese Actionism, is announced in the festival's program as follows: 'RICHARD KERN. *Submit to Me* or *From Sex to Death*, new film in progress. Performance with Brian Moran. *Manhattan Love Suicides.*' The short description for *Manhattan Love Suicides* is put in quotation marks, indicating that the filmmaker has written the text himself:

New York City 1985 — A churring world where the realities of poverty and sex among the desperate musicians, artists and scene makers dictate a mutated parody of normal lifestyles. Consumed with bitterness and hatred, the characters of *M.L.S.* stalk their objects of attention through the depths of the Lower East Side [...]. [T]his film contains four vignettes featuring NYC cult stars Nick Zedd, Bill Rice, Adrienne Altenhaus, David Wojnarowicz, Tom Turner and Amy Turner.[42]

While other film descriptions adopt a more sober tone (such as Manuel DeLanda's ISM ISM: 'Documents graffiti from 1975-1978'), Kern frames his films specifically as products of the Lower East Side and additionally supplies a narrative of its 'realities of poverty and sex and desperation.' Fittingly, the text is accompanied by a still from *Submit To Me Now*, depicting a half naked Tommy Turner. Tied to the floor as if crucified, sharp wooden sticks are goring his flesh. After mentioning that the film was shot in 'dazzling black and white Super 8' and includes a soundtrack by J.G. Thirlwell, Kern introduces its performers as 'NYC cult stars', half-mockingly alluding to the fact that the stardom of most of them, except maybe Wojnarowicz, is limited to the downtown scene.

Kern's first Super 8 film *Goodbye 42nd Street* in 1984 was only four minutes long. But since you 'needed 20 min. to be in a club,'[43] he began to collaborate with Brian Moran aka Blood Boy on live events. These sometimes incorporated Kern's later films such as *Zombie Hunger 1* and *Zombie Hunger 2* (both from 1984), which were screened while the men were 'on stage shooting up and fainting, or dying, whatever.'[44] Moran also appears as Blood Boy in Kern's *Submit To Me* (1985–86), of which excerpts were shown at the NYFFDT in 1985. Here, we watch the slender bodies of young women move and undress to the guitar sounds of the rock band The Butthole Surfers, their gaze is directed straight into the camera which circles around them. As the film progresses, we see scenes

---

[41] Carr, p. 75.

[42] The program appeared in the October 1985 issue of *East Village Eye*.

[43] Richard Kern, interviewed by Marie Sophie Beckmann, 4 October 2018.

[44] Richard Kern, interviewed by Jack Sargeant, in *Deathtripping: The Cinema of Transgression,* ed. by Jack Sargeant (London, San Francisco: Creation Books, 1995), p. 98.

of increasing violence, a couple is choking each other with tightropes until the blood gushes out, someone is 'overdosing,' and a naked male body, the head covered by a latex mask is held on a leash. In the final scene, we see a naked, blood covered Moran screaming silently.

What Carr described as Nick Zedd drifting across the stage with the 'gaze of a dying starlet […] accompanied by a schmaltzy soundtrack' is announced in the festival program as an 'Ordeal he co-wrote with Lydia Lunch.' This piece called *SHE* is based on a script originally entitled *The Perfect Woman*. Musician Richard Hell, who also starred in Zedd's *Geek Maggot Bingo* (1983), read the text on stage, while Zedd performed as Nichole Z., a drag character he sometimes assumed for a night out,[45] on stage (in his piece *ME MINUS YOU*), or in the film *Thrust In Me*, a collaboration with Kern. Excerpts of that film, in which Zedd plays both a suicidal woman and her necrophiliac boyfriend, were in turn used to depict a dream sequence in *ME MINUS YOU.*

Film and performance are interrelated in various ways here. Kern and Zedd made films specifically to be screened during performances, re-used existing material in a performative setting, or turned performance into film, with both director and performers appearing on stage as well as in the film. But film was also *acted out*. Nick Zedd stated that because he lacked the money to shoot a film in 1985, he decided to perform *ME MINUS YOU* as a 'live movie'.[46] After all, shooting on Super 8 is fairly cheap, but doing a performance is even cheaper. In the script for *ME MINUS YOU*, we find detailed information of when which tape should start playing, or which slide should be shown. For the other performers the script includes stage directions, indicating that certain lines should be spoken 'frustratedly,' or with an attitude that is 'impassive to the audience.'[47] But even with a script that leaves little to no space for improvisation, a live situation invites uncontrollable elements. When *ME MINUS YOU* was performed at the Pyramid, one performer forgot his script, was thrown off the stage by an enraged Zedd, and went on roaming the audience searching for his knife he had lost in the meantime. Though this part obviously wasn't scripted, Zedd said he was 'pleased that occured,'[48] because the confused audience couldn't tell whether the performance was still happening or not. Although the aspects of immediacy and incalculability of a live event was intriguing for both Kern and Zedd, the practice of performing a film live or combining it with live elements was often also a pragmatic or economic decision – similar to Hughes-Freeland and Troyano doing projections at the festival if the time for finishing a film was lacking.

---

[45] 'One night, after I got made up in drag, a bunch of us went to a girl named Tessa's apartment, high on dope, vodka and mushrooms.' Nick Zedd, *Totem Of The Depraved* (Los Angeles: Two Thirteen Sixty-One Publications, 1996), p. 54.

[46] Cf. Nicholas Zurbrugg, 'Nick Zedd: Living Performances/Filming Transgression. An Interview with Nicholas Zurbrugg', *Art & Film*, 49.11 (1996), 42–47 (p. 44).

[47] Cf. *Screenplay for 'Me Minus You', 1985*, Nick Zedd Papers, Series I, Subseries A, Box 2, Folder 27, Fales Library and Special Collections, New York University.

[48] Cf. Zurbrugg, p. 44.

Lastly, I want to suggest that we should take the dismissive tone of Carr's text as evidence for Kern's and Zedds acts being self-referential to a degree that makes them easy to dismiss in precisely the way that Carr did. Rather than valuing or devaluing them for being 'good' works of art or not, I'd argue that these films (and/as performances) must instead be understood as manifestations of a scene, in this case of collaborations within the loosely defined orbit of the *Cinema of Transgression*.[49] As such, they both create and result from a network in which images, narratives and characters appear and reappear on screen and on stage, and in which the same participants alternately take on the roles of director, performer and curator. In this sense, Kern's and Zedd's work fits well into the program of a festival that can be understood, with Elsaesser, as a 'moment of self-celebration of a community'.[50] But what do these images, narratives and characters signify once they leave their local context?

From Club To Kino: The NYFFDT On The Move

The first two editions of the NYFFDT were housed by the East Village clubs Limbo Lounge and 8BC respectively. Both venues were closed by 1985 in a wave of shutdowns ringing in the beginning of the end of the East Village.[51] In 1984, part of the NYFFDT's first edition program traveled to the Collective for Living Cinema in Tribeca/Soho, which despite that still being Lower Manhattan, was perceived as 'kind of a different thing.'[52] Alf Bold, who worked as film programmer at Berlin's Kino Arsenal, spent a year in New York as curator for the Collective, which was founded in 1973 as an artist-run cooperative and multi-disciplinary venue by film students from the Harpur College Cinema Department. After visiting the NYFFDT's first edition, Bold took a selection of its program and

---

[49] The founding of the NYFFDT coincided with the launch of *Underground Film Bulletin*, a zine issued by filmmaker Nick Zedd under the pseudonym Jerion Oriko. Through interviews and reviews, it predominantly featured downtown filmmakers and their work. In 1985, Zedd singlehandedly announced, 'a new movement is born' and called this movement the Cinema of Transgression. The now oft-cited manifesto was published in the subsequent issue. The filmmakers whom–whether they wanted or not–Zedd associated with the Cinema of Transgression were friends, collaborators or like-minded artists who had been making Super 8 films in the Lower East Side more or less since the late 1970s. These films explored forms of transgression and excess. Textually, this often meant the display of physical abuse, violent sex, and the squirting of body liquids both real and fake. Many of the films were produced on a low or with no budget at all, they were highly music-based, conceived as part of art installations or performances. The films were thus defiant not only because their content matter was meant to challenge the audience's aesthetic sensibility, but as they are by their nature extending into different practices, media, and genres, they are difficult to pinpoint. Both initiators of the NYFFDT belonged to the orbit of this grouping and the festival would become an important platform for the filmmakers associated with the Cinema of Transgression as well.
[50] Elsaesser, p. 95.
[51] Cf. Gross, p. 1.
[52] Tessa Hughes-Freeland, interviewed by Marie Sophie Beckmann, 13 September 2018.

showed the films at the Collective. Since the 1970s, Bold had been interested in the ongoings of the US-American film avant-garde and in 1978 he dedicated a weekly program at the Arsenal to Anthology Film Archives. After his return to Berlin, he expanded the Arsenal film collection around the focus on US avant-garde and underground film.[53] Viewed in this light, the NYFFDT became a node in the transatlantic network of institutions, curators and filmmakers. And in 1986, that network expanded further when the NYFDDT crossed the Atlantic itself. The NYFFDT entered Germany's *Kino*-circuit when German filmmaker Jürgen Brüning invited Hughes-Freeland and Troyano to take a selection[54] of the festival's second edition to Germany and organized their tour, starting in Berlin's Eiszeit Kino,[55] to Kommunales Kino in Hanover, Kino Lichtwerk in Bielefeld, Dusseldorf's Filminstitut, Mal Seh'n in Frankfurt/Main, Cologne's Filmhaus and Werkstattkino in Munich between March and April of 1986. Brüning had entered the downtown scene in 1983 when he showed his own Super 8 films and those from local Berlin filmmakers at the Pyramid Club. Troyano attended the screening and approached Brüning, remarking that the Berlin films were 'similar to what we do here.'[56]

'Super 8 activity there [in Germany generally and Berlin specifically] has no center. It has, rather, a multiplicity of centers which can be connected only by imaginary lines,'[57] writes filmmaker and theorist Keith Sanborn in the introductory text for *Super-8/Berlin. The architecture of division,* a group show he curated at Hallwalls in Buffalo in 1983. The various centers of this rhizomatic[58] structure were formed by the *Kinos,* many of which were equipped either for showing Super 8 alone or alongside 16 and 35mm, as well as by individuals or loosely structured groups providing the technical equipment,[59] and of course by the filmmakers themselves. Those were said to prefer Super 8 over 16mm

---

[53] Cf. *On the Collective for Living Cinema,* press text for exhibition, April 2007 <https://www.47orchard.org/exhibition/The_Collective.html>; *Edit Film Culture!*, press text for screening program, July 2018 <https://www.arsenal-berlin.de/en/arsenal-cinema/current-program/single/article/7299/2803.html> [both accessed 8 December 2018].

[54] The selection included films by Mary Bellis, Michael Oblowitz, Michael Mannetta, Ivan Gallitti, Manuel DeLanda, Richard Kern, Tessa Hughes-Freeland, Ela Troyano, Uzi Parnes, Erotic Psyche, Jo Andres, Tommy Turner, M. Henry Jones, W. Robinson, Edit DeAk, Sandy Tait, Julius Klein, Terry Stacey, Sokhi Wagner, Susan Pitt, Nick Zedd, Ellen Fisher, Ron Dumas, Cassandra Stark, and Penelope Wehrli.

[55] Eiszeit Kino was co-founded by Jürgen Brüning in a squatted building and moved locations in 1985. Next to the presentation of Super 8 films, Eiszeit also presented concerts and performances.

[56] Jürgen Brüning, interviewed by Marie Sophie Beckmann, 7 November 2018.

[57] Keith Sanborn, *Super-8/Berlin. The architecture of division* (Buffalo: Hallwalls, 1983), p. 2.

[58] Deleuze and Guattari conceive of the rhizome as a as a non-hierarchical structure with no predetermined beginning or end, without center, or rather, with multiple centers, multiple points of entry and ongoing potentials of multidirectional connectivity. Cf. Gilles Deleuze and Félix Guattari, *Rhizom* (Berlin: Merve, 1977), p. 21. Originally published by Les Éditions de Minuit in 1976.

[59] Sanborn refers to groups 'which were formed out of pre-existing friendships, common aesthetic and political interests, and sometimes sheer economic necessity' and notes that, though Berlin did not have its own own Super 8 film processing labs at the time, film could be send to to other West German cities. Cf. Sanborn, p. 2.

or video because of its affordability, convenient handling and because it had an existing *Kino* distribution. And since, as in the downtown scene too, 'many of the films [were] used in multi-media performances in clubs and cafés, [...] there [was] no particular fetishizing of "image quality"'.[60] In this sense, the films must have reminded Troyano of *what they did there*, not only because they bore resemblance in terms of their 'cheap' aesthetics, their non-commitment to genre, and their topical subject-matter (ranging from urban and night life documentation to comments on state violence), but also because they point to a collaborative and indisciplinary practice. For instance, similar to the collaborations between downtown musicians and filmmakers, we find the songs of German post-punk and new wave bands, such as Fehlfarben, DAF and Malaria, rhythmize Yana Yo's films; the artist collective Die Tödliche Doris collaborated on films, publications, performances and were also a band; and the filmmakers Axel Brand and Anette Maschmann became Brand-Maschmann, a 'two bodied system'[61] not unlike Bradley Eros and Aline Mare of New York's Erotic Psyche.

So what happened when the NYFFDT traveled from *here* to *there*? First, the shift from clubs to *Kinos* implied that the program itself became less messy and more pristine, meaning that the films were no longer part of an ongoing program in which they were mixed and blended with live performances, dance, and multimedia events, but were experienced within the more orderly conditions and specific spatial arrangement of the cinema hall. Second, as these screenings were attended by a local *Kino* audience and reviewed in local media, the films' images produced new imaginings of their place of origin.[62] From *Bielefelder Spiegel* to *Berliner Tagesspiegel*, from the West to the East, newspapers and magazines reacted with a multitude of reports and reviews. Bielefeld was excited to experience 'ein Streifzug für Entdeckungsfreudige durch die amerikanische Undergroundlandschaft' – 'a journey for explorers through the American underground landscape.'[63] While Berlin was glad to '[n]ot [see] the beautifully polished, melancholy poetry of Jim Jarmusch or Eric Mitchell [...], but the other, more original, direct, dirty New York.'[64] In New York, there had been little press coverage of the NYFFDT, except for announcements in the downtown papers and zines. The German media response, which was comparatively sweeping,

[60] Sanborn, p. 2.
[61] Ivi, p. 17.
[62] Bill Nichols suggests that once local/national cinemas and the work of individual filmmakers respectively enter a global film festival circuit and are exposed to new critics and audiences, new meanings will be produced which are inevitably different from those produced by an audience familiar with their local context. Cf. Nichols, p. 71.
[63] 'Ungewöhnliche Filme direkt aus New York', *Neue Westfälische,* 19 March 1986, p. 1 (my translation).
[64] Anke Sterneberg, 'Das ursprüngliche New York', *Der Tagesspiegel,* 16 March 1986, p. 64 (my translation).

reverberated to New York City and played no small role in the festival becoming a more recognized platform for exhibition as well as distribution.[65]

Further, the fact that most German newspaper articles, though some less enthusiastically than others, accentuated those films that would confirm New York City's, and especially the East Village's, reputation of being a gritty place where crime is high, drugs are cheap and sex is violent, hints to a yearning to see an 'original, direct, dirty New York.' And this yearning in turn brings us to conclusively think about the scene in yet another way, namely in terms of its imaginative structure. 'Scenes make the city a place,' writes Janine Marchessault, referring to scenic descriptions in books, scenes in films, but also cultural scenes. She mentions Flaubert, who turns Paris into a 'series of scenes,' and Warhol, who built a scene around his factory and who himself 'live[d] in a scene that he endlessly document[ed]',[66] directed at his own mythologization and, inevitably, that of New York City as well. A scene of/in a city thus makes that city *scenic*, fueling desire for an imagined place. Similarly, as the films of the downtown scene circulated, they made New York City visible in a particular way, creating images which anchor themselves more and more in the popular imagination, contributing to the city's perpetual mythologization.

The case of the NYFFDT therefore makes tangible not only how media and practices merge and inform each other within the framework of a local scene, but also how scenes overlap and connect to form an ever expanding network[67] in which people, institutions and events function as nodes and connectors, and in which images and imaginations are produced and reproduced, interpreted and reinterpreted as they circulate.[68]

---

[65] 'We got a ton of press. So when we came back, all of a sudden we were hot. Hot in this… whatever.' Ela Troyano, interviewed by Marie Sophie Beckmann, 7 September 2018. When the NYFFDT took place for the third time in New York in 1986, the 1 October issue of *International EYE* featured the whole program of the festival and noted that even though most filmmakers presented at the NYFFDT still hadn't received funding or grants for the production of their films and screening venues in New York City were becoming scarce, their films were increasingly screened in Europe, Canada and in other US cities, a development that was also due to the increasing success of the NYFFDT.

[66] All quotes taken from Janine Marchessault, 'Film Scenes: Paris, New York, Toronto', *Public*, 22.23 (2001), 59–75 (pp. 61, 67, 68).

[67] The network kept expanding when Brüning became film curator at Hallwalls Contemporary Art Center in Buffalo, he co-curated *Angles & Angels. The Buffalo Edition of the Fifth Annual New York Film Festival Downtown* (March 1989), a screening with selected films from the NYFFDT's 1988 edition. He also kept working with Ela Troyano, a.o. as a producer of her film *Latin Boys Go To Hell* (1997) and with Jo Andres, for whom he organized performances in Osnabrück and Budapest. Also Nick Zedd returned with solo screenings to many of the *Kinos* that hosted the NYFFDT and started to work closely with German distributor Uwe Hamm of artware.

[68] I want to thank Jürgen Brüning, Tessa Hughes-Freeland, Richard Kern and Ela Troyano for sharing their time and memories.

Cathode Mamma: Post-punk and Television in Italy
Francesco Spampinato, Alma Mater Studiorum - Università di Bologna

Abstract

Spanning from the late 1970s throughout the 1980s, the music-based subculture known as post-punk was characterized by an antagonistic attitude towards mass media and pop culture. This resulted frequently in acts of appropriation and parody, conducted through a multidisciplinary set of visual and performative forms of artistic expression that were complementary to music, namely film, video, performance, fashion, design and marketing. Borrowing tactics from historical and post-war avant-gardes – from Futurism to Situationism – and in line with the postmodernist ethos of such movements as the Pictures Generation, one of post-punk's recurring targets was television, blamed for its power to produce clichés with which viewers identified. While much has been written on American and British post-punk, little is known on peripheral scenes where this subculture assumed specific traits. This paper focuses on Italian post-punk and its unique 'response' to the epochal passage in Italy from state television to a privately owned, diversified, commercial mediascape. Although rooted in the 1977 counterculture, which harshly criticized mass media, Italian post-punk developed an ambiguous relationship with television, shifting from critique to complicity. For some, TV was the subject of sonic and visual parodies; for others, those who embraced the music video form, it became a useful medium. The paper reconstructs the cultural milieu of Italian post-punk in parallel with the diffusion of commercial television.

The Post-punk Gesamtkunstwerk *and The Early Case of Krisma*

Whereas the punk movement that arose in the late 1970s was characterized by a spontaneous, fiery and rude attitude against authority and the status quo, post-punk, which developed right after punk and throughout the 1980s, distinguished itself for its avant-garde sensibility based on a self-conscious, at times even programmatic attempt to reimagine the codes of individual expression and social behaviour. Centred on music, the post-punk subculture included also a diverse and multidisciplinary array of visual and performative forms of artistic expression, notably moving images, hybrid types of performance, visual communication and fashion design. Articulated in various subgenres (e.g. new wave, no wave, mutant disco, punk-funk, cold wave, goth, industrial, EBM, synthpop, minimal synth, new romantics etc.), post-punk sound and lyrics were evidently unable, alone, to fulfil the need for self-expression felt by the generation that came of age at that time, during an era marked by the rise of neoliberalism and the early proliferation of affordable, electronic technology.

Borrowing tactics and signs from both historical and post-war avant-gardes – Dadaism, Futurism, Situationism and Fluxus immediately come to mind – and in line with the postmodernist ethos of coeval art movements such as the Pictures Generation, the post-punk artists, filmmakers, performers and designers took advantage of music to develop forms of *Gesamtkunstwerk* that offered youth new perspectives from which to face reality. Music critic Simon Reynolds has highlighted the conceptual dimension of post-punk in his seminal book on the movement, as when he asserted:

> On a mission and fully in the now, post-punk created a thrilling sense of urgency. The new records came thick and fast, classic after classic. Even the incomplete experiments and interesting failures carried a powerful utopian charge and contributed to an exhilarating collective conversation. Certain groups existed more on the level of an idea than a fully realized proposition, but nonetheless made a difference just by existing and talking a good game in the press.[1]

In 1987, when post-punk was coming to an end, two books, curiously published by the same English publisher, Methuen, acknowledged the major influence that the art school education played on many rock musicians from the 1960s: Simon Frith and Howard Horne's *Art into Pop* and John Walker's *Cross-Overs: Art into Pop/Pop into Art*. 'Art-school trained musicians took ingredients from the avant-garde but changed the recipe', wrote Frith and Horne, and 'stirred Pop art ideas too – what we got was not art vs. commerce, but commerce as art, as the canvas for the musician's creativity, individuality, style'.[2] The history of rock is certainly also a history of image but 'art rock', the term these authors employed, is a much more hybrid phenomenon. By applying to music and its marketing, processes based on originality, experimentation and critical thinking learned in art schools, art rockers broke down, once and for all, the ideological dichotomy between high and low culture on which modernism relied. If in the modernist era the avant-garde defined itself in opposition to popular culture, now pop culture was embraced unapologetically, as an arena in which to develop metalinguistic discourses.

The conceptual nature of post-punk emerges clearly from its deconstructionist approach to mass media codes and clichés. Television, in particular, was often the target of acts of appropriation and parody, blamed for its subliminal

---

[1] Simon Reynolds, *Rip It Up and Start Again: Post-punk 1978–1984* (New York: Penguin Books, 2005), pp. 10–11.
[2] Simon Frith and Howard Horne, *Art into Pop* (London and New York: Methuen, 1987), p. 65.

power to elicit political consensus and induce consumerism. The multimedia production of bands such as Devo and Talking Heads in US, and Cabaret Voltaire and Psychic TV in the UK, is representative of post-punk's alignment with postmodernist thinking, which for what regards television is epitomized in Jean Baudrillard's idea of 'hyperreality', according to which television replaced reality with its *simulacrum*, not merely a copy of the real but a truth in its own right. While much has been written on American and British post-punk, little is known on peripheral scenes. A case in point is that of Italy, where the post-punk subculture developed a unique 'response' to the passage, that was epochal for the country, from the monopoly of state television Rai to a diversified, commercial mediascape. This allowed Silvio Berlusconi to establish his own media empire, Fininvest, and turn Italian television into a duopoly that, with some variations, still persists today.

Italian post-punk's relationship with television, which this article aims to map and explore, has been ambiguous, shifting over time from critique to complicity to autonomy. As a recurring subject of sonic and visual appropriations and parodies, for those who embraced the music video form, television also became the medium through which they developed metalinguistic forms of reflection. A quintessential case was that of Krisma – a duo composed of Maurizio Arcieri and Christina Moser, formerly known as Chrisma – who referred recurrently to TV in their lyrics, visual identity and music videos, but also made countless TV appearances, collaborated on TV programs and at some point even ran a TV channel. Their early thoughts on TV are summed up in the title-track of their 1980 album *Cathode Mamma*, whose lyrics state: 'I like television sets because they have voices for when you are alone […]. Cathode mamma kiss me, in my cable paradise […]. I like television sets. They fill my empty rooms with electronic stone […]. They never go to sleep but glitter through the night [….] They always stay at home and keep my bed so warm'.[3]

Krisma's song describes the TV set as a maternal presence in the home, able to keep company to the lonely viewer as if it was a real person. The 7-inch record cover, conceived by visionary art director Mario Convertino, shows seven flows of TV sets, each broadcasting an image of Christina, dropping down from the letters that form the band's name and disappearing into a dark void (fig. 1a). Portraits of the musicians taken from a TV screen appear on the cover of the album and the popular single *Many Kisses* (fig. 1b, 1c). The duo had already played with similar issues in 1979, via the 16mm promo for the song *Aurora B.* – when they still went by the name of Chrisma – directed by Sergio Attardo, which in fact could be considered one of the earliest 'music videos' ever produced in Italy. Scenes of the two in erotic moments that end with Maurizio's attempted suicide alternate with scenes of Christina in a dark room, singing behind TV sets that transmit her live image, while another one broadcasts the footage of a

---

[3] Krisma, *Cathode Mamma*, Polydor 1980, lyrics of the song retrieved from http://krisma.mayancaper.net/records/lyrics_cathode.html [accessed 12 December 2019].

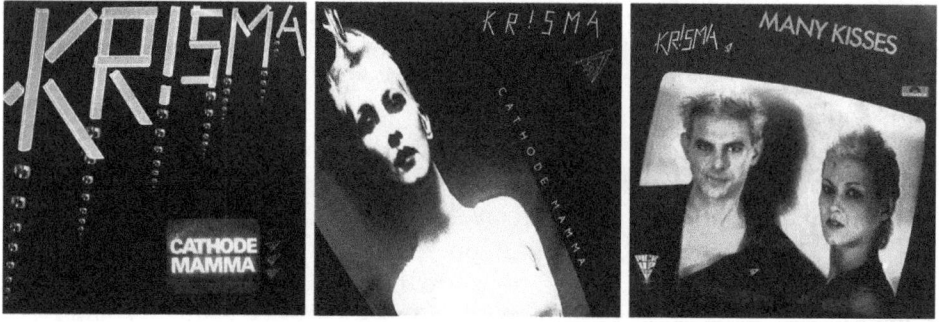

Fig. 1a, 1b, 1c: Krisma, record covers. From left: *Cathode Mamma* (7"); *Cathode Mamma* (LP); *Many Kisses* (7"). Polydor, 1980. Design: Mario Convertino.

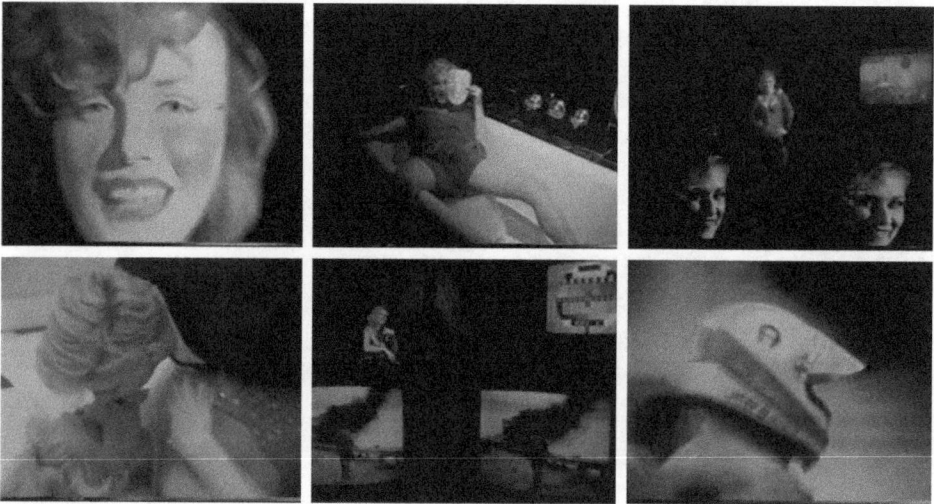

Fig. 2: Chrisma, *Aurora* B., 1979, 16 mm, 4'52", Color. Producer: Polydor. Director: Sergio Attardo.

Formula 1 incident, before setting on the Rai test pattern that appeared on the screen when no programming was broadcast, usually at night (fig. 2).

Post-1977 Bologna: Gaznevada, Grabinsky and the Stupid Set

Television was a major issue for various bands that emerged from Bologna, where Italian post-punk was literally born from the ashes of the movement of 1977, made of students and left-wing extra-parliamentary groups who demanded direct action. The reference points that allowed the birth of post-punk in Bologna were: the experimental university major in DAMS (Disciplines of Art, Music and Spectacle), the yearly Performance Week festival, the creative squat

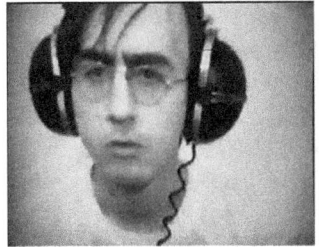 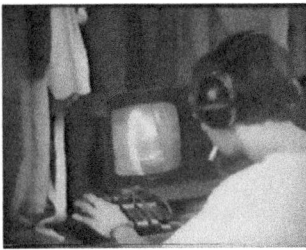 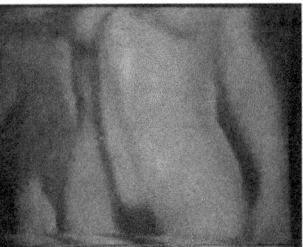

Fig. 3: Gaznevada, *Telepornovisione*, 1980, video, 7'35", b/w.
Producer: Italian Records. Director: Grabinsky. Courtesy: Oderso Rubini.

Traumfabrik, the pirate radio station Radio Alice, the music venue Punkreas, the record store Disco d'Oro, and Oderso Rubini's record label Harpo's Music, which later became Italian Records. Many people who gravitated around this network had been involved in the 1977 riots, culminating in the 'Conference Against Repression'. The event featured a performance by Bolognese punk band Centro d'Urlo Metropolitano (the 'Center for Metropolitan Screams'), whose song *Mamma Dammi la Benza* ('Mom Gimme Fuel'), with its indomitable pace and allusion to the Molotov bomb, became a late anthem of the uprising.

Rechristened Gaznevada, the group's earliest commentary on television was *Teleporno T.V.* (1979), a noise composition in line with the style of industrial music built around the still punk refrain: 'posso fare il guardone con la mia *telepornovisione*' ('I can be a voyeur with my *telepornovision*'). The song referred to those TV channels that used to broadcast pornographic content, but also the diffusion of CCTV in public spaces, as emerges in the music video directed by Grabinsky (Emanuele Angiuli, Renato De Maria and Walter Mameli), a group of videomakers also from Bologna. This shows a guy who tunes a TV set to the live images of a couple in intimate moments (fig. 3). Austrian scholar Klemens Gruber has noted that a trope for the 1977 *intelligentsia* was 'the relationship between the artistic avant-garde and mass media: two snakes who devour each other. The importance of media for a cultural transformation and the actuality of the historical avant-garde, submitted to the conditions of the information society, become determinant fields for their explorations'.[4]

As police repression, that resulted in the murder of student Francesco Lorusso, and some rioters' sympathies for the terrorist group the Red Brigades brought the movement to an end, the 1980 deadly bomb attack on the Bologna train station and the diffusion of heroin signalled the beginning of a new phase of cultural opposition to the dominant order. Unlike Radio Alice, a model of media autonomy at the core of the 1977 movement, which is the focus of Gruber's study, Gaznevada and Grabinsky developed a critical commentary on mass media from within a culture of commodities, namely the record industry, albeit

[4] Klemens Gruber, *L'Avanguardia Inaudita: Comunicazione e Strategie nei Movimenti degli Anni Settanta* (1989), trans. by Elfi Reiter (Genoa: Costa & Nolan, 1997), p. 16 (my translation).

one that was extremely 'DIY'. Gaznevada referred to TV again on the cover of the single *Nevadagaz* (1980), the first of Italian Records' releases, designed by Anna Persiani after inputs from the band's members, showing fading portraits taken off a TV screen (fig. 4), and the B-side song *Blue TV Set*. TV screens broadcasting musicians are the leitmotiv of the covers of their 1985 album *Back to the Jungle* and single *Living in the Jungle*, but at that point the band had already shifted towards a cheesy Italo disco style, a move that was harshly criticized by their early punk and post-punk aficionados (fig. 5).

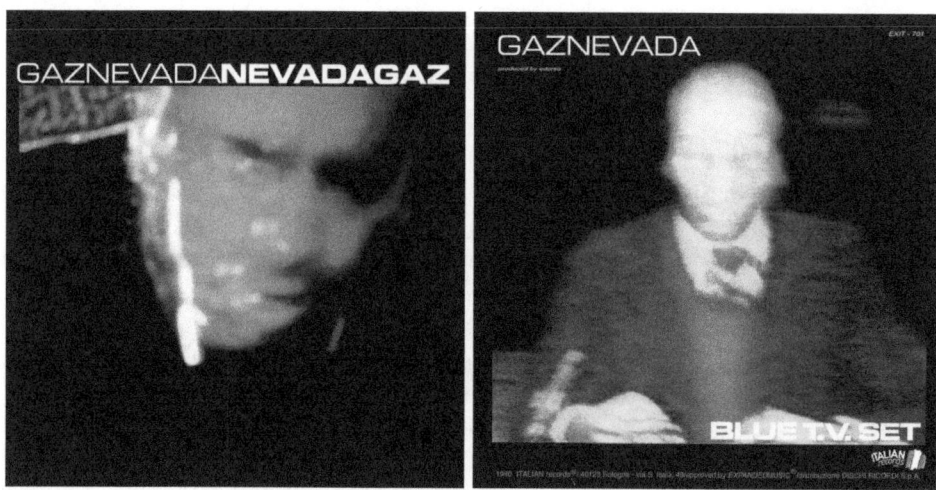

Fig. 4: Gaznevada, record cover (front and back): *Nevadagaz* (7"), Italian Records, 1980. Design: Anna Persiani. Courtesy: Oderso Rubini.

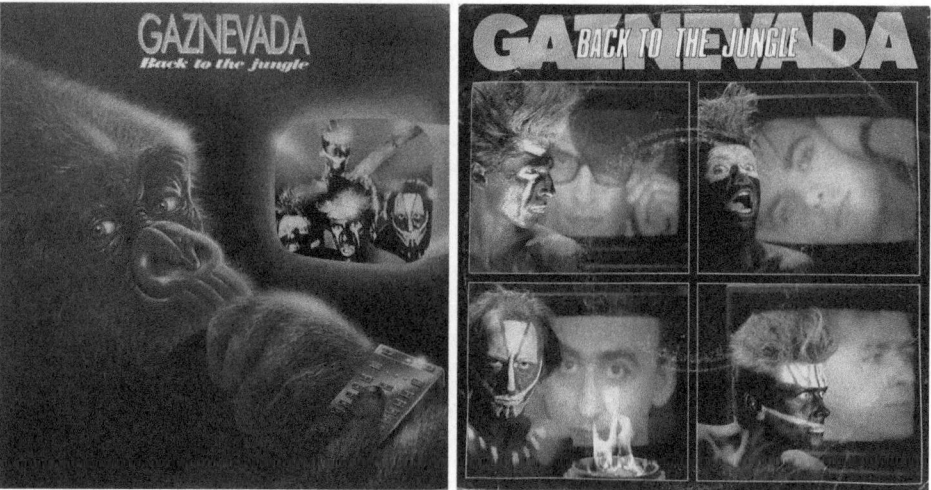

Fig. 5: Gaznevada, record covers. From left: *Back to the Jungle* (LP); *Back to the Jungle* (7"). Both EMI, 1985. Illustration (LP): Kenji Sumura.

Meanwhile, two of Gaznevada's original members, Giampiero Huber and Giorgio Lavagna, had formed the band and multimedia project Stupid Set. In the hilarious music video of *Hello, I Love You* (1981), a cover of a famous song by the Doors, directed by Grabinksy, the musicians are filmed as they perform the song inside an empty room, with TV sets in the place of their heads, broadcasting static and their zoomed in mouths (fig. 6). For the Stupid Set, Grabinsky realized also the *Tape Show* (1980), a wall of twenty TV sets, sponsored by Philips,

Fig. 6: Stupid Set, *Hello, I Love You*, 1981, video, 3'10", Color.
Producer: Italian Records.
Director: Grabinsky.
Courtesy: Oderso Rubini.

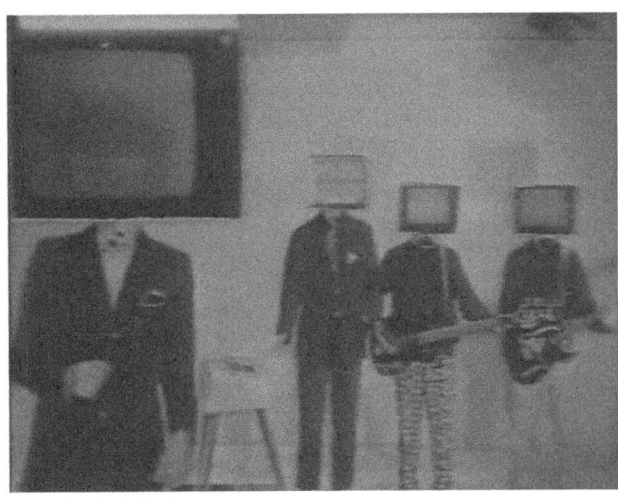

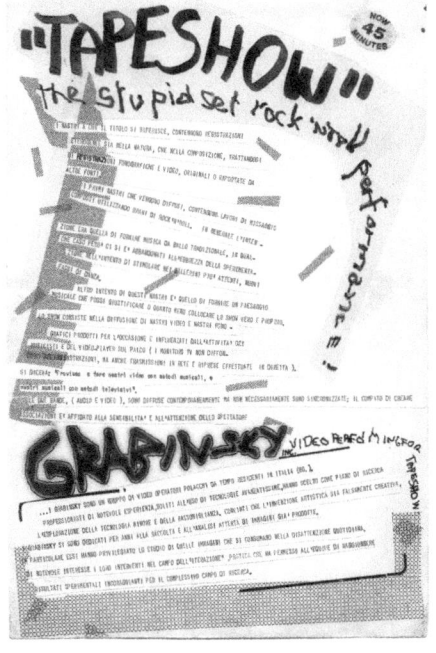

Fig. 7: Stupid Set and Grabinksy, *Tape Show*, collage for the flyer, 1980. Design: Giampiero Huber and Giorgio Lavagna. Courtesy: Oderso Rubini.

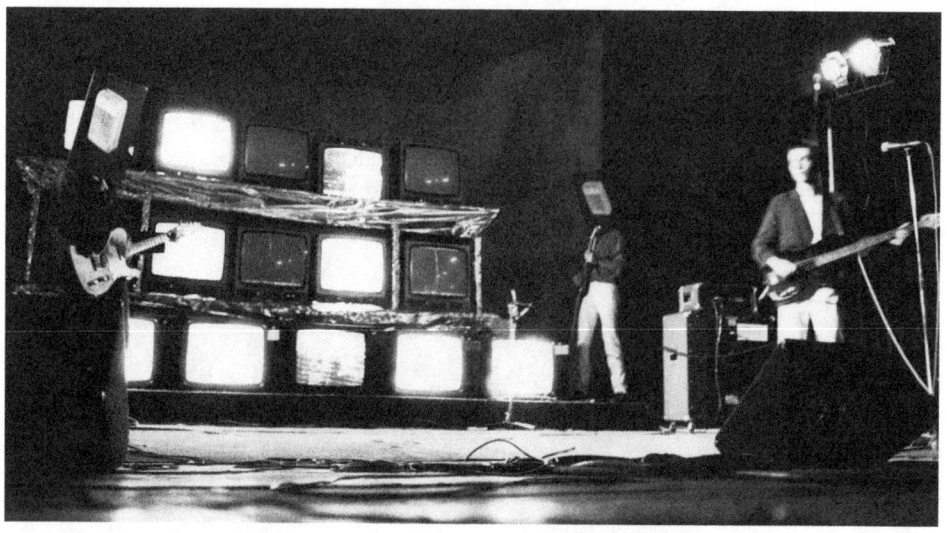

Fig. 8: Stupid Set and Grabinksy, *Tape Show*, performance and set,
IV International Performance Week, Bologna, 1980.
Producer: Italian Records. Performance: Stupid Set. Set Design: Grabinsky.
Courtesy: Oderso Rubini.

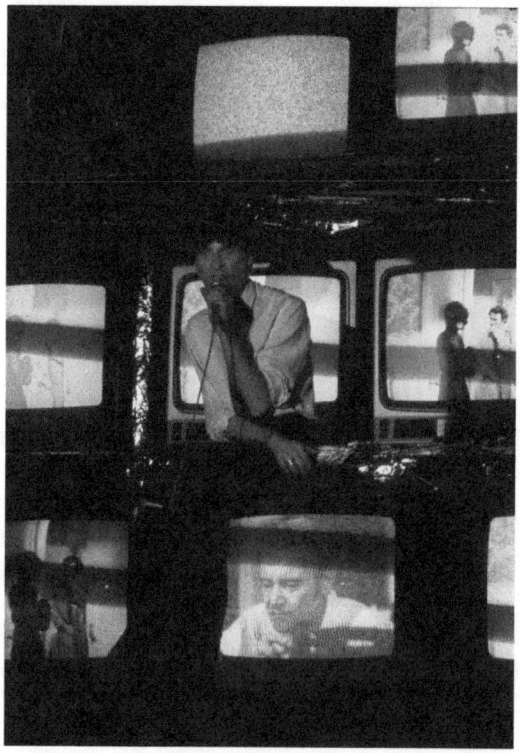

Fig. 9: Stupid Set and Grabinksy,
Tape Show, performance and set, IV
International Performance Week,
Bologna, 1980.
Producer: Italian Records.
Performance: Stupid Set. Set Design:
Grabinsky. Courtesy: Oderso Rubini.

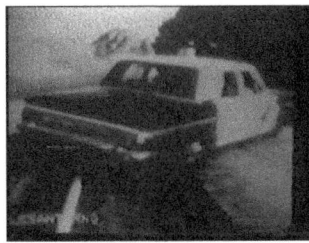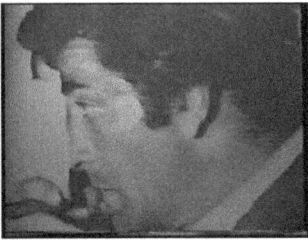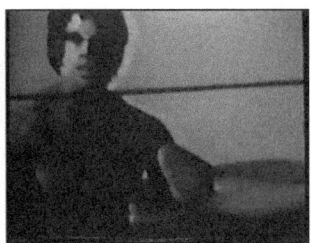

Fig. 10: Grabinsky, *Tape Show*, 1980, video, b/w.
Producer: Italian Records. Courtesy: Emanuele Angiuli.

broadcasting cut-up footage from popular TV series such as *Hulk* and *Columbo*, used as a backdrop of a live show by the band in Bologna's Piazza Maggiore (figg. 7, 8, 9). The *Tape Show* was also featured in the city's fourth edition of the 'Performance Week', when the group added toy instruments to their equipment. With a montage based on abrupt juxtapositions and obsessive loops, the *Tape Show* echoes the allegorical procedures of some American visual artists associated to the Pictures Generation, such as Jack Goldstein and Dara Birnbaum, and notably the latter's video *Technology/Transformation: Wonder Woman* (1978) (fig. 10). Employing TV sets on stage became a kind of trend at that time; other Italian post-punk bands that did so were Pale TV (who also referred to TV with their own name and in their 1981 song *B/W Television Shock-Show*) from Parma and Scortilla from Genoa.

The Stupid Set invoked television again in the song *Basset*, the B-side of the 12-inch *Soft Parade* (Mmmh Records, 1981), based on a text recited over the audio of an episode of the TV series *Hunter*. The group's ultimate project on TV was *Soul of Trade*, recorded in 1980–1981 but released only in 2015 by Spittle Records: a series of sound compositions that were supposed to be performed within another multimedia installation. Equally inspired by the Residents' deconstructionist parodies of muzak and William S. Burroughs' cut-up technique, as it emerges from his seminal book *The Electronic Revolution* (Berlin: Expanded Media Editions, 1970), the project was based on 'the use of video/audio recordings of commercials and newscasts', to be employed 'as harmonic material for some pop songs'.[5] For the live show, the group had envisioned a performance from behind a Venetian blind onto which TV footage and slides would be projected, while a CCTV system would transmit the live images of the performers on two TV sets in the apron.

The Stupid Set's interest in the subliminal nature of mass media and the automation implied in 'video/audio recordings' and editing techniques is also at the centre of their last project, which was presented at the 1982 'Contaminazioni' festival in Bologna. *Psychodisco* consists in a series of cut-up compositions

---

[5] The Stupid Set, 'The Silent Generation (nota privata)', undated text appearing in the liner notes of the vinyl release of *Soul of Trade* (Milan: Spittle Records, 2015), unpaged.

based on appropriated samples (recorded in 1982 but this one too released only in 2015 by Opilec Music), paired with a video directed by band's member Umberto Lazzari. Less a music video than a video art project in its own right, the 34-minute amalgam contains: illustrations of Maya gods; pixelated animations (i.e. a deserted landscape with a cactus and a buffalo skull, a skyline, and a guy watching TV at home) made with a Commodore 64 computer by Francesco Chiarini; and footage recorded by Lazzari from Dutch and Italian television: mostly commercials featuring children smiling, eyes blinking, a choreography of women on a beach, and fragments typical of the iconography of ads for household products (fig. 11).

The Rise of Music Videos: The Peculiar Case of Mister Fantasy

The music video is usually intended as a short promo film for TV that integrates a song with imagery, whose birth could be situated around the mid 1970s. According to the writer Pier Vittorio Tondelli – who has acknowledged the innovative impact of Italian post-punk culture in many of his writings – this peculiar type of media genre soon evolved 'from a simple means of distribution and promotion of an album to a product [...] that recalls the avant-gardes' old dream of total art: cinema, music, theatre, poetry, computer art that interact in

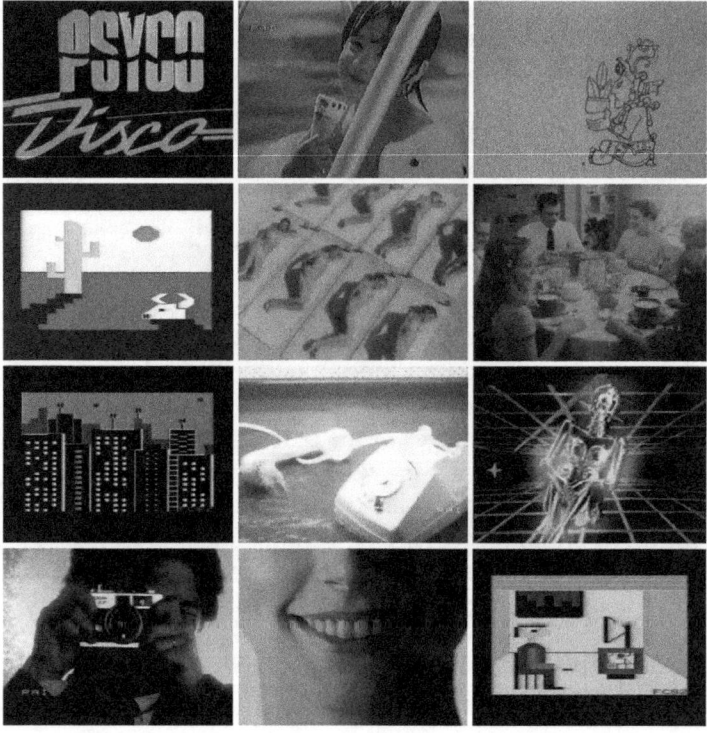

Fig. 11: Stupid Set, *Pyschodisco*, 1982, video, 34', Color. Director: Umberto Lazzari. Courtesy: Oderso Rubini.

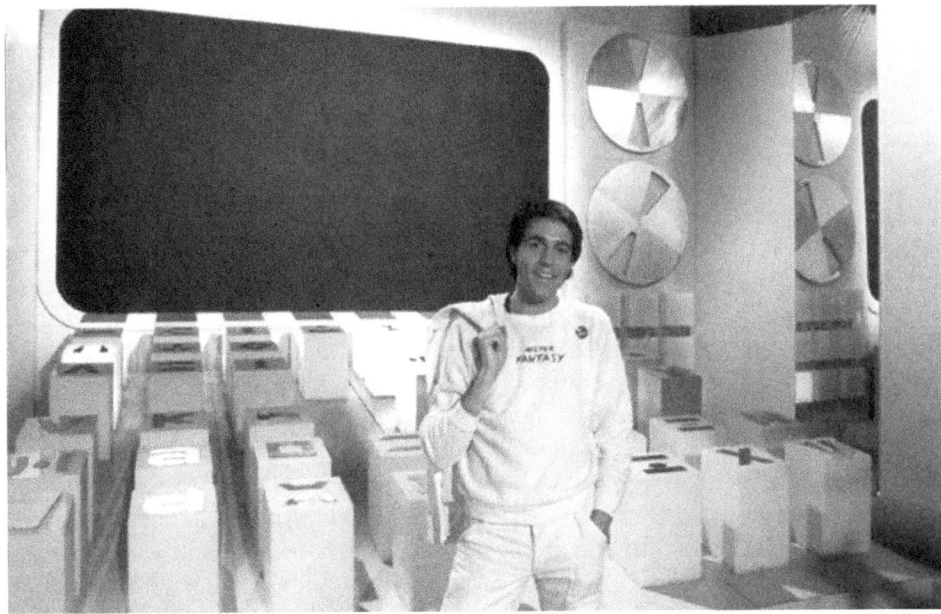

Fig. 12: Carlo Massarini in the TV studio of Mister Fantasy, Rai 1, 1981.
Design: Mario Convertino.

the space of a few minutes'.[6] As this was evident for Grabinsky's production and Lazzari's video of *Psychodisco*, which circulated in art circles and clearly aligned with that of contemporary experimental filmmakers and visual artists working with video, performance and installation, it was less immediate for Attardo's film for Chrisma's *Aurora B.* (1979), because this was made expressly for TV, which is rarely considered a context in which artistic forms of critical thinking are experimented. This preconception changed with the arrival of *Mister Fantasy* on Rai 1, the first Italian TV program to be exclusively dedicated to music videos, which debuted on May 1981, three months before the launch of MTV in the U.S.

Conceived by TV producer Paolo Giaccio and hosted by Carlo Massarini, the program developed a distinct postmodernist style based on effects of fragmentation and pastiche thanks to the space-age studio, Convertino's videographics, and the music videos directed by a roster of emerging practitioners (fig. 12). Massarini defined *Mister Fantasy*'s studio without audience a 'hyperspace […] empty, aseptic, out of time and space'.[7] Strictly related to Baudrillard's idea of 'hyperreality', the concept of 'hyperspace' was theorized by Fredric Jameson,

[6] Pier Vittorio Tondelli, 'Videosexy', *Alter Alter*, 6 (June 1984), p. 28 [repr. in Pier Vittorio Tondelli, *Un Weekend Postmoderno. Cronache dagli anni Ottanta* (Milan: Bompiani, 1990)], pp. 218–219).
[7] Carlo Massarini, 'Il Fantasy Lessico. L'Iperspazio è Abitato da Creature della Notte', *Segnocinema*, 8 (May 1983), p. 26 [reprinted in *MTV. Il Nuovo Mondo della Televisione*, ed. by Domenico Baldini (Rome: Castelvecchi, 2000), p. 174].

another key postmodernist thinker, as a space that transcends 'the capacities of the individual human body to locate itself, to organize its immediate surrounding perceptually', and that for this reason is a symbol of 'the incapacity of our minds, at least at present, to map the great global multinational and decentred communicational network in which we find ourselves caught as individual subjects'.[8] As a hyperspace, *Mister Fantasy* epitomized the process of media integration that television entailed and its alienating and disorienting effects.

Active until 1984, in its 100 episodes the program featured also 80 original music videos produced in-house, alongside music videos mainly from the US and the UK. Although these were mostly made for Italian pop singers and songwriters, and a handful of post-punk acts, *Mister Fantasy* was not only responsible for bringing the post-punk aesthetics to TV: inspired by the post-punk *milieu*, it also manufactured a postmodernist *Gesamtkunstwerk* in the form of a commercial product. This, however, had a double effect: while challenging the language of TV, it also helped to reinforce its persuasive power. Indeed, on the one hand *Mister Fantasy* broke with traditional notions of media entertainment and turned mainstream television into a context for artistic expression and experimental communication. On the other, the program exemplified what Umberto Eco called 'Neo-Television', a new type of television that emerged in the 1980s, which was self-referential, based on an obsessive audiovisual flow, the juxtaposition of different layers of communications and, precisely, the convergence of various media.[9]

At the core of Neo-TV, as media scholar Gianni Sibilla argues, the music video is based on a kaleidoscopic merging of various elements and 'is aware of its role, its position within the music and audiovisual context and does not miss the opportunity to expose its proper communication modes'.[10] Interestingly enough, some music videos produced by *Mister Fantasy* adopted self-referentiality as a deconstructionist tactic as in the case of the 1982 video trilogy realized for Krisma's songs, by a team that included the video directors Piccio Raffanini and Attardo, the photographer Edo Bertoglio, and the art director Convertino. Filmed in Bali, the trilogy opens with the *Miami* video, based on a scene with Maurizio wondering on a paradise beach, armed and threatening, intercut with flashes of a TV set tuned to the new-born channel Rete 4 broadcasting the Vietnam War movie *The Soldier's Story* (Ian McLeod, 1981) (fig. 13). The anti-war ethos, based on the dichotomy beauty/cruelty, persists in the videos of *Water* and *Samora Club*, where Christina's glamour clashes with the shadows of

[8] Fredric Jameson, *Postmodernism, or, the Cultural Logic of Late Capitalism* (Durham, NC: Duke University Press, 1991), p. 44.
[9] Umberto Eco, 'TV: Transparency Lost' (1983) in *Telegen: Art and Television*, trans. and ed. by Dieter Daniels and Stephan Berg (Munich: Himer Verlag GmbH, 2015), pp. 207-218.
[10] Gianni Sibilla, *Musica da Vedere. Il Videoclip nella Televisione Italiana* (Rome: RAI – ERI, 1999), p. 43 (my translation).

a submarine in the first, and of Maurizio in military attire and anxious to use his knife in the latter (figg. 14, 15).

Along with this explicit anti-war reading, another interpretation emerges: in manufacturing a hyperreality based on criteria of entertainment and advertising, television desensitizes its audience regarding the world's real problems such as war, notably the Cold War that was ongoing at that time, while producing

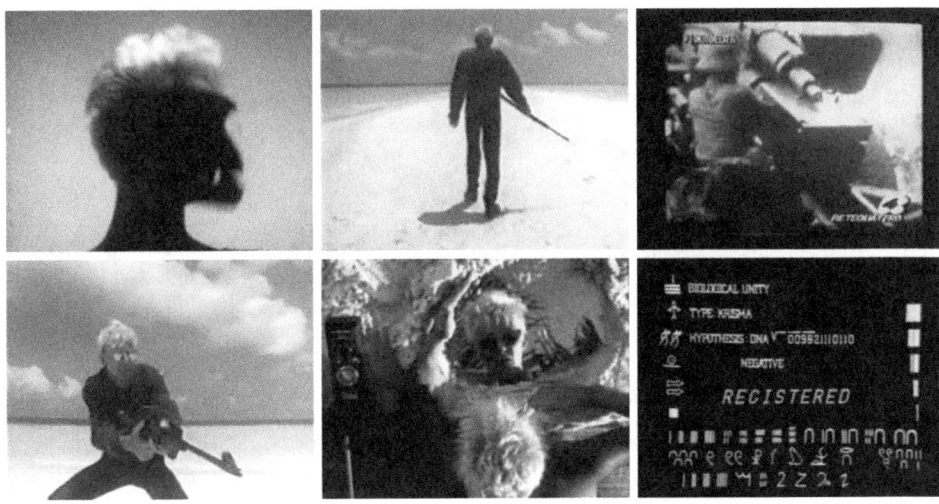

Fig. 13: Krisma, *Miami*, 1982, video, 3'57", Color.
Producer: Mister Fantasy, Rai 1. Directors: Piccio Raffanini and Sergio Attardo. Photography: Edo Bertoglio. Art Director: Mario Convertino.

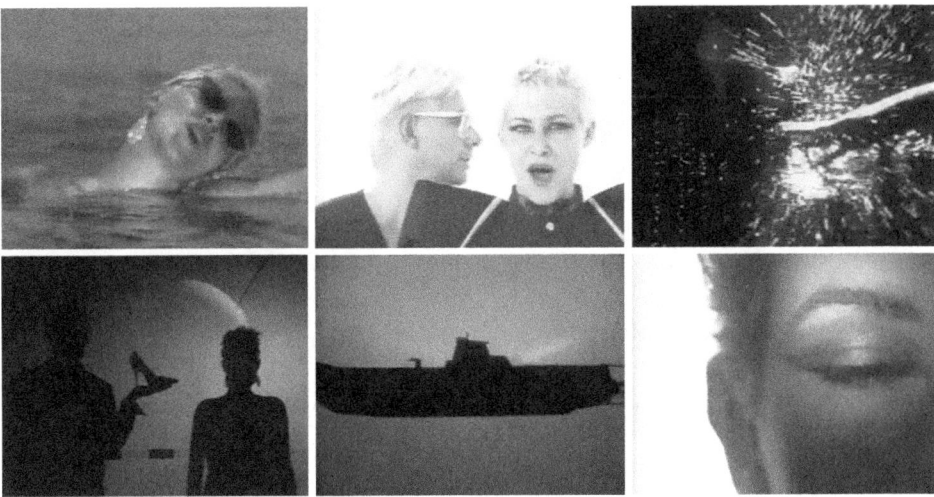

Fig. 14: Krisma, *Water*, 1982, video, 4'25", Color.
Producer: Mister Fantasy, Rai 1. Directors: Piccio Raffanini and Sergio Attardo. Photography: Edo Bertoglio. Art Director: Mario Convertino.

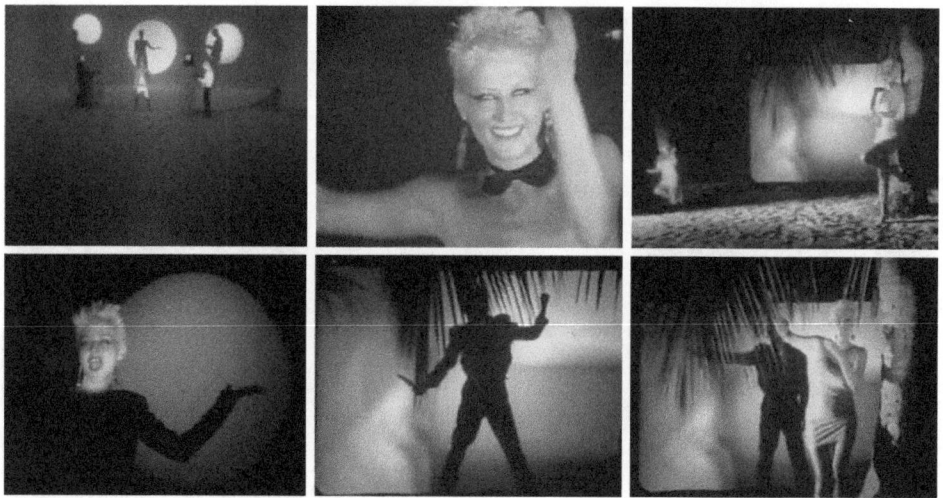

Fig. 15: Krisma, *Samora Club*, 1982, video, 3'25", Color.
Producer: Mister Fantasy, Rai 1. Directors: Piccio Raffanini and Sergio Attardo. Photography:
Edo Bertoglio. Art Director: Mario Convertino.

subtle forms of propaganda. By juxtaposing original scenes with TV footage and Convertino's infographics, exposing elements of the backstage (e.g. a backdrop) and playing on the ambiguity between reality and its double (e.g. the shadows), this trilogy elicits a metalinguistic reflection on the media's power to manipulate reality. *Mister Fantasy* produced also the video for Krisma's *I'm Not in Love* (1984), directed by Giancarlo Bocchi, although this was less concerned with television per se than the propaganda of totalitarian regimes at large. Along with Krisma, the only other 'proper' post-punk act featured in the program was Garbo. Out of the three music videos produced for him by Mister Fantasy, the one for *Radioclima* (1984), directed by Raffanini, is characterized by the presence of radios and TV sets, alluded to as media able to produce stereotypes with which the audience unwillingly identifies.

Less post-punk than pop, but similarly interested in facing issues of media representation and influence through visuals and performance, is the video for Matia Bazar's *Il Video Sono Io* (*I Am the Video*, 1983), this one too directed by Raffanini. In line with the geometrical set designed by postmodernist design group Alchimia co-founded by Alessandro Mendini, the musicians perform a theatrical choreography based on mechanical moves. The highlight is the presence of six totems, each made of four piled TV sets, which alternate the face with the fractured full-length figure of the glamorous singer Antonella Ruggiero (fig. 16). Loosely labelled 'videosculpture', this peculiar mode of display was employed at that time by artists such as Friederike Pezold and Studio Azzurro to allegorize how media can fragment the viewer's subjectivity. Andy Warhol's film *Outer and Inner Space* (1966) also comes to mind, but unlike Edie Sedgwick, who tries to

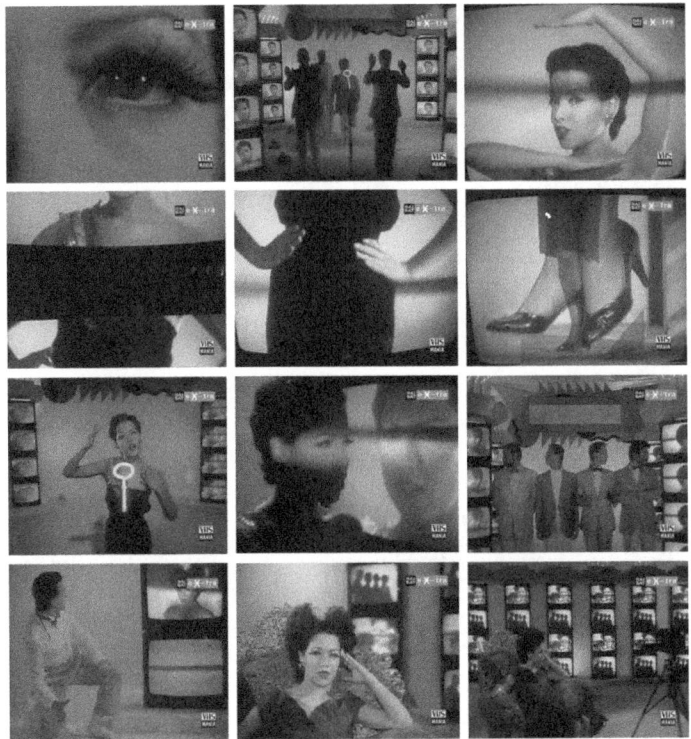

Fig. 16: Matia Bazar, *Il Video Sono Io*, 1983, video, 2'40", Color. Producer: Mister Fantasy, Rai 1. Director: Piccio Raffanini. Set Design: Alchimia.

get hold of her media duplicate, Antonella, like Christina in Chrisma's *Aurora B.*, seems disinterested in interacting with her double; self-confident and in control, their media image coincides with their own selves.

The Italian Post-punk Music Video

Examples such as these prove that the music video could not only challenge the modernist dogma, according to which art is defined by the fact of being displayed in an artistic context and in opposition to popular culture, but that they could also trigger an even more radical deconstructionist effect than art, because it criticizes the media from within. This was not always the case of course. Indeed, most music videos have neither the ability nor the intention of challenging media and, as Dick Hebdige has written, they could 'be seen as a further congealment/commodification of "authentic" culture into "inauthentic" (packaged) product in a process which leads to the primacy of the televisual: the simulacrum'.[11] Interestingly, visual and performative forms of critical thinking

[11] Dick Hebdige, *Hiding in the Light: On Images and Things* (London and New York: Routledge, 1998), p. 237.

in line with the visual arts are more often developed by people associated with the loosely-defined 'alternative' music genres, that is genres whose very existence is legitimated by being oppositional to the status quo. In this sense, being coincidental with the rise of music television, post-punk had a major responsibility in bringing procedures rooted in critical thinking from the arts to pop culture via the music video form.

Italy has always been at the forefront of the evolution of forms of convergence between music and moving images. As popular music was so ingrained in Italian culture, from its launch in 1954, Rai produced several programs in which music, visuals and performance converged, notably the live broadcast of the Sanremo music festival, as well as dozens of variety shows and short films. In the late 1950s the Società Internazionale Fonovisione produced the Cinebox, a coin-operated 16 mm film projector jukebox, which was sold worldwide and installed in public places like cafes, following in the footsteps of the Scopitone, its French precursor. The idea of pairing songs with a movie expanded into a film genre called 'musicarello', a type of musical movie that became highly popular in the 1960s. Italian music video scholars Domenico Baldini, Bruno Di Marino and Domenico Liggeri all dedicate considerable space to the evolution of the music video in Italy in their publications. However, aside for *Mister Fantasy* and Krisma, they fully ignore Grabinsky as well as the rest of the Italian post-punk videography.

Examples of post-punk music videos produced in Italy in the 1980s that deserve to be rediscovered and re-contextualized, within both the evolution of media and the arts, are: Tony Verità's video for Litfiba's *Dea del Fujiama* (1981); Toni Occhiello's for Doris Norton's *Psychoraptus* (1982); Corso Salani's for Litfiba's *Der Krieg* (Guerra, 1982); Giancarlo Onorato's for Underground Life's *La Tempesta* (1983); Alessandro Furlan's for Jo Squillo's *Bizarre* (1984); Paul Allman's for Ruins' *Fire!* (1984); Carlo Isola's for Neon's *Isolation* (1986); Metamorphosi's for Maurizio Marsico's *Mefisto Funk* and *Lovely Racers* (both 1986); Giovanotti Mondani Meccanici's for their own *Et Maintenant* (1986) and for Alexander Robotnik's *C'est la Vie* (1987); and Massimo Gasparini's for Plasticoast's *Canzone Dada* (1988). The Italian Records videos for Gaznevada's *Antistatico Shock* (1982), Hi-Fi Bros' *The Line* (1983), and N.O.I.A.'s *Do You Wanna Dance* (1984) are still uncredited. The same is true of those for KKD's *I Need Help* (1981), Frigidaire Tango's *Recall* and *Vanity Fair* (both 1983), Diaframma's *Siberia* (1984), and HAKKAH's *No Way Out* (1986). This is just a handful of music videos that returned to public attention thanks to the internet, uploaded by their directors, the bands or their fans, but hopefully more obscure examples are on the way.

Other music videos still offer commentaries on television and its subliminal power. Luca Setti and Marina Spada's video for Maurizio Marsico's *Frisk the Frog* (1982), at the crossroads of new wave, rap and Italo disco, whose lyrics have been written by comic artist Massimo Mattioli, alternates an Intellivision frog videogame with the soap-opera-styled scenes of a couple singing. The broken

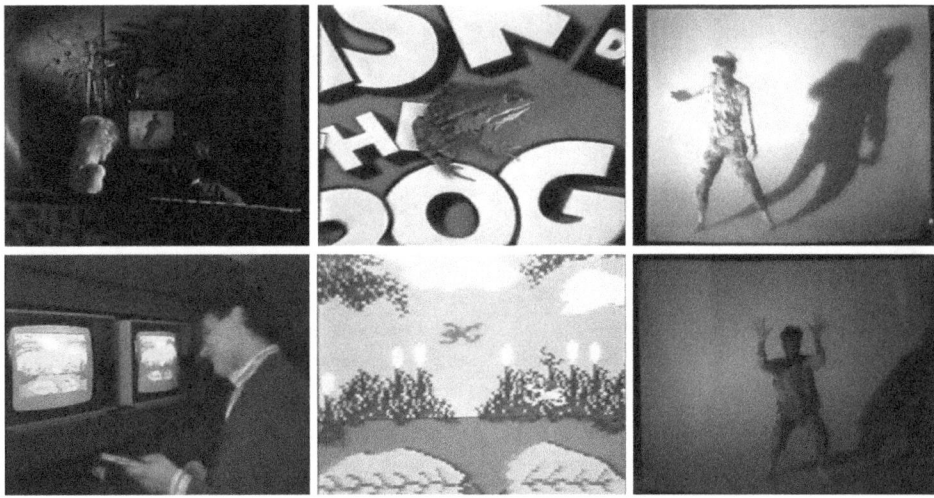

Fig. 17: Maurizio Marsico, *Frisk the Frog*, 1982, video, 5'13", Color.
Directors: Luca Setti and Marina Spada. Photography: Toni Meneguzzo.

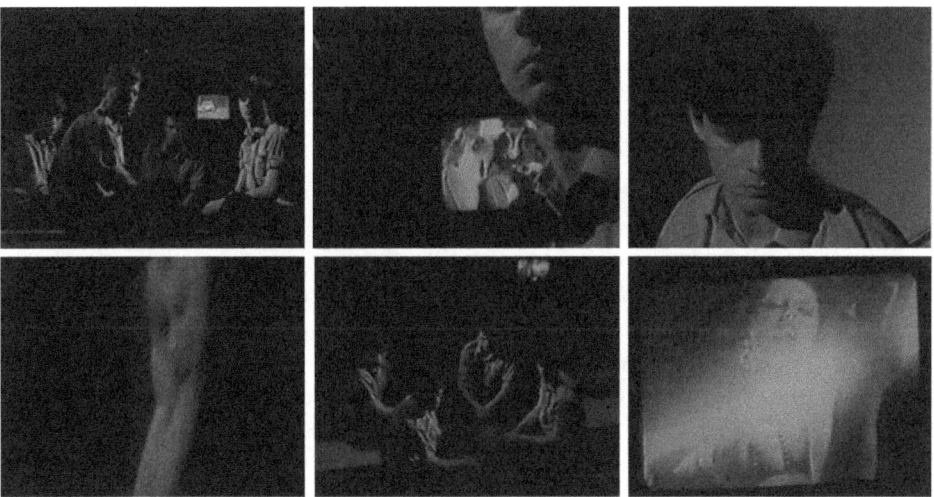

Fig. 18: Diaframma, *Altrove*, 1983, video, 5'22", Color.
Producer: Contempo Records. Director: Tony Verità.

narrative is punctuated by a TV set broadcasting images of a breakdancer in an empty room who, among other moves, mimes to push the TV screen from the inside as if trying to escape from a prison (fig. 17). Not so much hilarious as it is conceptual, Tony Verità's video for Diaframma's *Altrove* (1983) depicts the four band's members sitting motionless in a dark room, looking severely into the camera (fig. 18). In the background a TV set broadcasts an unidentified erotic

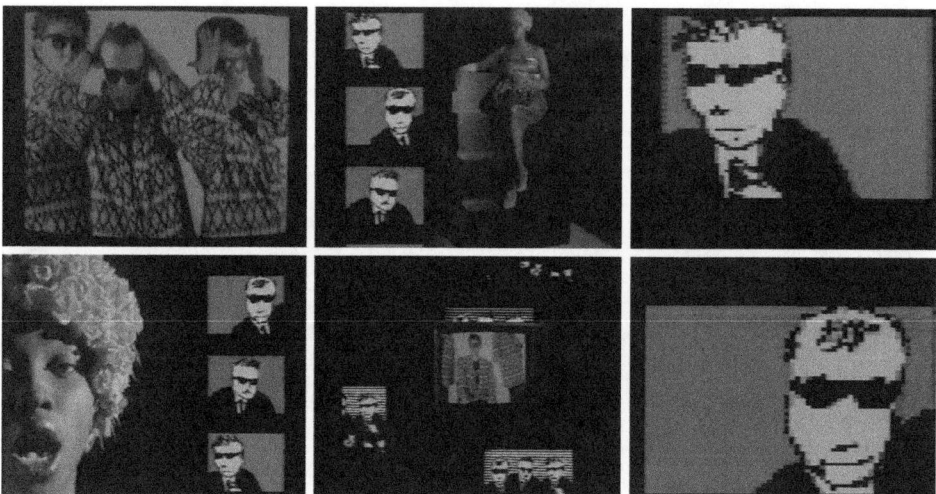

Fig. 19: GMM feat. Alexander Robotnik, *Don't Ask Me Why*, 1985, video, 3'15", Color.
Producer: Materiali Sonori. Directors: Giovanotti Mondani Meccanici (GMM) and Studio
Azzurro.

movie, illuminating the environment with its typical bluish luminescence. The
four's impassive stillness is clearly an act of resistance to television and the very
nature of the pop music video, which is traditionally based on lip-synching.

One more post-punk music video that refers to TV is that by multimedia
collective Giovanotti Mondani Meccanici (GMM), directed in collaboration
with the likeminded group Studio Azzurro, for *Don't Ask Me Why* (1985): a
hybrid new wave/Italo disco track made by GMM with their associate Alexander
Robotnik (fig. 19). The video juxtaposes the performance of the singer Irene
N'Jie, images of the electronic alter egos of the three GMM – the notorious
protagonists of various computer comics and video works – and of the three
artists in trendy clothing and black sunglasses as they dance and struggle with
finding the perfect pose in an empty room, a scene that is also broadcast by a
TV set. The frenetic multiplication of these two types of images, media persona
and electronic duplicates, ironizes on the effects of media's fragmentation of
subjectivity. With its emphasis on collaboration and through references to media
and the personal computer, the video tackle issues of depersonalization and
anonymity in relation with media and information technologies, at the core of
both GMM and Studio Azzurro's practice.

The Representation of Post-punk in Italian TV: A Search for Autonomy

During the 1980s the programs that featured music videos multiplied on both
public and private TV channels in Italy, another highly popular one being *Deejay
Television* (1983–1990) on Canale 5; like *Mister Fantasy*, this also produced in-

house music videos, mostly for Italo disco acts. Shortly after *Mister Fantasy* ended its transmissions, in the wake of MTV in the US, a proper music channel was launched. *Videomusic* (1984–1996) transmitted music videos, documentaries, live concerts, interviews all day long, with 8 minutes per hour of commercials. According to Baldini, only 200 music videos were produced in the whole decade of the 1980s by Italian record labels, while in US this was the number for one month.[12] It is not clear what are the sources Baldini uses for this data, nor how authoritative they are, but it is certainly true that this number does not include the post-punk music videos, which had an extremely low visibility on TV and sometimes, as in the case of Grabinsky, circulated only in art or experimental film and video festivals.

More than music videos, Italian post-punk became visible on TV through live performances. In 1982 Gaznevada put their reputation on the line by competing, unsuccessfully, in the selections for the populist Sanremo music festival on the family-oriented variety show *Domenica In*. Only the most pop-oriented post-punk acts performed in the media event of Sanremo: Garbo (1984) and Denovo (1988). Diaframma, Litfiba, Neon and Underground Life all performed at *L'Orecchiocchio* (1982–1986) on Rai 3, maintaining intact their credibility, like those featured in the *Mister Fantasy* documentaries on the scenes of Bologna and Pordenone or on Videomusic. Krisma and CCCP – Fedeli alla Linea performed on several generalist TV programs, injecting them with the threatening as much as appealing deviancy proper of the outsiders. A truthful, backstage image of Italian post-punk emerges from the documentary *L'Ultimo Concerto* (1984) directed by Piergiorgio Gay on Frigidaire Tango for Rai 1, which, as band member Carlo Casale has recounted, 'told the problems of an independent band, on the edge between the need to express their art and the conditional integration into a society that was becoming that monster thirsty for money, arrogance and power that distinguished the 1980s'.[13]

A quintessential representation of Italian post-punk identity can be found in *Pirata! Cult Movie* (1984), a low-budget film directed by Paolo Ciaffi Ricagno, featuring post-punk acts Art Fleury, Jo Squillo, Gaznevada and the Great Complotto (fig. 20). Set in a dystopian future, it tells the story of a 'pirate' on roller skates arising against the totalitarian regime of the 'Sognatore Supremo' (Supreme Dreamer), who enacts his power through television and a violent armed force. In the name of the 'video-negativi' (video-negatives), an obscure movement of resistance, the pirate steals the 'cappello dei sogni' (hat of the dreams) from the dictator; then is chased through Turin's foggy streets and nightlife venues by guards and his own mother. He eventually infiltrates the TV station from where whoever owns the hat can divulgate the dreams that keep the population under control. But as he tries to disrupt the system, he remains

---

[12] Domenico Baldini, *MTV. Il Nuovo Mondo della Televisione* (Rome: Castelvecchi, 2000), p. 167.
[13] Carlo Casale, 'Il Tango era nel Congelatore' in *Gli Altri Ottanta. Racconti dalla Galassia Post-Punk Italiana*, ed. by Livia Satriano (Milan: Agenzia X, 2015), p. 40.

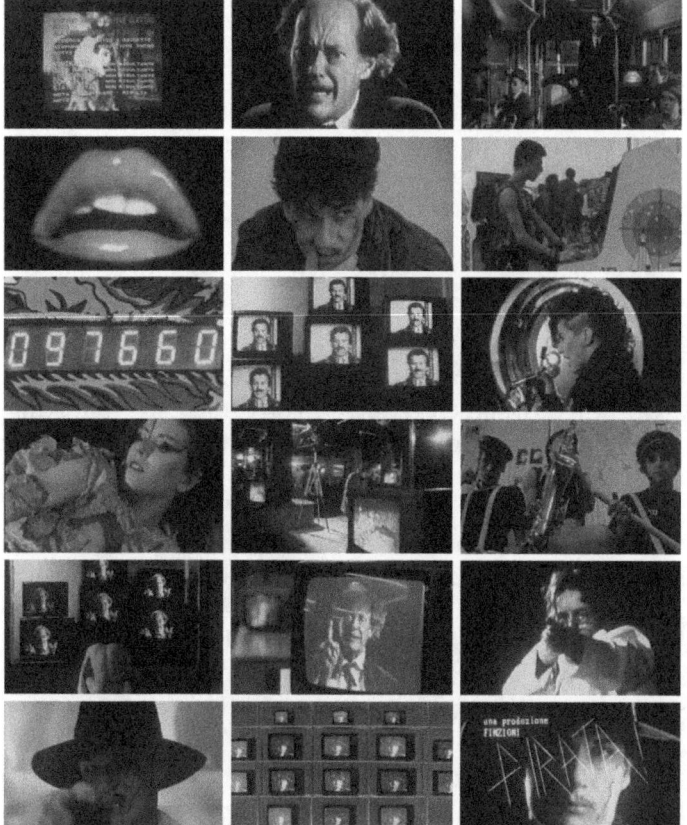

Fig. 20: *Pirata! Cult Movie*, 1984, 35 mm, 95', Color. Director: Paolo Ricagno.

embedded within it and his image broadcast. The most successful achievement of the film, which media scholar Rossella Catanese has defined 'an interesting model of cinematic remediation of comic book and video culture',[14] is its ability not only to represent media technologies but to accelerate their alienating effects, exposing the mechanism of fictionalization enacted by media.

Around the mid 1980s, post-punk bands faced the ethical choice of either compromising with the mainstream or disbanding. Those who compromised tried to maintain as much autonomy as possible. CCCP – Fedeli alla Linea, for example, which self-defined as a 'filo-Soviet punk' band, staged performances at the crossroads of political forums and vaudeville shows, glorifying left-wing values while parodying mass culture with their aesthetics and lyrics. Their blurring of political faith and parody reached a point of no return in 1989, the year they performed in Moscow, which was also the year of the fall of Communism and of the Berlin Wall. For the release of their album *Canzoni Preghiere Danze del*

---

[14] Rossella Catanese, 'Pirates: The Punk and Post-Punk Scene in Italy', *Bianco e Nero. Rivista Quadrimestrale del Centro Sperimentale di Cinematografia*, 585 (November 2016), 51–59 (pp. 52–53).

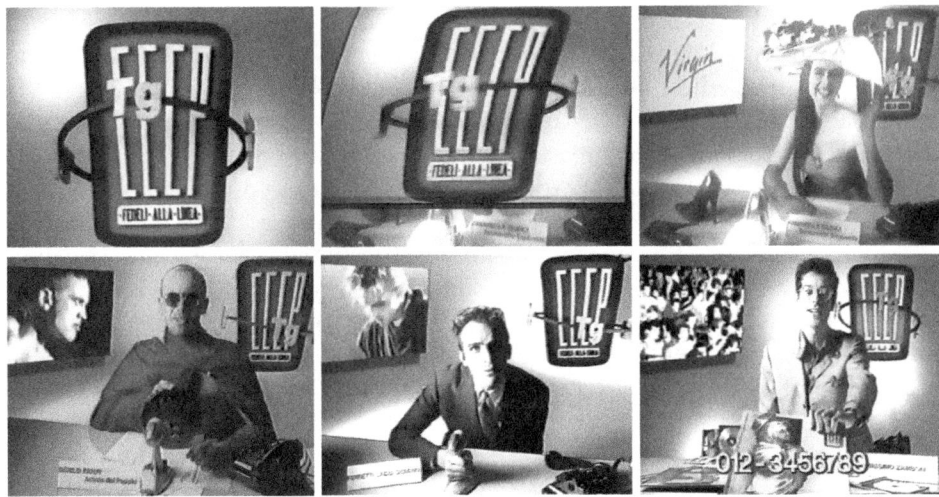

Fig. 21: CCCP – Fedeli alla Linea, TV commercials for the release of the album
Canzoni Preghiere Danze del II Millennio – Sezione Europa, 1989.
Producer: Virgin Records.

II Millennio – Sezione Europa (Virgin 1989), their label produced four sarcastic
TV commercials for Videomusic, in which each of the band's members offers a
hilarious parody of a promotional video, filmed in a studio that recalls that of a
real TV newscast, merging a propaganda agenda with the style and language of
TV news and shopping channels (fig. 21).

Although made in the late 1990s, way beyond the timespan discussed,
two late projects by Krisma provide the ultimate examples of post-punk's
deconstructionist approach to television. One was their nightly TV program
Sat Sat (1995–1996) for Rai 3, made of chaotic cut-ups of various TV channels
from across world. The other was the satellite channel *Krisma TV* (1998–2002),
produced by Eutelsat Communications, made of live footage from the Cocoricò
club in Riccione (where the duo worked as DJs) and disorienting loops of
samples from a variety of sources, distorted through fisheye and other lysergic
editing techniques, on a hypnotic techno soundtrack. After almost two decades,
Krisma were finally able to establish their own *Cathode Mamma*. Interestingly
enough, during the same timeframe a 'Supreme Dreamer' named Berlusconi
expanded from the small TV channel Telemilano 58, which he had bought in
1978, to the three-channel empire Fininvest (later Mediaset) comprising Canale
5, Italia 1, and Rete 4. Through TV, Berlusconi developed impressive strategies
of consensus-building, which he then applied to political marketing, forming the
centre-right political party Forza Italia and eventually becoming Prime Minister
for nine years between 1994 and 2011.

Berlusconi became a target for artistic and political resistance only in the
1990s. In retrospect, however, it is interesting to note how Italian post-punk's
deconstructionist approach to television prophesized the risks implied in the

manipulation of mass media under neoliberalism. To this extent, Mark Fisher's considerations on Manchester band Joy Division, a quintessential incarnation of the post-punk ethos, are illuminating: 'Listen to JD now, and you have the inescapable impression that the group were catatonically challenging our present, their future. […] It has become increasingly clear that 1979-1980, the years with which the group will always be identified, was a threshold moment – the time when a whole world (social, democratic, Fordist, industrial) became obsolete, and the contours of a new world (neoliberal, consumerist, informatic) began to show themselves'.[15] The same is true, albeit with some variations, for Italian post-punk, whose schizophrenic relationship with television is symptomatic of how artistic forms of critical thinking were no longer exclusive domain of the visual arts but could be employed to dismantle mass media from within.

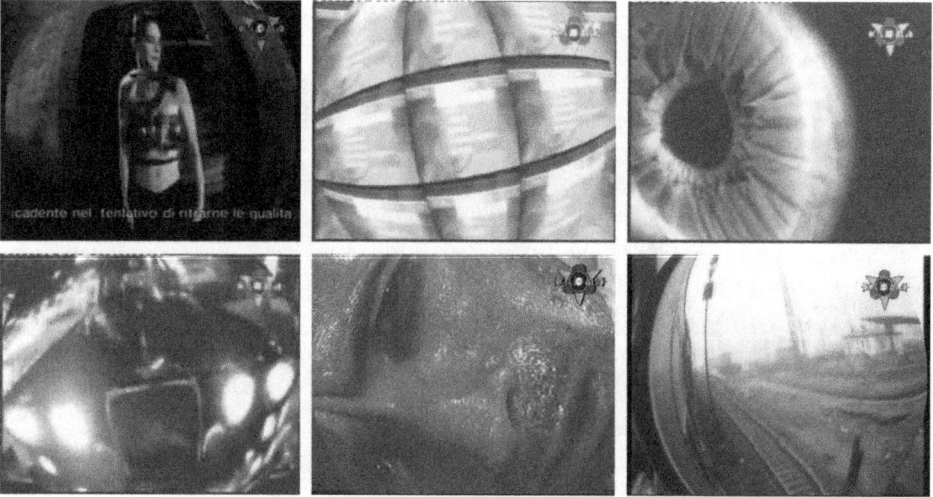

Fig. 22: Krisma, *Krisma TV*, 1998–2002. Stills from the satellite TV channel Krisma TV produced by Eutelsat Communications.

[15] Mark Fisher, *Ghosts of my Life: Writings on Depression, Hauntology and Lost Futures* (London: John Hunt Publishing, 2014), p. 50.

The Avant-Garde Roots of Video Game Music and Algorithmic Culture

Donal Fullam, University College Dublin

Abstract

The enclaves of post-industrial capitalism are surrounded by audiovisual panoramas that have emerged from European and American avant-garde experiments in composition and multimedia experience. Avant-garde approaches towards the technologization of music and democratic media choice were transformed within the consumer culture of the 1980s, and are now consolidated as commerce within modern algorithmic culture. More than any other medium, video games most fully reproduce the encompassing, participatory ideal of the postwar avant-garde, but transfused with a relentless commercialism. Video games surround the player with choice, but the impetus to design these enveloping audiovisual environments does not come from the attempt to democratize culture — it comes from an overarching consumerism and the rationalization of computer logic. Avant-garde experiments in participatory art, named 'democratic surrounds' by Fred Turner, and interactive music in games share a genesis in the politics of media participation that developed after World War 2, but also in the logic of computerization. The modularity and automation of new media that creates a panorama of uniquely individuated audience experiences is not new, but the meaning of media interaction has been radically transformed within a hyper consumerism that developed towards the end of the millennium.

Introduction

Interactive multimedia has emerged as a critical means for cultural engagement in the twenty-first century. Video games, websites, social media, advertising, new media art, and all kinds of apps and software now feature integrated media elements — sound, music, video, images — that users can engage with through different kinds of interaction. By employing a degree of choice, users are each granted different encounters within defined sets of parameters, structuring media experiences as individual and unique. Video games present a convergence point for all kinds of media, and video game music, as an aspect of the multimedia form, can be analysed according to the potential to individuate player experience through the historical conditions of its development. Using Fred Turner's concept of the 'democratic surround',[1] and Ted Striphas' 'algorithmic culture',[2] it is possible to evaluate video game music as an aspect of contemporary multimedia that is deeply connected to twentieth century avant-garde composition. Video games are the product of a complex history of converging technologies, but also converging political and economic conditions. Game history is normally treated chronologically and the interactive nature of games is often treated cognitively, and sometimes critically, but almost never in terms of cultural history. What are the historical conditions through which this industry and increasingly popular hobby has emerged, and what can they tell us about the current conditions of gaming? By describing the formal and cultural connections between these different musical approaches in terms of technology, algorithmic culture and art history, the machine logic at the heart of modern media and the relay from mid-century experimentalism to modern commerce can be disclosed.

Twentieth century European and American avant-garde composers approached musical composition in different but ultimately convergent ways — as a totally determined parametric system, but also as aleatoric experiences of chance and interaction. Taking inspiration from Arnold Schönberg (1874-1951), composers associated with serialism wanted to completely control all musical parameters to create objective 'integral' systems,[3] conflating composition with research, in imitation of the new technical work carried out in postwar laboratories.[4] Following John Cage, another school of thought emerged, where composition could be a work of interactive multimedia — immersive and subjective, with elements of chance and choice presenting a sense of democratic participation. These avant-garde approaches are often placed on opposing ends of the compositional spectrum due to their extreme formal differences, but they both arise within similar conceptual and cultural contexts. For both sides of the twentieth century avant-garde, music was a technology that enabled the composer to create automated pieces and processes for audiences to experience subjectively.

Video games represent a kind of modern *gesamtkunstwerk*, combining video, animation, stagecraft, modelling, architecture, lighting, narrative, game mechanics and, of course, sound effects and music. In these terms they can be categorized as multimedia — the combination of disconnected media sources into homogenous, all encompassing media experiences. Music can operate as a facet of multimedia because it has been historically theorized within European art music as an auditory object, comprised of parametric elements, and

[1] Fred Turner, *The Democratic Surround: Multimedia and American Liberalism from World War II to the Psychedelic Sixties* (Chicago: The University of Chicago Press, 2015).
[2] Ted Striphas, 'Algorithmic Culture', *European Journal of Cultural Studies*, 18.4-5 (2015), 395-412.
[3] Markus Bandur, *Aesthetics of Total Serialism: Contemporary Research From Music to Architecture,* (Basel: Birkhäuser, 2001), p. 11.
[4] Georgina Born, *Rationalizing Culture: IRCAM, Boulez, and the Institutionalization of the Avant-Garde* (Berkeley and London: University of California Press, 1995), p. 1.

organized through a technical system. The abstraction of music as a system of parameters allows it to be placed within incongruous formats but also allows it to be automated — it is the ability to automate the system that forms the nexus between twentieth century avant-garde experiments and contemporary video game music. Automated, algorithmic compositional techniques emerge at different times, from different contexts, and according to different political, aesthetic, and technological conditions. They reflect ideological assumptions but also refract these assumptions in new ways. What becomes clear from looking at the emergence of these approaches during different times is that, while formal aspects radically change, underlying technical structures remain the same. The concept of music as a technical system that can be algorithmically organized underpins these seemingly disparate approaches, and while the political aims of twentieth century avant-garde composers were discarded, their technical inventions were retained and rearranged to suit the new circumstances of our panoptic, panaural algorithmic culture.

Music In Technology/Technology in Music

The concept of music that emerges from what is generally called Western classical, or European art music, is a technical system of modular parts that can be organized through sets of parameters — in other words, a technology. The word 'technology' entered the English language during the seventeenth century, coming from the root *techne* (create) and *logos* (ordering).[5] Logos, and the sense of ordering that it implies, can be understood as logic, 'in series of steps in order, and reasoning also in steps'. When *techne* and *logos* are combined as technology, the word is understood to 'refer to a "creation of order" (as in skill or art used to create order-yielding work), or that in which order is created'.[6] Technology can be defined as 'a system created by humans that uses knowledge and organization to produce objects and techniques for the attainment of specific goals'.[7] Contemporary perceptions of technology tend to reduce the concept to specific material objects, but historically the word did not necessarily signify the objects themselves, rather, the skill of doing things and the abstraction of logical skill into a system.

Music is a complex human activity, and although it can be abstracted as theory and reified as a recorded object, it is still normally conceptualized as art, rather than product or technology. Still, music as a social practice and expressive medium has always been entangled with *techne* and *logos*, with musical instruments thought to be among the earliest technological objects, and evidence

[5] La Shun L. Carroll, 'A Comprehensive Definition of Technology from an Ethological Perspective', *Social Sciences*, 6.4 (October, 2017), 1-20, (p. 6).
[6] Ivi, p. 6.
[7] Rudi Volti, *Society and Technological Change* (New York: Worth Publishers, 2018), p. 29.

of abstract musical theorization since before 1500 BCE.[8] Musical instruments are a kind of technology but musical material is traditionally conceptualized as an artistic, expressive medium, not usually thought to be technological. Along with the introduction of the word technology, seventeenth and eighteenth century European theorists and composers began to conceptualize music as a form of technology,[9] by abstracting and quantifying acoustic material as the fundamental musical element and systematically organizing tonal, rhythmic and formal elements. These projects were generally intended for pedagogical use[10] but they also asserted the understanding of music as acoustic material that could be abstracted according to fundamental laws.

Musical-theoretical literature during the eighteenth century reflects profound changes in European intellectual thought due to the upheavals in science and philosophy[11] occurring at the time. The beginnings of an overarching project by theorists to 'rationalize the system of harmonic tonality'[12] can be understood as a pedagogical necessity for practical guidance but also as a deeper ideological analogue with movements towards philosophical rationalization. What emerges with the detailed organization of music into an apparently universal system is the conception of music as a kind of technology: rational, impartial and autonomous. In many ways music was already thought of in this sense, but large scale projects of theorization during the eighteenth century allowed this form of thinking to cohere among the theoretically literate and proliferate amongst amateur musicians and the public. Students of theory and analysis of tonality are normally taught the foundations in the same way — how the four part harmonic rules of counterpoint are used to write chorale music through voice leading, chord progression, cadential treatment, and so on, and how these parametric aspects are organized within larger forms. This is a systematized way of understanding music as an objective classification of parts, that are easily replicated as an overall totality. This kind of system presents many different kinds of benefits — works are easily reproducible with the correct information; the different parts have been schematized, making it user friendly; it is modular, so parts can be reorganized and recycled; new, unique instances can be created with similar material, and the methodology and stylistics of the system can essentially be reduced to an algorithmic determinacy. When the complex social processes of music are excised in favour of the abstraction of musical material into a technical system, it is essentially conceptualizing music as a kind of technology. twentieth century European composers associated with the avant-garde brought the rationalization

[8] Sam Mirelman, 'A New Fragment of Music Theory from Ancient Iraq', *Archiv für Musikwissenschaft*, 6.1 (2010), 45-51 (p. 45).
[9] Robert W. Wason, 'Musica Practica: Music Theory as Pedagogy', in *The Cambridge History of Western Music Theory*, ed. by Thomas Christensen (Cambridge: Cambridge University Press, 2002), 46–77 (p. 55).
[10] Ibidem.
[11] Ivi, p. 53.
[12] Ivi, p. 54.

of music to an unprecedented degree, ushering in a new age of mechanistic musical control. One of the main benefits of this systematic concept of music for twentieth century compositional practices and the development of video game music is the level of parametric automation it allows. Interactive music in video games has roots in the early configuration of music as a modular, technological system, but the realization of immersive 3D sound worlds is possible because of the configuration of music and sound as a more total parametric science during the twentieth century.

European Avant-Garde - Serialism

In 1921 Arnold Schönberg famously invented a new formal technique called twelve-tone music, which seemed to present an original conception of the fundamentals of music itself. In order to create a sense of atonal balance and to disrupt the hierarchy of nineteenth century tonal theory, twelve-tone music uses each of the twelve notes of the chromatic scale within a 'row', which becomes the main musical material. The row is subjected to a number of transformations — retrograde, inversion, and retrograde-inversion — in lay terms, backwards, upside down and backwards-upside down. The formal aspect of the technique is more complex than can be described within this essay, but essentially, it is an algorithmic process that uses musical parameters as its input, and produces atonal musical material as its output — the row transformations constitute the algorithm, 'a formal process or set of step-by-step procedures'.[13] Further developments in Europe led to total serialism: the attempt to micro-manage and control every aspect of musical sound and to organize it algorithmically.

Olivier Messiaen (1908-1992) set the prototype with *Mode de valeurs et d'intensités* (1949) while Pierre Boulez (1925-2016) developed the technique towards what became known as total, or integral serialism. For integral serialism, timbre, duration, frequency, and amplitude, the dynamic characteristics of sound, became organizational fragments rather than expressive attributes.[14] Karlheinz Stockhausen (1928-2007) attempted to create a parametric measure of all musical dynamics, not only as a way to more tightly control these aspects, but to also combine them all into one integral system.[15] He applied serial methods to pitch, rhythm, dynamics, timbre, density, and time to assert an overarching sense of unity, as a musical unified field theory in line with Einstein's groundbreaking theory of relativity.[16] A vast new terrain had been opened and composers saw themselves

---

[13] Striphas, p. 403.
[14] Paul Griffiths, *Modern Music and After* (New York: Oxford University Press, 1995), p. 29.
[15] Robert P. Morgan, 'Stockhausen's Writing on Music', *The Musical Quarterly,* 61.1 (January 1975), 1-16 (p. 3).
[16] Thom Holmes, *Electronic and Experimental Music: Technology, Music, and Culture* (New York and London: Routledge, 2008), p. 124.

as a vanguard heralding a progressive new era, with the creation of a completely new music unencumbered by antecedent relationships, representations, symbols or structures – an objective, rigorously scientific approach that might expose reality rather than emotion.[17] Schönberg's approach and ensuing theories of everything were attempts to further technologize music, to remove it from social context and treat it as an object of scientific scrutiny. The organization of music purely as a set of acoustic parameters granted composers a new level of control, allowing them to manipulate music and sound at the microscopic level.

Composers had identified where power was centralizing and were busy molding themselves and their craft into forms more hospitable to these institutions and their characters; the analysts, the specialists and the technocrats, around whom new loci of power were beginning to whirl.[18] Composers followed the technologizing impulse to its logical conclusion in the hope of discovering universal forms, and to position music within the sphere of technical fields that were providing new ways of understanding the world. The radical reconfiguration of composition as a tonal science during the middle of the twentieth century was characterized by its exponents as a progressive strategy to rethink musical form, and while the approach was popular within intellectual circles, the formal and structural aspects quickly became redundant.[19] The extreme contortions that traditional compositional forms endured through serialism put most listening audiences off and the music never gained popularity outside academia. However, the dissolution of traditional form and the freeing of dissonance led by Schönberg and the serial composers is not as important as the academic literature implies. Most modernist or avant-garde composers did not completely embrace total serialism or completely deterministic models of composition, so it is not possible to characterize the entire oeuvre of Boulez or Stockhausen in opposition to previous or contemporaneous styles. What was embraced, and what remains the most relevant characteristic of serialism, was the idea that music could be completely quantified as sets of parameters. Purely rational integral serialism pursued the idea of music as a parametrically organized material to a merciless degree. The concept that musical sound could be organized as discrete sets of parameters and automatically generated within algorithmic systems was taken up and transformed by American avant-garde composers in the second half of the 20th century, and the total organization of musical values continues. The quantization of musical sound that began during the 18th and 19th centuries, and reached an apex within the 20th century avant-garde, now saturates the contemporary world of music.

---

[17] Reginald Smith Brindle, *The New Music* (London: Oxford University Press, 1975), p. 23.
[18] Born, p. 100.
[19] Joseph N. Straus, 'The Myth of Serial "Tyranny" in the 1950s and 1960s', *The Musical Quarterly*, 83.3 (Autumn, 1999), 301-343 (p. 302).

American Avant-Garde - Democratic Surround

The American postwar avant-garde centered around John Cage (1912-92), 'possibly the most influential musician in the world'[20] at the time. On the surface Cage and his followers seemed to be doing the opposite of the European serialists — where they were closed, Cageans was open, where serialists sought determinacy and the systematic, Cageans seemed to counter with indeterminacy and chance. Their similarities went deeper than their differences however, as both groups "sought 'automatism,' the resolute elimination of the artist's ego or personality from the artistic product".[21] Cage described his chance methodology as a way to remove the composer's hand and thus the composer's ego, so music could simply reveal itself, but the outsourcing of composition to systems of chance and computers is also symptomatic of a much broader cultural and technological shift that occurred during the twentieth century. Cage wanted to create processes that could be experienced, and to create platforms for other people to interact, offering up 'a view of artistic practice as a leveled collaboration among artist, audience, and materials'.[22]

Cage is popularly known as the composer of *4'33* (1952), in which a pianist opens a piano and sits silently for four minutes and thirty three seconds. The ambient sounds of the auditorium, creaks and squeaks, people moving, coughing, and whispering are the musical material, meant to be heard subjectively by each audience member. Cage advocated for the emancipation of noise and the appreciation of all sound as musical and meaningful - a stance normally attributed to his study of Zen Buddhism, but which can also be understood as a reaction to media politics during the twentieth century. *4'33,* as with much of Cage's work, is intended to immerse audience members in a visual and auditory experience that extends beyond the stage, giving audience members a sense of participation. Cage considered it to be his most important work of chance and indeterminacy, and it set the format for his experiments in multimedia participation and happenings.

Following Cage, American composers began experimenting with the use of space and indeterminacy during the middle of the twentieth century — these experiments were encouraged by a national drive to create participatory, democratic forms of art, in opposition to perceived fascist and authoritarian modes of top down communication.[23] Fred Turner coined the term 'democratic surround' to describe these new media models — multi-image, multi-sound source environments created by artists associated with the 1960s counterculture, designed to model and produce a more democratic society.[24] The practice of

---

[20] Richard Taruskin, *Music in the Late Twentieth Century: The Oxford History of Western Music* (Oxford: Oxford University Press, 2010), p. 55.

[21] Ibidem.

[22] Fred Turner, *From Counterculture to Cyberculture: Stewart Brand, the Whole Earth Network, and the Rise of Digital Utopianism* (Chicago: The University of Chicago Press, 2006), p. 47.

[23] Turner, *The Democratic Surround*, p. 28.

[24] Ivi, p. 143.

creating visual panoramas was not new, but American artists and composers associated with the counterculture used emerging technologies to create more fully panoptic and panaural multimedia experiences and happenings that gave audience members a sense of participation by allowing degrees of choice.

John Cage's *HPSCHD,* a juxtaposition of chance procedures with computer technology, was premiered to an audience of 6000 on May 16, 1969, at the University of Illinois. The event featured seven harpsichord players arranged around the auditorium, playing seven solo pieces created from randomly processed music by Mozart, Beethoven, Chopin, Schumann, Schönberg and Cage. Slides and films were projected on giant screens hanging from the ceilings and on the walls, and computer generated sounds played from fifty-two PA speakers.[25] Lasting for about five hours, it was a huge event — a hypnotic environment of sounds and images where audience members were encouraged to move in and out of the building, around the hall, and through the performing area to experience unique interactions of sound, music and visuals. Audiovisual aspects 'were meticulously and systematically randomized so that it was left to the spectators to fill in the space between sound and image with their random noises and movements'.[26] People were encouraged to think of all the sound and noise they heard as important as the snatches of music that could be heard through the cacophony, presenting them with an overwhelming audiovisual encounter that used elaborate algorithmic planning and procedures to allow participation through choice.

The kinds of multimedia experiences that Cage and many others were creating became a fixture of American artistic and cultural life during the 1960s and beyond.[27] Artists and musicians staged elaborate events with huge, all surrounding PA systems, projectors, lighting, and performances that became known as human be-ins or happenings. Many other composers associated with the American and European avant-garde embraced the turn towards chance systems and democratic participation too. Serial composition systems share aspects of aleatoric design, although they were not necessarily created in the pursuit of new forms of agency. Indeterminacy and choice are characteristic of Cage's work but composers who are primarily associated with the strict ordering of serialism also adopted choice based forms that feature player-indeterminacy. Stockhausen's *Klavierstücke XI* (1956) allows the pianist to choose tempo and dynamic levels, and which order to play nineteen modular sections from a large single page score,[28] and different orderings of Boulez's *Third Sonata* (1958) can be chosen by the pianist during performance.[29] Composers associated with the American avant-garde more fully

[25] Stephen Husarik, 'John Cage and LeJaren Hiller: HPSCHD, 1969', *American Music*, 1.2 (Summer, 1983), 1-21, (p. 15).
[26] Ivi, p. 1.
[27] Turner, *The Democratic Surround*, p. 147.
[28] Elliott Antokoletz, *A History of Twentieth-Century Music in a Theoretic-Analytical Context,* (New York: Routledge, 2014), p. 397.
[29] William G. Harbinson, 'Performer Indeterminacy and Boulez's Third Sonata', *Tempo. New Series*, 169, (June 1989), 16-20 (p. 1).

embraced Cage's reconfiguration of performer and audience hierarchies. Terry Riley's *In C* (1964) grants musicians control over different decisions as the piece is performed — how long to play sections for or whether to play them at all — making modules available as choices within a loose but ultimately stable framework. La Monte Young's *Dream House* (1993) produces droning environmental sounds that adapt according to the listener's position in a room by utilizing the complex harmonic arrangements of sound reacting with itself in three dimensional space. These kinds of interactive characteristics can be traced through European classical musical developments from the middle of the twentieth century as a gradual process of ceding control — opening an interactive space between composers and performers, but also between composers and listeners.

John Cage was always willing to go a step further and it is in his work that the inherent contradictions become most apparent. He created musical and multimedia platforms that gave performers a sense of their own autonomy and allowed audiences to value their subjective experiences, but also to participate as equals. Freedom of interpretation and movement was meant to emulate and produce a broader sense of freedom within a democratic society, as, according to Michael Nyman, 'with all those parts and no conductor, you can see that even this populous a society can function without a conductor'.[30] The impulse to create modular, indeterminate and aleatoric pieces realized by Boulez, Stockhausen, Cage, Riley, and others during the period can be framed according to an emerging media culture that values open, interactive forms within rule-based frameworks. The use of these compositional techniques can be seen as reactions to media politics but also as composers displaying a precocious grasp of what was on the threshold — a culture of media creators providing platforms for others to interact. In theory, avant-garde composers and artists were attempting to democratize composition, but inherent contradictions radically altered the practical results. Cage suggested that his approach was more participatory and thus more democratic than previous methods but he was still dictating the compositional parameters, the audience's relationship with the composition and the audiences relationship with the composer. Audience members were not really granted an equal status but allowed to participate within the boundaries set by Cage. The top-down media methodologies that composers and artists attempted to bypass were reproduced as less strict but nonetheless stable hierarchies. Avant-garde techniques meant to demonstrate democratic potentials through audience choice became structured as managerial hierarchies, and were quickly used in the design of commercial products. By failing to inoculate the new techniques from commercialization, they were easily appropriated within the explosion of commercial culture during the 1970s and 1980s. The algorithmic control of music as parameters and the inclusion of audiences through chance and choice within multimedia experiences circumscribes the logic of new media, most explicitly in video games.

---

[30] Richard Kostelanetz, *Conversing With Cage* (New York: Routledge, 2003), p. 263.

Video Games

Video game sound and music is dynamic, it adapts in response to the actions of the player and is contextually generated according to the needs of particular events and gameplay states. This fundamental characteristic differentiates game audio from that of film and other traditionally passive forms of sonic representation in entertainment. Game music is usually process driven, supporting the 'temporal structure of the game narrative and gameplay'[31] and while these structures are immensely variable, the systems that control them are logical and predictive. Changes are managed according to physical processes of input by players who are in turn responding to in game action, flexible interchanges that must be absolutely tracked and predicted by the game engine to create a coherent experience.

Early games featured simple looped monophonic melodies and crude noise effects which, despite the limitations of relatively primitive technology, displayed the basic elements that have come to define audio aspects of the medium — contextual generation of music and player evocation of sounds. Failure to reach the end of a level in *Super Mario Bros.* (1985) before the countdown timer has reached one hundred will trigger a tempo shift in the music that tells the player to move faster. Entering certain pipes will trigger the pipe sound and then the famous underground theme, communicating to the player that an environmental boundary has been crossed according to their actions.[32] These kinds of musical changes in early games are often accomplished by simple horizontal switching but they nevertheless respond to the player and progress in real time response to their actions, or lack of action. Later games present more complex musical interactions and soundscape cues that are carefully balanced, faded, transformed through effects and generated by the game according to player input and changing events. In *Tomb Raider* (1996) sound and music emerges differently for every player, creating soundscapes and musical developments that are precisely individuated for each instance. Moving from a cave system to the lost dinosaur valley replaces ambient sounds of echoing wind and dripping water with the roar of a waterfall and angry snarl of Velociraptors. A tense nondiegetic orchestration quickly fades in as a Tyrannosaur enters the scene and fades out as soon as it is defeated.[33] No two players will hear the same combination of sounds or exact appearance of music — audio is tailored to individual experience. *Spore* (2008) features a complex generative system created by Brian Eno and Paul Chilvers that creates an 'ever changing, musically cohesive dynamic soundtrack"[34] using

---

[31] Isabella van Elferen, '¡Un Forastero! Issues of Virtuality and Diegesis in Videogame Music', *Music and the Moving Image*, 4. 2 (2011), 30-39 (p. 34).

[32] Nintendo, *Super Mario Bros* (1986), N.E.S.

[33] Eidos, *Tomb Raider*, (1996) Microsoft Windows and other platforms.

[34] Tim Summers, *Understanding Video Game Music* (Cambridge: Cambridge University Press, 2016), p. 22.

a computer model called cellular automata.[35] In *Portal 2*[36] (2011) music is structured around the player's activity — horizontally switched when moving to new areas, or vertically re-orchestrated through modular systems when puzzle pieces are assembled. At an abstract but more fundamental level, all audio in *Portal 2* is interactive — game systems that control sound and music are continually modifying parameters according to player action, creating a coherent acoustic space and a sense of enveloping verisimilitude.

A video game is a machine with many interlocking and interdependent parts — in complex, first person perspective games, audio aspects are determined by technical systems relying on banks of parameters of myriad microscopic gradations. If the player turns their avatar ninety degrees left, the systems controlling sound will react so that the acoustic space reflects the new position. Sonic events heard previously from the front of the player will now be heard on the right with all degrees in between accounted for. Audio emanating from in front of the player is not actually playing from a spatial position — parameters of panning, volume, reverb and frequency are adjusted so that audio appears to be coming from a position relative to the player. In *Portal 2* (2011) puzzle pieces that add additional layers of music will be heard by each player differently, as they individually arrive at solutions but also as they move around the 3D space. The modular organization of audio as parameters allows it to be controlled and deployed according to specific conditions, individualizing listener experience. Interactive, dynamic and procedural music and sound in video games is possible because of these processes — the theoretical rationalization of music has allowed it to be conceptualized as a modular system of interlocking and interdependent acoustic parts. Sound is generated through complex algorithmic structures and precomposed modular parts are reconfigured in accordance with each player's actions.[37] These systems create highly individualized musical experiences, within the parameters set by the game's designers and composers. No two players of the same game are ever likely to hear exactly the same audio combinations and contiguities, even if the music and sound heard by each is broadly similar.

Video games are part of a modern media culture that is characterized by interactivity, audience participation and a blurring of boundaries between consumers and producers, but they are produced in a more commercial context than earlier avant-garde experiments. The interactive nature of game sound and video games in general can be understood as the expression of an impulse that characterizes modern media production and consumption — an increasing necessity for input from audiences, mediated by algorithms. The idea

---

[35] Ian Steadman, 'Brian Eno on music that thinks for itself', https://www.wired.co.uk/article/brian-eno-peter-chilvers-scape [accessed 21 December, 2018].

[36] Valve Corporation, *Portal 2,* (2011), Microsoft Windows and other platforms. Composed by Mike Morasky.

[37] Elizabeth Medina-Gray, 'Modularity and Dynamic Play: Video Game Music and its Avant-garde Antecedents', paper presented at Ludomusicology conference, Liverpool University, 12-13 April 2013.

that producers and consumers share collaborative duty is common, so much so that the term 'prosumer'[38] was coined to designate the new role consumers play. Analysis often places players somewhere between the subject position of 'author/ producer and audience/consumer'[39] but the term only applies to one side, as the producers subject position has not changed. Producers are keen to develop an 'all in it together' mentality, aligning consumers with the task of production but in terms of consumer culture, rather than twentieth century experiments in subjective meaning making and democratic inclusion. The political intentions of earlier avant-garde approaches have been mostly abandoned, but, within the context of consumer culture, the concept of music as a technological component and the individuating power of interactivity have been retained and radically transformed. Modern approaches are directly connected to practices that emerged around the middle of the twentieth century in Europe and America but are also expressions of something different — a 'commercial surround.' We are surrounded by media and music but not in the way that Schönberg or Cage envisioned. The impetus to design contemporary multimedia environments does not come from the confrontation with top down modes of media — it comes from an overarching consumer and algorithmic culture.

Algorithmic Culture

Algorithms are at the heart of modern media use and it is the potential to individualize media interaction through parametric ordering that is the connective tissue between musical composition, cultural interaction, consumer subjectivity and the contemporary media culture in which we have become enmeshed. Video games are an expression of this context that Alexander Galloway and Ted Striphas term 'algorithmic culture', a societal movement towards the use of complex automated systems to create and mediate cultural products. The overwhelming power of computerization seems to place algorithms within the realms of the occult, but a definition is not complex — algorithms are step-by-step processes used to complete tasks, and can be carried out by people or automated using machines — particularly computers. In contemporary use "an algorithm is any well-defined computational procedure that takes some value, or set of values, as input and produces some value, or set of values, as output. An algorithm is thus a sequence of computational steps that transform the input into the output."[40] In video games a simple algorithm can take the player action as input, and horizontally switch one music track for another or add new vertical layers of harmony or melody, as

---

[38] Alvin Toffler, *The Third Wave* (New York: Bantam Books, 1980).
[39] Karen Collins, *Playing with Sound: A Theory of Interacting with Sounds and Music in Video Games* (Cambridge, MA: The MIT Press, 2013), p. 11.
[40] *Introduction to Algorithms,* ed. By Thomas H. Cormen and Charles E. Leiserson (Cambridge, MA and London: The MIT Press, 2009), p. 5.

output. Complex systems can output music using computational models and more complicated structures of code, in response to the players input, individualizing the experience of virtual worlds. This kind of composition is not new — the impulse to treat music as an algorithmically determined system can be traced back through the twentieth century avant-garde and further, to the foundations of functional harmony. Western perceptions of musical tonality itself can be described as a type of algorithmic schema and an expression of a broader impulse to systematize aspects of cultural articulation. Algorithmic culture does not necessarily arise from the twentieth century, but the increasing mechanization and computerization of societies has spurred its development and pervasiveness.

The necessity for input from users and the feedback that generates individualized experiences might paint algorithmic culture as a triumph of democratic public culture,[41] but there are hidden dangers. Algorithms are used to structure cultural life and artistic expression in increasingly labyrinthine configurations, with all kinds of modern musical interaction tending to come within the algorithmic domain. Spotify's *Discover Weekly* uses machine learning to individually structure user listening habits[42] and YouTube's recommendation algorithm uses deep neural network architectures to order, rank and tailor each users feed.[43] According to Striphas, "part of what is at stake in algorithmic culture is the privatization of process: that is, the forms of decision making and contestation that comprise the ongoing struggle to determine the values, practices and artifacts — the culture, as it were — of specific social groups."[44] In video games, the goals of the avant-garde have materialized in unexpected ways — the individualization of experience has been expanded, but within the context of consumerism, it is also transformed. Sound and vision is structured around activity, and participation engenders new forms of subjective experience in an infinite field of digital choice, but participation within algorithmic culture is increasingly managed according to the dictates of commerce.

Conclusion

Video game sound and music is a convergence of both European and American twentieth century avant-garde compositional approaches — the parametric and the interactive — transformed as an aspect of commercial culture. The invention and refinement of serial composition by European composers during the twentieth century framed music as a technological material that could be precisely measured

---

[41] Striphas, p. 407.
[42] Sophia Ciocca, 'How Does Spotify Know You So Well?', https://hackernoon.com/spotifys-discover-weekly-how-machine-learning-finds-your-new-music-19a41ab76efe [accessed 22 December 2018].
[43] Alex Giamas, 'How YouTube's Recommendation Algorithm Works', https://www.infoq.com/news/2016/09/How-YouTube-Recommendation-Works [accessed 22 December 2018].
[44] Striphas, p. 406.

and manipulated as sets of parameters. Beginning with Schönberg's twelve-tone music and culminating in integral serialism, composers created methods that could generate music by treating notes as autonomous parameters within an algorithmic system. To automate composition, music had to be expressed as information, so composers began to more fully quantize musical values — from a system of notes, to a system of every available acoustic attribute. The formal concepts of the European avant-garde are now largely abandoned but serial composers were harbingers of the technical and digital transformation of music into an automated multimedia component. The hardware, theoretical concepts and organizational procedures that engrossed composers and technicians during the first half of the twentieth century were continually iterated on and developed through the proceeding decades, and the conception and implementation of music as a system of parameters is now more relevant than ever. Contemporary musical practice of all forms is totally saturated by technology that works through the organization of audio into parametric systems. Musicians, composers, sound designers and technicians who use any digital instruments, effects, recording or reproduction technology are engaging with the parametric organization of musical sound. The quantization of music as a system of acoustic parameters allows it to be used as a component within many forms of multimedia today, especially in video games. In games, the parametric management of acoustic elements has reached a level of sophistication that Schönberg or Stockhausen could barely have imagined.

Composers associated with Cage and the American avant-garde took seriously Marshall McLuhan's theory that the medium, rather than the content, is the message. They wanted to manufacture subjectivity by presenting randomized, automated systems to individuate experience, creating the conditions for audience members to see themselves as aesthetic and political actors within a spectacle. Following Cage, American composers and media artists combined music, sound and visuals within spatial multimedia assemblies to grant audience members a range of choice, and a sense of participation. Offering choices creates a sense of shared production, increasing the perceived value of the experience. By sharing the task of production, alienation from artistic or entertainment experiences can be diminished, as participation includes audiences as co-producers. This is the theory, but in practice the distance between artists and audiences can also increase, the connection occluded by interactive frameworks and managerial hierarchies that are mediated through algorithmic processes. The impulse to treat music according to algorithmic systems can be detected throughout the history of European music — in medieval isorhythmic composition,[45] twentieth century musical dice games,[46] and more recently in serial and avant-garde techniques, but it is particularly apparent within twentieth century and contemporary

[45] Keith Muscutt, 'Composing with Algorithms: An Interview with David Cope', *Computer Music Journal*, 31.3, (Fall, 2007), p. 10.
[46] Stephen A. Hedges, 'Dice Music in the Eighteenth Century', *Music & Letters*, 59. 2 (April 1980), 180-187.

media culture. The intertwined histories of European and American avant-garde composition can reveal the underlying threads that constitute the warp and weave of our current algorithmic audio culture. The serialists parametric organization and algorithmic control of music converged with the interactive multimedia of the American avant-garde, forming the logic of music and sound in new media towards the end of the millennium.

Rather than a direct line of descent between video game and avant-garde composition, the similarities and differences between approaches can be characterized according to related musical tools used to facilitate the application of choice within an emerging algorithmic culture. In the democratic surrounds, freedom was presented as choice within frameworks designed by specialists, rather than a dialectic between participants exercising equal power. Participants had no access to Cage's algorithmic methods of musical organization, but could instead choose from within a range set by the composer. Still, Cage was usually physically present during performances and the public nature of the surrounds did present levels of media participation that were not usually available. Video games present infinite fields of possible choices and music that responds to player behavior, but the interaction between players and composers, or consumers and producers, is mediated through the black box of machine and code. Avant-garde experiments pointed towards an increasingly public level of engagement but the current model of algorithmic culture seems to be instigating the 'gradual abandonment of culture's publicness and the emergence of a strange new breed of elite culture purporting to be its opposite.'[47] We are surrounded by sound and vision but not in the way that twentieth century avant-garde composers and artists envisioned. The automatism[48] they sought is ubiquitous, but as an element of consumer culture it becomes a method of social organization that structures consumer choice, rather than an escape from hierarchy towards democratic participation.

[47] Striphas, p. 1.
[48] Taruskin, p. 37.

Imaginary Video Landscape: John Cage, Mugam Music, Video Art

Sandra Lischi, Università di Pisa
Matias Guerra, artist[1]

Abstract

The essays focuses on a video by Robert Cahen and Matias Guerra, *Imaginary Video Landscape. For a random number of cuts from 14 archive videos*, 2017. This short work, presented in some international festivals, is based on *Imaginary Landscape n.5* by John Cage (1952), and offers a profound and interesting intersection between the avant-garde and popular music. Moreover, this "dialogue" is articulated and represented in electronic images by the French video-artist Robert Cahen and the Chilean multimedia artist Matias Guerra. The artists conflate their respective video archives: the images and the music produce a "video landscape" intertwining two different musical experiences, two different approaches and identities. The essay offers a critical analysis of this artwork in relation to John Cage's influence on video-art, the several existing versions of his musical work, Robert Cahen's *musique concrète* as well as to Guerra's multimedia approach and to the composer Jahangir Selimkhanov's studies and music inspired by Mugam musical tradition in Azerbaigian.

The correlation between musical research and video art develops on various levels starting from an electronic intuition, a sort of affinity, between sound and visual signals: one of the first discoveries made by artists experimenting with video recording equipment (available on the market since the mid 1960s) was that 'images and sound were coming from the same source: images were formed by tension and frequencies and sound too, at least the electronic ones or those coming from an electronic equipment. The most important thing was that image and sound differed only in the way tension and basic frequencies were organized in time. This unicity was the most interesting discovery', as Steina and Woody Vasulka have observed.[2] According to Bill Viola: 'video is closer to sound than to

---

[1] As an artist and music expert, Matias Guerra co-authored the project with Sandra Lischi and contributed to the essay by writing its more specifically musical parts and by providing a general revision.
[2] Steina and Woody Vasulka, interview in Galleria Flaviana, Locarno (Switzerland), October 4,

film or photography, you find the same relation a microphone has with the person talking. A microphone, and suddenly the voice travels through the room [...]. A dynamic living system, an energy field. There isn't an instance of discontinuity, of immobility of time.'[3]

The members of the Fluxus movement, in which Nam June Paik and Wolf Vostell formed, are considered the 'founding fathers' of video art; within it the role of the musical experience goes from desecrating performances, 'silence', noise and disturbance to an openness to chance and to the unpredictable, simple playfulness. Paik had started as a musician: he played the violin and had written his university dissertation on Schönberg. Steina Vasulka was a violinist too, Vostell was a painter, but also author of sculptures and *oeuvres* that produced sound effects. Bill Viola himself declared the importance of music at the beginning of his career; Cahen, too, whom we'll discuss further subsequently, was educated as a musician. Among these few examples – of many, even if we limit ourselves to Fluxus – it is also worth recalling the collaboration between the video artist Gianni Toti with Cage: the composer realized the sound concept for the video-poem *Tenez Tennis* (1992, 15'), based on the sound of tennis balls during a game.

Considering the relationship between music and video, alongside the "incubator" of Fluxus outlined briefly here, we might also recall *Musique concrète* (a term coined in 1948 by the theorist and composer Pierre Schaeffer). Fluxus embraced the beginning of video art with ephemeral act poetics, with the casual combinations and the mocking of myths and rites of the classical show; *Musique concrète,* composed without a score and exists only in recording – it's in fact from these recordings that sound is re-created, processed and modified – indicating methods of transformation for the material fixed on tape, methods that will be applied by video artists to the recording of images. These provide two different, almost opposing views, since the playful transiency, the dispersion, the ways of Fluxus are far from the "concrete" (concretely fixed on tape), meditated, elaborated and structured construction of the research and works of *Musique concrète*. The derivations and complex entanglements we briefly mentioned here form a multidisciplinary and undisciplined whole in video art: music, cinema, theatre, painting which together transcend definitions and borders.

An equally complex plot intertwines art experiences like video (long considered "avant-garde" or "experimental", with all the necessary terminological precautions) and popular culture. According to a misleading theory, video art was born in opposition to television: this is can be undoubtedly true for single episodes and some counter-informative approaches, but inaccurate when you consider the several artist residencies in television structures and the

---

1984, in *Catalogue V International Videoart Festival* (Locarno, 1984). Repr. in *Techno-Graphia* (Locarno: Videoart festival, 1993), 71 (our translation).
[3] Bill Viola quoted in Raymond Bellour, 'La sculpture du temps (entretien avec Bill Viola)', *Cahiers du Cinéma* 379.1, January 1986, 35-44 (our translation).

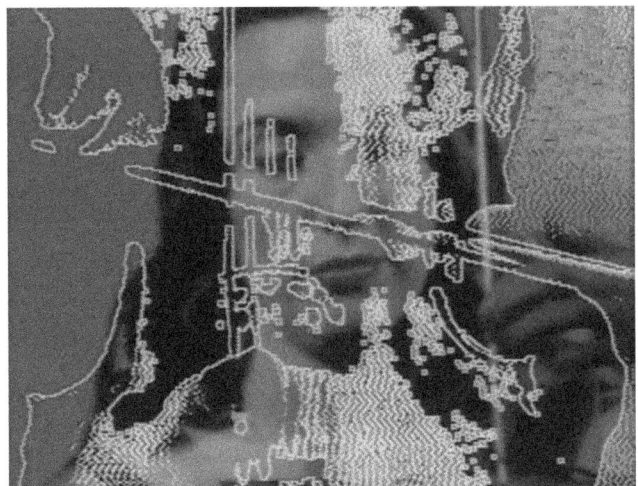

Fig. 1: Nam June Paik, *Global Groove*, 1973

importance of experiences such as those of RAI's Studio di Fonologia in Milan or ORTF (Office de Radiodiffusion Télévision Française), the public radio television broadcast in France (in which in fact Pierre Schaeffer developed his research). This is further troubled by figures such as Ernie Kovacs in the USA, who put artistic experimentations and popular television genres in dialogue; or Jean-Christophe Averty's career, which started in ORTF documenting jazz concerts, combined pioneering electronic effects and surrealist fascinations with traditional TV genres, and renewed musical TV programs by introducing avant-garde aesthetics for songs, long before the music video, by singers like Yves Montand, Jane Birkin, Serge Gainsbourg; the same can be said of certain significant production experiences in television, especially during the eighties.

Besides experimental niches and single events, some artists came close to the television medium in its actual popular and homogenized values. Without calling Warhol or Schifano into question, let us consider Cage's participation in the popular Italian TV show *Lascia o raddoppia* in 1958.[4] Paik himself took advantage of the TV medium in several ways, playing with daily TV images as sources for fascination and unusual combinatory practices, or creating anthropomorphic families with TV monitors and programs such as Global Groove in 1973. This programme takes (and elaborates) a patchwork of images from the television universe: *Global Groove*'s non-linear structure includes tap dancing, ice-skating, Native American drumming, a Pepsi commercial, and Allen Ginsberg chanting – all gliding through a video landscape processed by the Paik-Abe Video Synthesizer.'[5] (fig.1) In *Good Morning Mr. Orwell* (1984), the live split-screen satellite transmission from Paris to

[4] See Marco Senaldi, *Arte e televisione. Da Andy Warhol al Grande Fratello* (Milan: Postmedia, 2009).
[5] John Hanhardt, *Nam June Paik Global Groove 2004*, ed. by John Hanhardt and Caitlin Jones (Berlin: Deutsche Guggenheim, 2004) p. 33.

New York plays with television conventions, entertainment and electronic effects (we could say "mass culture" and "avant-garde interventions"). These are only a few of the many examples of Paik's works on and with television, even in the most strictly commercial and mainstream terms, with assembled references, quotations and compresence of visual stimuli. These characteristics make this artist the main figure in post-modern art, according to Fredric Jameson (though we will not enter into this slippery territory).[6] Collages of popular television images also appear in Paik's video dedicated to the composer, *A Tribute to John Cage (1973-1976, TV Lab WNET/Thirteen, 29').*[7]

Video art hence formed and grew in dialogue with music and television, even in its more widespread and popular forms. If the music video (in its commercial declination since the 1980s) owes much to certain video art experiences, video art has in turn dealt with types of music that cannot be considered 'cultured'. This is evident in the work of an artist like Dara Birnbaum, not only with her *Technology/Transformation: Wonder Woman* (1978-79), a pop development from the TV series of the same name, but also in her music videos that put together pop musical and cultural icons. For the series *Pop-Pop video* "she mashed together a shootout from the crime drama Kojak with a commercial for Wang Laboratories computers to make Kojak/Wang (1980)", as Alex Greenberger writes, recalling also Birnbaum's experience on MTV, "creating a work that involved the MTV logo, a Max Fleischer cartoon, and blurred images of a female animator all in a matter of 30 seconds. It showed at the time on airwaves shared with "antic music videos" by the likes of U2, Whitney Houston, Madonna, and Bon Jovi".[8] *In different ways, other authors who are also considered part of the video art field, like Pipilotti Rist, have dealt with pop images and music, and Zbigniew Rybczynski, animation cinematographer that turned to video,* dedicated an entire season of his career, between 1984 and 1989, to the creation of music videos (some of which are distinctly avant-garde in reference to the electronic effects and the visionary staging) even for mainstream and pop groups and musicians (the likes of Art of Noise, Lou Reed, Simple Minds, Cameo, Mick Jagger, Yoko Ono and John Lennon).[9] The most recent video works in which avantgarde and pop-

[6] Fredric Jameson, *Postmodernism, or the Cultural Logic of Late Capitalism* (Durham: Duke University Press, 1991). In the part regarding Paik and the spectator to whom the impossible is asked, that is, to watch all the screens at the same time, Jameson also quotes David Bowie in *The Man who Fell to Earth* (Nicolas Roeg, 1976). The considerations on Paik had appeared also in a smaller text of the same name published in *New Left Review*, 1.146, July-August 1984.
[7] See also the chapters devoted to Paik, Cage and "Fluxus" in Inkyung Hwang, *Il lungo treno di John Cage* (Milano: O barra O, 2007).
[8] Alex Greenberger, 'ArtNews', March 27 2018, http://www.artnews.com/2018/03/27/icons-dara-birnbaum/ [accessed 7 December 2019].
[9] On the relation between music video and video art see Alessandro Amaducci and Simone Arcagni, *Music Video*, (Turin: Kaplan, 2007) and, more recently, Giacomo Ravesi, *Occhi tagliati che danzano. Forme sperimentali della videomusica italiana degli anni Duemila*, in *Fuori norma. La via sperimentale del cinema italiano*, ed. by Adriano Aprà (Venice: Marsilio, 2013); Bruno Di Marino, *Segni, sogni, suoni. Quarant'anni di videoclip da David Bowie a Lady Gaga* (Milan:

culture meet include the case of *Your body must be heard*, by Özlem Sariyldiz (Germany, 2018, 10'), a sort of re-imagining of Peter Campus' video art classic *Three Transitions*, 1973. Here, the chroma-key inlay is revealed by fragments of scenes from old movies (from Turkish melodramas), assembled also as collages and in split screens with popular songs and music.

Imaginary Video Landscape

Within this context, a further interesting instance is found in the collaboration between two artists with different backgrounds and origins, Robert Cahen and Matias Guerra, facing the proposal of Jahangir Selimkhanov to work on the video part of his piece based on *Imaginary Landscape n.5* by John Cage (1952). The subtitle indicates: *for magnetic tape recording of any 42 phonograph records. Imaginary Video Landscape* is hereby born.[10] Here two experiences intertwine what we can, with due caution, define as avantgarde (Cage's piece and the video art) and a popular musical tradition, that of Mugam music from Azerbaijan, which is revisited over an entire century from the 1920s until today. The meeting between Cahen and Selimkhanov happens in Azerbaijan, where the French video artist held a video workshop in 2016, after other invitations in the precedent years. Cahen writes: 'Thanks to Jahangir Selimkhanov I discovered Baku jazz. He is well aware of the music of Cage, Schaeffer, Stockhausen and Boulez and we've talked about contemporary music. He once came to Strasburg for an Azerbaijani music concert…'.[11] Selimkhanov is a musician and musicologist, cultivator of the traditional Azerbaijani music, expert in the music of the 1900s and cultural organizer; he involved Cahen in the creation of a version of *Imaginary Landscape n.5* based on Mugam music, taken from various recordings. In asking Cahen to take care of the video part of Selimkhanov's project, the latter writes:

Meltemi, 2018); Luca Quattrocchi, *Musica per gli occhi. Interferenze tra video arte, musica pop, videoclip* (Milan: Silvana, 2018) catalogue for the art exhibition held in Santa Maria della Scala, Siena, 10 august-4 november 2018). Concerning the relationship between image and sound (up to video and video art a reference to Michel Chion's work) remains crucial, first of all *L'audio-vision. Son et image au cinéma* (Paris: Nathan, 1990) and, on music and video art in particular, *Suono nel cinema, suono nel video,* in *Cine ma Video*, ed. by Sandra Lischi (Pisa: ETS, 1996). For the relation between experimental cinema and sound see *The Music and Sound of Experimental Film*, ed. by Holly Rogers, Jeremy Barham (Oxford: Oxford University Press, 2017); Holly Rogers, *Sounding the Gallery: Video and the Rise of Art-Music,* (Oxford: Oxford University Press, 2013). Again, regarding the relationship between video art and music, and with references to Cage and Paik, see Marco M. Gazzano, *Kinēma. Il cinema sulle tracce del cinema*, (Roma: Exorma, 2012), in particular the chapter 'Comporre audio-visioni. Suono e musica sulle due sponde dell'Atlantico, alle origini delle arti elettroniche'.

[10] *Imaginary Video Landscape*, Azerbaijan-France, 3' 48", 2017. HD 1080p video; Video editing and post-production: Matias Guerra; Footage: Robert Cahen, Matias Guerra; Music: Interpretation of John Cage's *Imaginary Landscape n.5* with Mugam music of Azerbaijan, conceived by Jahangir Selimkhanov

[11] Robert Cahen to Sandra Lischi, e-mail correspondence, 3 April 2018.

I'm working currently on a music performance project where the traditional Mugam music will be put into the context of electronic sounds - from noises to recorded sounds of the planets, and with some music references in between (including generative music based on samples from Mugam and also a reconstruction of Alvin Lucier's experiment on revealing the sound portrait of a particular room through circular recording onto two recorders). One of the electronic 'interventions' I'm planning to do is to make a version of *the Imaginary Landscape n.5* by John Cage based on the bits of Mugam music – both in the pure form and electronically processed. I came to an idea in this regard which I dare to share with you. Do you think it might be interesting to precisely follow the Cage's score which he composed for 42 scrapes of music and make a parallel video score with 42 scraps of video [...] Wouldn't it be interesting for you (it's a sort of hommage to your idea to convey the logic and techniques of *Musique Concrète* to the medium of moving image)?[12]

Robert Cahen (Valence, France, 1945) is one of the most important and well-known artists and pioneers of international video art, he was trained at the end of the 1960s within Pierre Schaeffer's *Musique Concrète* school,[13] at the Paris Conservatory and at the radiophonic studios of the public radio and television in France. A cinematographer and photographer, too, Cahen's first video dates back to 1973, inspired by the desire to experiment the electronic effects obtained with the *Musique Concréte*'s method, recording first and developing afterwards, testing the effect generators of the TV studios that were next door to the radio ones. From his formative years, his path was marked by a particular emphasis on the relation between image and sound design (often authored by Michel Chion) in almost total absence of speech. He experimented in this way both in his own videos and in musically inspired ones (*La recherche instrumentale à l'IRCAM* (1983), *Boulez-Répons* (1985); *Instantanés* (1987), portraits of three IRCAM musicians, *Compositeurs à l'écoute* (1998); *Le deuxième jour* (1988), with the music of John Zorn). The video installation *Le Maître du temps - Pierre Boulez dirige* Mémoriale, 2011, is dedicated to Pierre Boulez, whilst *Hong Kong Song* (1989) is the result of interdisciplinary and international research on the sound of urban spaces (fig. 2). Work on John Zorn's composition *Godard ça vous chante? Tribute to Jean-Luc Godard*, commissioned as an international co-production for an author video music series, shows the search for non-linear and variable rhythmical correspondences with the musical composition, and the succession of urban images linked also with constant variations of space and time. Music penetrates all of Cahen's work: aside from the composers with whom he collaborates and to whom he has dedicated the aforementioned works, he uses music from different times and styles, both famous and unknown, and often only via quick evocations: Schumann, Crumb, Chopin, Strauss, Ravel, Verdi,

---

[12] Selimkhanov to Robert Cahen, e-mail correspondence, June 2017.
[13] See Robert Cahen's *Compositeurs à l'écoute*, 1998, outcome of a visual montage (drawing mainly on photographs of yesterday and today) starting from compositions from various *Musique Concrète* authors, and produced on occasion of the 50 years since 1948.

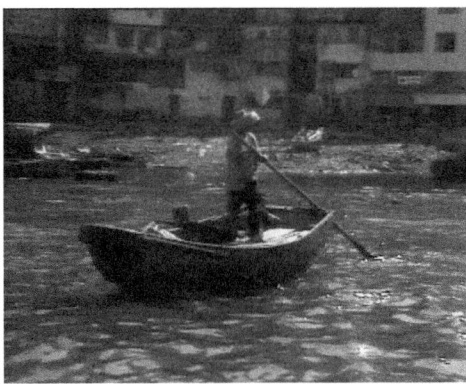

Fig. 2: Robert Cahen, *Hong Kong Song*, 1989

Max Roach, Bartók. For some videos he also worked as sound designer, mainly in the first period of his career.

In a different way, Matias Guerra (1973, Santiago, Chile) also works on the relationship between music and image; he is a painter, musician and author of works that dialogue with music, cinema, the electronic image as well as literature and astronomical references. Regarding the latter, a musical composition and sound installation (one permanent and two temporary) from 2016 within the "Moby Dick" festival at Piane di Bronzo (Tuscania) are worth mentioning.[14] Guerra has an education in information technology and philosophy, and a particular attention to science. His research marks works with rich networks of references, which are not presented as explicit quotations but as structural and deep affinities with the matter in question: this is very pertinent in *Nekrotzar. Following the rainbow,* with a study of the works of Stanley Kubrick as its starting point (paint on canvas, digital prints, video, sound, collective work and research and more- fig. 3). This same piece has also a sound and video-loop installation version.

Compendium K for soundscape, electric guitar, live electronics and sometimes video, *Nekrotzar*, is part of a series of pieces called *Compendia*, namely live musical performances and elements, such as video or painting, reflecting a specific knowledge. *Compendium K* (the K stands for Stanley Kubrick) puts together soundscapes, live music performance and a video with a fixed duration and narrative. [...] It is not a montage-film, it's not by any means a film. It's another mechanism for sense and non-sense, an instrument to play with. Each device pertains a certain quality of my vision of Stanley Kubrick's work. The video work can be ideally divided in four macro scenes as in *Der Grosse Makabre* of the Ligeti/Meschke libretto, where quotations, cites and references to past musical styles are the devices to create its pastiche form. The choice here of Ligeti is manifest, but maybe the choice of the libretto as a baseline for the narrative is less obvious, as occult and evident are certain routes of Kubrick's vision.[15]

[14] http://www.matiasguerra.com/moby-dick.php [accessed 9 December 2019].
[15] M. Guerra, "Nekrotzar. Video and Performance", http://www.matiasguerra.com/nekrotzar.php

Fig. 3: Matias Guerra,
*Nekrotzar. Following the
rainbow* (2016-2017)

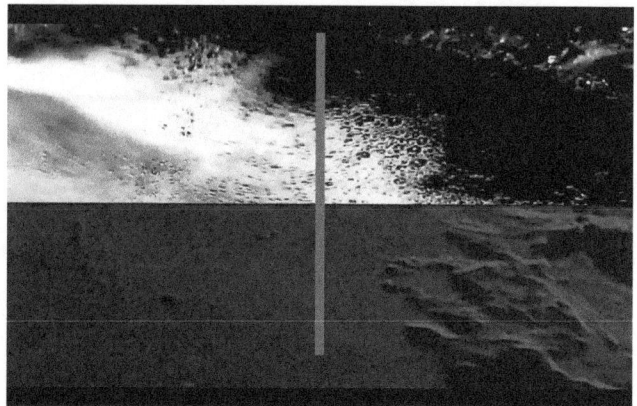

Guerra also wrote the musical score and contributed to the editing of Andrea Semerano's film *Dedalo 2018* (2018), radically and decisively experimental and rich in loving, existential and cinematographic visions. Cahen and Guerra had met for the realization of a video, *This is an Unknown Surface* (2014) from an idea and a text by Alessandro De Francesco – another artist that is comfortable with different media, but mainly with the formal elaboration of language and *augmented writing*.[16] Also thanks to this collaboration Cahen decided to call Guerra, by Jahagir Selimkhanov's invitation, writing to the French artist,

> That would be so great to visualize Cage's score! I thought that 8 levels of sound volume (equivalent to pp to fff) in his score could be applied to 8 levels of opacity of video images, so that landscapes appearance vary from extremely blurred, as in a fog, to very bright, as under sunshine, and the zones of complete silence represented by TV screen 'white noise' [...]. We are working now on sonorization of the score with 42 fragments from recorded samples of Azerbaijianian music of all genres – folk, traditional, symphonic, jazz – up to underground synth-pop. A sort of imaginary soundscape of the national music in 3 minutes...[17]

Cage, Mugam Music, Video

Imaginary Landscape n.5 was composed by Cage in 1952, constituting the last of the *Imaginary Landscapes* series, the first of which is dated 1939. *Imaginary*

[accessed 9 December 2018].
[16] https://docplayer.fr/14932490-Alessandro-de-francesco-portfolio.html [accessed 9 December 2018]. On the international collaborations of Cahen and Guerra, see S. Lischi, 'Videoarte nomade. Cinema, immagine elettronica, musica, scrittura. Percorsi, dialoghi e intrecci planetari (e cosmici): dalla Patagonia all'Azerbaigian, con echi di Cage, Kubrick, Ligeti', *Alias* (*il Manifesto*), 14 April 2018, https://ilmanifesto.it/videoarte-nomade-dalla-patagonia-allazerbaigian/ [accessed 9 December 2018].
[17] J. Selimkhanov to R.Cahen, e-mail correspondence, June 2017.

Landscape n.5 is for 42 records to be re-recorded on tape, as Cage's version was originally composed for a dance piece by Jean Erdman, *Portrait of a Lady*, using 42 jazz records to be played in eight simultaneous tracks. The score indicates that any type of recording can be used, focusing in fact on the length of the excerpts being played and further characteristics such as amplitude, *crescendo* and *diminuendo*, and changes of records, all notated on block graphic paper forming a graphical score that anticipates not only the musical concept of sampling but also its graphical presentation – in fact, Cage's score resembles the interface of any modern audio sequencer software. The final piece is a set of indications or rules that create a system where the sound content produced will vary according to the records used, and the recording of such system will create a different, set *musical object* every time. As a result, there have been many different versions of the score, of which the most interesting to date is Michael Barnhart's, on the prestigious Mode record label, using recordings of Cage's music.[18]

Jahangir Selimkhanov, as one can understand, is interested in national music, a theme on which he often writes and to which he is dedicated as a musicologist and curator of events and festivals, also with the Musicians' Society of Azerbaijan. His work consists, among other aims, in revamping popular musical traditions including Mugam, and also circulating them abroad: dissemination that becomes easier and wider after 1989.[19] The artistic value of Azerbaijani Mugam and its cultural importance was acknowledged in 2003 by UNESCO, when it included Azerbaijani Mugam on The Representative List of the Intangible Cultural Heritage of Humanity. It is worth noticing that the video, which premiered at the Baku Festival (International Symposium on Azerbaijani Carpet, from October 17 to 20) was projected for the first time at an evening with live performed Mugam music.

> Mugam is not merely the main form the national music tradition – one could say it's one of basic cultural values which constitute national identity of Azerbaijan people. Historically and in contemporary use, this term has various meanings – it may simultaneously refer to specific categories of tone scale, melodic pattern and genre. The history of mugam dates back to ancient times. Azerbaijanian mugam bears similarities with various forms of Eastern music – the common principles of modal composition and melodic elaboration could be observed in Indian raga, Iraqi maqam, Magreb noubah, Uzbek and Tajik Shashmakom, Iranian destgah [...]. Since early 20th century Azerbaijanian mugam started to attract the attention of listeners beyond the circle of devoted connoisseurs. Many music groups perform mugam regularly

---

[18] The are many renditions of the score and concept of *Imaginary Landscape n.5*, too many to count, nevertheless to our knowledge there has never been a video realization that has actually taken into account the score, the concept and the principle of Cage's work in the process of creating images. The video is hence not merely an accompaniment to the music, but more similar to a transposition, where the conceptual and artistic value of the piece is inherent to the relation between sound and image.

[19] See Jahangir Selimkhanov, 'Music: Then and Now', *Azerbaijan International*, 3.1 (Spring 1995), 36-37, 45.

in festivals and concert programs all over the world [...]. The Azerbaijani Mugham is a traditional musical form, characterized by a large degree of improvisation. The Mugham, though a classical and academic art, draws upon popular bard melodies, rhythms and performance techniques and is performed in many venues throughout the country.[20]

Thus Selimkhanov turned to Mugam music for his interpretation of *Imaginary Landscape n.5* by Cage, summarizing the operation in the following way:

The 'collage' made out of bits of Azerbaijanian music is a precise realization of the *Imaginary Landscape n.5* (1952) by John Cage, a seminal work in the history of electronic music. The composer has created a graphic score, where 42 scraps of magnetic tape to be chosen randomly are given the precise indication of duration, dynamic level and are distributed between 8 channels. There are countless renditions of this 'author instruction', which differ quite substantially, however, the composer's intention was not to present a final 'product' completely under his control, but rather to initiate a situation allowing to show contemporary soundscape which is disruptively simultaneous, non-linear, fragmented. The idea to use 42 fragments of recordings of Azerbaijanian music from archive recordings of 1920-ies up to very contemporary ones was related to the desire to show a condensed landscape of the national music in all its variety - traditional and new urban folk, jazz, rock, pop, classical and contemporary classical. This fragment of recorded sound appears all of a sudden - as an expression of forced 're-formatting' all the musical perception of the participants of the performance.[21]

As Selimkhanov had written to Cahen, the reference to the performance is due to the version of which this experimentation, entitled *Bahariya*, with the sound artist Farhad Farzaliyev.[22] This inspired the idea to call Cahen, who had been trainedin the *Musique concrète* school:

I thought about a precise 'translation' of the score intended for 42 sound fragments into 42 video fragments to be constructed following the indicated length and intensity of each fragment - in a way, that might be a parallel to what Cahen did in the Seventies – a `translating` approach to sound into the realm of vision [...] Robert Cahen replied very enthusiastically, however, he didn't choose to follow the exact instruction of the Cage`s score, and rather has constructed his video work created jointly with Matias Guerra as an evocation to the music piece we have sent to him. Most important point is that the authors of the video have picked up the historical spirit of an archived memory which is felt in our rendition of the Cage`s piece, and Robert and Matias have decided to attract their own early works as layers into the translucent, polyphonic imagery of this piece.[23]

---

[20] J. Selimkhanov to S. Lischi, e-mail correspondence, 11 December 2018.
[21] Ibidem.
[22] https://www.youtube.com/watch?v=JqaMomtwp6I&t=10s [accessed 18 December 2018]
[23] J. Selimkhanov to Sandra Lischi, e-mail correspondence, 11 December 2018.

'For a random number of cuts from 14 archive videos'

Robert Cahen and Matias Guerra therefore worked together on the video score, analysing first Jahangir Selimkhanov's musical montage. They retrace their archives, intertwining different fragments, including those of their faces on camera today, and in fact the subtitle indicates *For a random number of cuts from 14 archive videos*. Guerra's account is useful here:

> This short work, presented in a few international festivals by now, is based on *Imaginary Landscape n.5* by John Cage (1952), and offers an interesting intersection between avant-garde and popular music (in this case between Cage's score and the Mugam musical tradition, here re-created by the Azerbaijani musicologist and scholar Jahangir Selimkhanov). Moreover, this 'dialogue' is articulated and represented in electronic images by the french video-artist Robert Cahen and myself. Our video-strategy actualizes the fragments, which in a new time and space create unexpected micro-narratives. We have chosen excerpts from our respective video archives to create a 'video landscape' intertwining two different musical experiences, two different approaches and identities, two different histories and aesthetics. The main elements in play become the key references within the images, like the small narratives that open up from second to second and the recognizable repetitions which not only give a rhythm but a semantic context too. We were commissioned the piece and had the music given to us first, instead of focusing on the Azerbaijani *Imaginary Landscape n.5* version we decided to go back to the root, thus not analysing specifically actual 'mugam' distinctive marks like it's tempo or 'mood' but studied the original score breaking down elements of main interest to follow the score not blindly but as a transposition for video, in the end the score was for sound and not image, where the principle and the baseline ideas from Cage's work are respected.[24]

Cahen has commented on this collaboration with Guerra,[25] highlighting the necessity to adopt a pre-existent piece of music (with a commissioned work: two characteristics that recall his work at the end of the 1980s on the music of John Zorn in *Le Deuxième Jour*), but deciding to 'fabricate a mosaic' with pre-shot images that were not filmed for the occasion and opting for less recent and more geometric videos, with saturated colours: what he calls 'the primitive côté of the first video gestures transformed in image (figg 4 - 5). Also in Cage, as a matter of fact, we find great liberty in composing a piece done with scraps of other works. A correspondence of assemblies'. With this approach in place, the editing was done

---

[24] M. Guerra, http://www.matiasguerra.com/imaginary-video-landscape-n5.php (accessed 18 December 2019). See also *Origini/Origins*, catalogue 27th edition of the festival *Invideo-Video e cinema oltre*, 16-19 November 2017. The video was presented at its world premiere at the Festival ISAC, BAKU 2017; then at the INVIDEO 2017 Festival, Milan; at Nasimi Festival, Baku, 2018; at cinema Arsenale, Pisa April 2018, during *Ondavideo, Paesaggi sonori*. On this topic and the relation between sound and image, Guerra held a master's class at the IED in Milan (November 2017), and Cahen and Guerra held a seminar (again on this work) at the University of Pisa, Dipartimento di Civiltà e forme del sapere, in April 2018.

[25] Cahen's statements were collected by S. Lischi, in Pisa on 1 November 2018.

Figg. 4,5: Cahen-Guerra, *Imaginary Video Landscape*, 2017

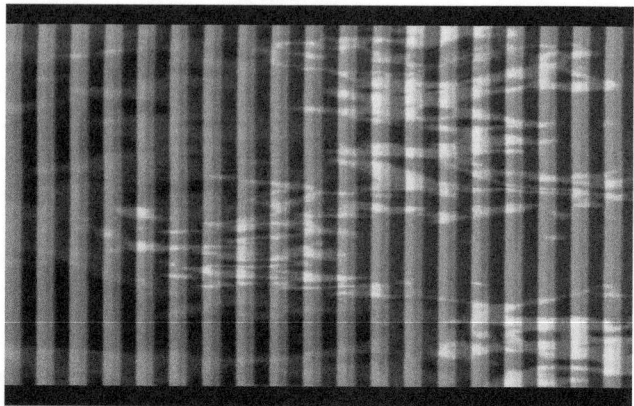

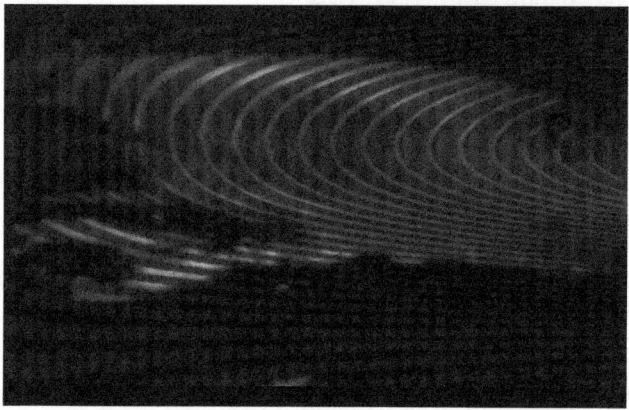

intuitively and enriched by inserting the faces of the authors – or rather the details of their faces, a sort of identification of the author with non-archival clips that were filmed in the moment. 'The alive aspect', Cahen observes, 'which allows the author to escape the gesture expressed uniquely by his creation'. This reminds Cahen of Cage himself, 'his face, his laughter, his gestures – as those of his performances, like the closing of the piano [in *4'33"*, 1952]'. This ensemble in the end takes on 'a micro-coherence of sense', even if its fundamental impetus, Cahen concludes, is that of playfulness: to play with the archive images, to play with details of faces and the correspondences between the music and the visual score.

On the other hand, while writing to Jahangir Selimkhanov, Guerra comments as follows:

> We thought that by using our archives we could match Cage's principle and not go too far from our own aesthetic directions. The historical progression line within the works is strong but I feel it vanishes, making the fragments contemporary, which to me means mainly that they don't have a firmly marked time distinction (the time the video was made as a distinctive element), as the main elements in play become the key references

within the images, like the small narratives that open up from second to second and the recognizable repetitions which not only give a rhythm but a semantic context too. I've watched it without music and I think it works too, as one can ride along according to what marker each person can find or wants to find or simply receives. Anyhow it's a *paysage vidéo* that interlaces two different types of work, two identities which are put in discussion by the work itself.[26]

As already stated, the score wasn't specifically followed and Guerra remarks:

The 3" tape unit of measure could be applied and transposed to video but it would create in some instances a convulsive visual effect that doesn't happen in sound, the score wasn't meant for film so we decided to avoid a blind faithful approach, instead, we took 14 videos, 7 of Robert and 7 mine, they were divided in units of 3 minutes taking what we recognized as having moments that visually could pertain to Cage's indications of, for example, amplitude, *crescendi* or *espressivo*, by choosing colour, rhythm, subject and narrative movements. For example a *crescendi* of 4 to 6, as per the score, in some instances is simply given through a clip with an intense colour change or upwards frequency modification, whereas a set amplitude is given by choosing an arbitrary mix of narrative, movement and colour within the clip. We re-created an eight track system in the editing software were we placed the chosen clips, to be then cut to a minimum of 1 second, the lines from 1 to 3 from the original score can be easily identified by length and as a sort of baseline for the cross-dissolving shorter clips. In a very early stage we had quite an accurate transposition of the score and it was tempting to settle for it, but the insertion of the details of our faces, if I recall properly, changed radically our approach and led us to focus on the rhythm and semantics of the video, leaving the timings chosen and a baseline, but drastically changing the resulting order, I guess that once we had a system in place given by a context and a set of rules, playfulness prevailed, not so much as in determining the ending video but as in playing around with the clips: it was like having a set of puzzle pieces that can create a different final image each time according to where you place them, they will all somehow by chance fit (thanks to the system chosen). I think that in this way we have maintained the underlining philosophy of the composition.[27]

Two different approaches, then, to video composition, two different poetics that relate to each other, two video archives and two 'self-representations' with new footage, inserted in an architecture of images that is transformed by the irruption of eyes, mouths, the creases of the faces, hair, beards, ears and the texture of the skin (fig. 6). It is like a double signature or a vital and 'present' element that insinuates itself here and there in the brief video sequences of the archive footage (from the past) of the two authors. An element of surprise or mystery that in fact has radically changed the approach to the visual score, adding the touch of an apparently unexpected form of study and research. The video opens with a detail of eyes and proceeds by showing, in fast succession and

[26] M. Guerra to J. Selimkhanov, e-mail correspondence, September 2017.
[27] M. Guerra, specifically written for this text.

Fig. 6: Cahen-Guerra, *Imaginary Video Landscape*, 2017

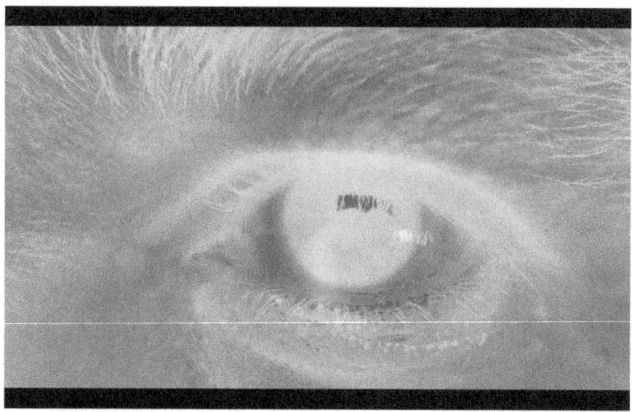

sometimes superimposed, fragments of other works: landscapes, abstract images, a browsed book, trains and gestures, sometimes in black and white and at others in colour, solarizations, sometimes lush colours 'pop' like the first effects and the first chromatic electronic canvases, rarely they are naturalistic. Then sea reflexes, incumbent seas that seem to invade and force the surface of the image, that make the crest of the seafoam dance. Someone passes by, runs, arrives, we go forth through a green pathway, we see train tracks from above. Sometimes it is a suspension, sometimes a correspondence between sound and image, like the short sequence in which a black and white geometric grid – almost a keyboard – appears alongside piano notes in the music composition. At times, even the faces are taken in the archive images with the use of superimposition, occasionally in a single image we find two superimposed details: an eye, a mouth (fig. 7).

The audio track consists specifically of a succession of Mugam clips: a kind of music which was transmitted generation after generation, and which changed over time, interbreeding with other musical genres but maintaining its tradition and broad popularity. It is usually sung (by a female or male voice) and accompanied by musicians that play traditional instruments such as the *kamancha* (a four-string spiked fiddle), the *tar* (a long-neck lute), and the *daf* (a type of large tambourine).

Selimkhanov's composition, even though it consists in a set of brief, sequential cuts, maintains the melodic character of the music as audible, recognisable and driven by a well consolidated tradition. Nevertheless, its fragmentation and, in particular, its development through an extremely experimental video score modifies sense and perception, making space for an audio-vision made also of dissonances and deviations, not only within the musical part but also in the video. The procedure of confronting an avant-garde work (Cage's) with popular and traditional music finds a sort of enhancement in the union of sound and image (which is also inherent in Cage's system, considering the use of jazz, a popular music, in relation with the score and way the sound is conveyed), mainly because the visual idea avoids a 'blind faithful approach', to paraphrase Guerra.

The artwork includes definitely experimental images and definitely popular

Fig. 7: Cahen-Guerra, *Imaginary Video Landscape*, 2017

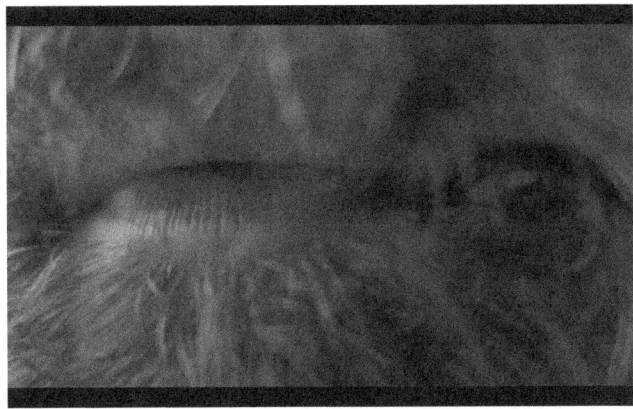

music, weaved into Cage's avant-garde and the reflections of another avant-garde – which produced the well-known declaration *The Future of Sound* in 1928 (signed by Eisenstein, Pudovkin e Alexandrov). Also known as *Statement on Sound*, the latter sought to avoid the dominance of sound over image – it was produced at the advent of sound in cinema, and it feared in particular the possible use of speech – and over editing, with all the latter's dialectic and creative power. To avoid the shoals of the illustrative dimension equates to create a "new orchestral counterpoint" between image and sound.[28] *Even in this orchestration,* the encounter between avant-garde and popular music finds in *Imaginary Video Landscape* an example of a profound research, one rich in echoes.

---

[28] Sergej Ejzenštejn, Vsevolod Pudovkin, Grigorij Alexandrov, 'Il futuro del sonoro. Dichiarazione', in Sergej M. Ejzenštejn, *Forma e tecnica del film e lezioni di regia*, ed. by Paolo Gobetti (Torino: Einaudi, 1964), pp. 523-524.

Tuning into the Radio in Experimental Films from India

Gauri Nori, English and Foreign Languages University, Hyderabad

Abstract

In India, the nexus between the film, music and radio industry ensured that every film included several songs, which in turn were broadcast on the radio. By aligning their commercial interests, the broadcast media endorsed each other and propagated the same content. Kamal Swaroop's *Om Dar B Dar* (1985) and Vipin Vijay's *Hawa Mahal* (2003) subversively employed this repetitive audio-visual excess produced by the mass-media industries to trace the impact of economic liberalisation and the uneasy transition of India into a capitalist society. In both films, the radio is used as a metonym to critique the aural experience in broadcast media. Whereas commercial cinema emphasises the visual, in these experimental films the acousmatic nature of the radio (as an unseen sound) helps to concentrate the focus on the auralscape. By inverting the conventions of commercial cinema and exploring different permutations, Swaroop and Vijay disrupt any possibility of synchrony between the audio and the visual track. This article intends to listen for the ways in which both films upend the hierarchies that plague film sound, allowing instead for a reduced mode of listening as theorised by Pierre Schaeffer and Michel Chion.

Introduction

Although the sense of hearing is first activated in the womb and vision becomes possible only after birth, in the evolution of the cinematic medium, this order was reversed. Films remained 'silent' for more than three decades and when sound was finally synced to the visuals, it was regarded as a mere accompaniment. Now, after a century of filmmaking, we cannot imagine a film without sound and yet the audience continues to pay more attention to visual storytelling than to auralscape. While it is profitable for conventional films to preserve this status quo, avant-garde and experimental filmmakers have sought to explore the possibilities of the medium (both visual and aural, often separately) by challenging these preconceptions of the cinematic audience. For instance, Mani Kaul, a pioneering avant-garde filmmaker, sought to formulate a visual design that was deeply entrenched in the musical tenets of *Dhrupad* (one of the oldest styles of Hindustani classical music).[1] The next generation of experimental filmmakers in India was more aware of the hegemony of 'classical' aesthetics and instead focused their investigations on the persuasiveness of popular culture propelled by mass medias.[2] Kamal Swaroop's fictional film *Om Dar B Dar* (1985) incorporates numerous radio tropes including film songs along with their *farmaishes*,[3] snippets of film dialogue and advertisement jingles to evoke the emptiness that lies at the core of capitalistic excess. Similarly, Vipin Vijay's film essay *Hawa Mahal* (2004) tunes into various histories, memories and events that are associated with the radio. More importantly, Vijay's film interrogates the evolution of broadcast media like the radio and film in the way that each incorporates the conventions of the other. Through the trope of the radio, both films critique the hierarchies and limitations of the aural experience in commercial cinema. Adopting Pierre Schaeffer's understanding of acousmatic sounds and reduced mode of listening, along with Michel Chion's theory of film sound, this paper seeks to listen for ways in which both films effectively address the lacuna of aural studies of cinema.

Film studies has primarily been concerned with the visual aspects of cinema and has rarely articulated an analysis of sound design.[4] One reason for this may be that the human mind tends to spontaneously fuse the audio and visual content when they are played together, making it difficult for us to concentrate solely on the aural track of the film. Swaroop and Vijay sought to prevent this synchresis[5] by creating a disjunction between the audio and the visual. Their films also address the emphasis on the verbal and the musical in commercial film sound. Most films tend to depend on the dialogue to convey the story while music is often used to cover up the visual flaws, drowning out any possibility of creatively using ambient sounds. Instead, the cinematic experiments of Swaroop and Vijay creatively reuse the audio-visual excess produced by commercial mass-medias to produce a critique of it. Furthermore, conventional cinema encourages either a

---

[1] Mani Kaul, *Uncloven space: Mani Kaul in conversation with Udayan Vajpeyi*, trans. by Gurvinder Singh (Quiver: New Delhi, 2013).

[2] Shai Heredia, 'In conversation with Kamal Swaroop', in *The Cinema of Prayoga: Indian Experimental Film and Video 1913-2006*, ed. by Brad Butler and Karen Mirza (London: Wallflower Press, 2006), pp. 101-106.

[3] Traditionally, in live music performances, *farmaish* were requests made by patrons for songs they wished the artist to perform. Subsequently, radio listeners were encouraged to send in their requests via postcards. The RJ would often read out the sender's name and address before playing the film song that was requested.

[4] For examples of studies having theorized aspects of film sound extensively, see James Buhler, David Neumeyer, and Rob Deemer. *Hearing the movies: music and sound in film history* (New York: Oxford University Press, 2010) and Brian Kane. *Sound unseen: Acousmatic sound in theory and practice* (Oxford University Press, USA, 2014).

[5] 'Synchresis' is a term coined by Chion, who combined the words synchronism and synthesis, to suggest the forging of an immediate relationship between something one sees and something one hears at the same time.

'causal listening' which seeks to connect the sound to its source or a 'semantic listening' which allows languages to be decoded. Alternatively Schaeffer and Chion have sought to adopt and analyse what they have called a 'reduced mode of listening', which "focuses on the traits of the sound itself, independent of its cause and of its meaning".[6] The term 'reduced listening' was first coined by Schaeffer (2004 [1966]) who, inspired by Edmund Husserl's phenomenological reductions, sought to build an awareness about and subsequently reduce our dependency on causal and semantic listening.[7] To encourage this reduced mode of listening, Swaroop and Vijay highlight acousmatic sounds, like that of the radio, where the source of the sound is hidden from the spectator's sight, making the soundtrack independent from the visuals. By inverting the conventions of cinema, their films become an exercise in film phenomenology, pushing their audiences to question their cinematic conditioning.

From Classical Music to Popular Film Songs on the Radio

During the silent film era, American studios established their monopoly over the Indian market through the construction of cinema theatres that only screened foreign films.[8] Within this context, the advent of sound challenged this monopoly and contributed immensely to the development of the Indian film industry because Indian audiences wanted to 'hear' films made in their own languages.[9] India has always had a strong oral tradition and songs were vital to any kind of performance including religious ceremonies, folk drama and staged theatre. Recognising this commercial potential, the music industry hired musicians to produce box-set gramophone recordings of popular theatrical musical dramas. The musicians in these recordings became prominent celebrities overnight. Stephen Putnam Hughes demonstrates how the Tamil film industry appropriated this celebrity status of the musical stars and borrowed the heritage of classical music to gain popularity amongst the Indian upper classes.[10] With the rise of the talking films, the Indian film studios collaborated with the music industry to produce filmed versions of the box set recordings. While the actors of silent cinema required considerable training to adapt to the advancement in technology, musicians were already used to having their voices recorded. Hence,

---

[6] Michel Chion, *Audio-vision: Sound on Screen*, trans. by Claudia Gorbman (New York: Columbia University Press, 1994), p. 29.

[7] Pierre Schaeffer, 'Acousmatics', in *Audio Culture: Readings in Modern Music*, ed. by Christoph Cox and Daniel Warner (New York: Continuum, 2004), pp. 76–81.

[8] Kristin Thompson, *Exporting Entertainment: America in the World Film Market 1907-34*, (London: British Film Institute, 1985), p. 144.

[9] Kaushik Bhaumik, *The Emergence of the Bombay Film Industry,1913-1936* (Oxford: Oxford University Press, 2001).

[10] Stephen Putnam Hughes, 'Music in the Age of Mechanical Reproduction: Drama, Gramophone, and the Beginnings of Tamil Cinema', *The Journal of Asian Studies*. 66.1 (2007), 3-34 (p. 25).

early sound films of the 1930's were almost entirely composed of songs. In this way, traditional live musical performances were commodified into gramophone recordings which in turn were incorporated into cinema in the form of film songs.

Gregory Booth's study of the evolution of the Hindi film song industry shed light on the immense competition that existed between lyricists and musicians, who were constantly expected to produce songs that could fit into any narrative. Booth suggests that the aim to make songs fit outside of their initial filmic setting was so that they could: 'live an independent existence and take on personalized emotional meanings that might supersede or simply ignore their dramatic context'.[11] This independence of the film songs from their role in the cinematic narrative also proved useful when they were played on the radio which became more widely available from the 1950's onwards. Bhaskar Chandavarkar also found that repetition was a key factor to the success of film songs.[12] The lyricists tended to use a small set of words over and over, each time adding another connotation that would broaden its definition. Chandavarkar further observed that the form of the film song required that the first two lines called the *mukhda* or refrain be repeated after each of the 3-4 *antharas* (three-line verses) and the last words of each line had to rhyme. This constant repetition within the song with the addition of a catchy melody made it possible to commit the lyrics to memory. Unlike classical music, the repetitive formula of the film song also allowed for repeated broadcasting on the radio. Since radio was present in a large number of home, the songs reached a much larger audience. The radio could also be consumed less attentively and so it became the constant background score to household chores or social gatherings. If the song was popular among radio-listening audiences then the film could be guaranteed success at the box office, suggesting a direct correlation between the radio and the film audience. This nexus between the radio and the film industry further established the popularity of Hindi film songs.

In 1953, the newly appointed minister of the Information and Broadcasting Division (IB), Dr. B. V. Keskar, made the unpopular decision of banning film songs from being broadcast on the All India Radio (AIR). Film songs were deemed unworthy because of their innuendo-ridden lyrics and incorporation of Western melodies. Instead, Keskar envisioned the radio as a tool to spread awareness of and an appreciation for Indian classical music. According to David Lelyveld, this decision reflected a desire, on the part of the government, to compensate for the neglect that Indian music faced during the British colonisation as well as a move to clampdown on musicians of the erstwhile Muslim rulers who, in Keskar's view, had diluted the religious force of *Carnatic* music by creating the

---

[11] Gregory D. Booth, *Behind the Curtain: Making Music in Mumbai's Film Studios*. (New York: Oxford University Press, 2008), p. 31.
[12] Bhaskar Chandavarkar, 'The Power of the Popular Film Song', *Cinema in India* 4.2 (1990), 20-25. (pp. 23-24).

more secular variant *Hindustani*.[13] Lelyveld identified that Hindi film songs often mimicked the *Hindustani* rhythms, thereby fuelling the perception that this ban was an attempt by the subdominant Hindu upper class to (re)assert its ideology. [14] The new government also took complete control of the market by nationalising all industries and levying heavy taxes on the private radio and film studios. In her article 'Re-embodying the Classical', Shikha Jhingan identifies how the industry officials pushed back against this 'highbrow' attitude of the state, arguing instead that films finally made 'classical' music available to the common man.[15] As it turned out, the radio audiences summarily rejected Keskar's 'educational' impetus and switched over to a station that catered to their film song requests, the privately-owned Radio Ceylon. The shift in popularity from public to private radio stations was so pronounced that AIR's ban lasted only five years (1953-1957) before it was once again forced to play the week's most popular film songs. The immense popularity and the social impact of film songs could no longer be denied.

Previously, classical musicians depended on the patronage of the wealthy, performing mostly to private audiences, and were expected to perform any *farmaish* requested. The tradition of the *farmaish* continued with the patrons of the radio sending their requests via postcards on which most often only the first line of the film song was written. The radio jockeys would then announce the name of the sender and the place from where it was posted. This democratisation of the *farmaish* allowed everyone to have a few seconds of relative fame. Privately-owned radio companies also favoured following the countdown system or song requests format because it enabled them to play advertisements between two songs. Here, broadcasting classical music presented an additional practical problem: the compositions were not of fixed length and each piece was unique to the person rendering it. Unlike set compositions in Western Classical music, Indian Classical music encouraged a more fluid approach where the interpreter of the piece, considered a maestro, would spontaneously meditate on a *raaga* (melodic mode). AIR's solution to this problem was to commission renowned musicians such as Pt. Ravi Shankar and Ustad Amjad Ali Khan to compose short and light *Hindustani* pieces that were primarily aimed at displaying artistry.[16] This approach proved popular among radio audiences, and from adhering to the time limitations of gramophone recordings to composing light classical

[13] Carnatic is a system of music associated with the southern part of the Indian sub-continent while *Hindustani* music is considered a North Indian musical style. *Carnatic* was developed in the fifteenth and sixteenth century during Bhakti movement, while *Hindustani* synthesizes Vedic chants with Persian Musiqu-e-Assil traditions.

[14] David Lelyveld, 'Upon the Subdominant: Administering Music on All-India Radio', *Social Text* 39 (1994), 111-127 (p.117).

[15] Shikha Jhingan, 'Re-embodying the "Classical" The Bombay Film Song in the 1950s', *BioScope: South Asian Screen Studies,* 2.2 (2011), 157-179 (p. 160).

[16] B. N. Goswami, *Broadcasting: New Patron of Hindustani Music* (New Delhi: Sharada Publishing House, 1996) p. 20.

compositions for the radio, classical musicians were ultimately forced to cater to populist demands.

In the 1960's and 1970's, filmakers like Satyajit Ray sough to counter the commercial impetus of the entertainment industries that threatened the space in which classical arts could flourish. Ray's *Jalsagar* (The Music Room 1958) was one of the first films to feature performances of renowned artists of Indian classical music, including Ustad Vilayat Khan who composed the film's score. The narrative follows a former landlord losing everything in one last chance to host a grand soirée. To convey the society's sudden shift from tradition to modernity, Ray includes various audio metaphors such as the grating noise of the young neighbour's electrical generator that interrupts the feudal protagonist's enjoyment of the sombre classical notes of the *surbahar* (a plucked string instrument played by the renowned Ustad Imrat Khan). While Western audiences were enthralled by the refinement that the classical performances offered, Indian audiences found it tedious and Ray was criticised for indulging in bourgeois nostalgia.[17] By contrast, avant-garde filmmakers of the time, such as Mani Kaul and Kumar Shahani, sought to apply the tenets of classical music to the cinematic medium. Having studied the way *Dhrupad* emphasises each note, Kaul's camera would force his audience to meditate on a single shot and by doing so achieved a non-representational mode of cinema. Additionally, Shahani aspired to synthesise the various elements of sound in cinema including the musical, verbal and ambient sounds as observed in the tradition of *Khayal Gayki* music.[18] However, these avant-garde auteurs were accused of indulging in elitist experiments and were criticised by both the commercial industry and ironically, by Satyajit Ray.[19] Learning from these experiences, Kaul and Shahani's successors chose instead to interrogate the persuasiveness of popular aesthetics.

The Trope of the Radio in Experimental Films

By the end of the 1980s Rajiv Gandhi had set in motion the liberalisation of the economy and soon foreign goods flooded the market. After years of being denied access to these items, Indian consumers enthusiastically started going after them. Kamal Swaroop, once Kaul's assistant, recognised that at the heart of this consumerism was a never-ending desire for more and dealt with these pressing issues of modernity in his films. In *Om Dar B Dar*, Swaroop traces the India's society shift from Gandhi's model of *swadeshi* (self-reliance) and *satyagraha* (non-violent resistance) to a model of heady capitalist consumption through the

---

[17] Andrew Robinson, *Satyajit Ray: The Inner Eye: The Biography Of A Master Film-Maker*, (London: IB Tauris, 2004) p. 113.
[18] Kumar Shahani, 'Notes for an Aesthetic of Cinema Sound', *Framework. The journal of Cinema and Media*, 30-31 (1986), p. 91.
[19] Satyajit Ray, *Our Films, Their Films*, (New York: Hyperion, 1994) p. 105.

life of a small-town family. The film loosely follows the adolescent adventures of the protagonist Om (played by Aditya Lakhia and Manish Gupta) whom, the spectator learns, has a special ability to hold his breath for hours under water. He runs away from home after misplacing diamonds that were given to his father for safekeeping, only to be trapped by priests who use his talent to advertise a water-resistant electronic watch. Through surrealist imagery, witty metaphors and Dadaist style, Swaroop exposes the fallacy of capitalism that offers material products as a solution to spiritual problems.

As its title suggests, *Om Dar B Dar* highlights the life and struggles of those who are close to Om, all of whom are tragically trapped in their petty desires. In doing so, the film evokes themes of small-town aspirations and the uneasy shift from the neo-modernity of the independence movement to the capitalist modernity ushered in by the opening up of India's economy. The protagonist's sister, Gayatri (Gopi Desai) desires independence but is only able to achieve it superficially. As she boldly goes to the movies on her own, she attracts the attention of Jagdish (Lalit Tiwari). Jagdish is introduced as a private tutor who hails from Jhumri Telaiya, a small city that radio audiences would immediately recognise as the place from which the greatest number of film song requests were sent: Rameshwar Prasad Barnwal, a mica-mining tycoon from Jhumri Telaiya, sent numerous postcard requests to radio stations, leading to the city's name being announced on the radio and generating enthusiasm from a large number of its residents.[20] This episode established Jhumri Telaiya's reputation in the popular imagination across the country and while residents from other towns tried to compete with Jhumri Telaiya's fame by sending as many post-cards, many urban audiences assumed it was a fictional place that symbolised small town aspirations. In the film, Jagdish portrays a typical radio fan, whom film scholar Aswin Punathambekar has characterised as being the median between a rowdy character and a *rasika* (aesthete).[21] From the film dialogue, it is evident that Jagdish identifies with the tragic-fatalist lover more than the macho hero of popular Hindi cinema. By revealing the way in which these characters consume popular culture, Swaroop reminds his audience of its pitfalls: Jagdish's mediocrity stems from his limited exposure to Hindi cinema while Gayatri's curtailed aspirations epitomises the empty promise of the capitalist consumer culture.

Kamal Swaroop used the excess of sounds and images produced by commercial cinema and radio to reveal its inherent banality. This kind of experimentation opposes popular aesthetics by using its raw materials to

[20] Sanchari Pal, 'Of Music, Mica and Mithai: The Fascinating Story of How Jhumri Telaiya Became a Legend', in *The Better India,* https://www.thebetterindia.com/91535/jhumri-telaiya-koderma-jharkhand-mica-radio-kalakand/ [accessed 7 December 2018].

[21] Aswin Punathambekar, 'Between Rowdies and Rasikas: Rethinking Fan Activity', in *Fandom: Identities and Communities in a Mediated World,* ed. by Jonathan Gray, Sandvoss Cornel, and C. Lee Harrington, 2nd edn (New York: New York University Press, 2007), 198-209 (p. 198).

produce a radically subversive alternative. Although sound is more abstract than images, conventional filmmakers tend to solidify the aural track by synching it to the corresponding visuals in their films. In critiquing the limitations of sound design in conventional cinema, Chion experimented with creating a wholly different musical genre. His practice of musique concrète liberated mundane recorded sounds from their concrete causal connections to compose highly abstract pieces that necessitate a reduced mode of listening. Similarly, *Om Dar B Dar* can also be read as Swaroop's objection to commercial films, whether aimed at entertaining or advertising, for creating a surplus of repetitive audio and visual materials. His riposte was to take this excess and recycle it in order to understand it.[22] The film is replete with the surplus created by mass medias including film songs, radio *farmaishes*, over-the-top film dialogues and advertisement jingles, so as to reveal how persuasive their illusion is. The film continuously parodies the marketing of religious miracles and capitalist commodities. Just as the *farmaish* shows were often named after their brand sponsors such as *Binaca Geetmala* and *Colgate Cibaca Sangeetmala*, the film repeatedly alludes to the *Promise* toothpaste brand that became very popular in India (and was second only to Colgate in terms of the market share) because it claimed to include clove oil which is traditionally used to treat dental ailments. While this parodies the oral hygiene product placements that used to take place on the radio, the choice of brand conveys Swaroop's insight into the rise of capitalism in a society that is still deeply attached to traditional values.

Jagdish and Gayatri's romance is advanced primarily through the radio and, accordingly, the film is continuously punctuated by a radio jockey (RJ) announcing the request for their favourite song *Babloo from Babylon*. The way in which the radio *farmaish* expresses exactly what the characters are thinking and feeling is aimed at representing a near-telepathic connection between the characters. Chion observed that on-the-air sounds that are electronically transmitted via acousmatic devices such as the radio do not need to adhere to the 'natural' laws of propagation in cinema and, especially in the case of broadcast music, offer filmmakers the freedom to transcend the limitations of the onscreen and offscreen space.[23] Since the radio is often heard but rarely seen in the film, the RJ takes on the role of the omnipresent and omnipotent narrator of the film. After their encounter at the movies, the RJ notes that Jagdish changed his address from Jhumri Telaiya to Ajmer, in an obvious attempt to have his name read-out alongside Gayatri and Om. The lovers seem to be convinced that they are soulmates simply by requesting the same song and hearing their names together on the radio. Here Vebhuti Duggal's investigation of the *farmaish* phenomenon

---

[22] Kamal Swaarop, 'Kamal (Om) Dar B Dar's Googlies and Life in General', *Deep Focus*, 2.1 (1989), 12-20 (p. 16).
[23] Michel Chion, *Audio-vision: Sound on Screen*, trans. by Claudia Gorbman (New York: Columbia University Press, 1994), p. 77.

provides insights into the relationship between the RJs and their audience. [24] The audience not only forms a personal connection with generic songs but, through the *farmaish,* also hopes to gain public acknowledgment from the RJ. The *farmaishes* most often came from small cities and towns and would be ornamented or written in verse as if addressed to a lover who lives in a faraway city. The mostly urban RJ had to rally together this large dispersed audience while simultaneously bestowing on each individual *farmaish* the recognition that they sought. As a result, tAt a result, through this practice, radio as a form produced a peculiar intimacy in anonymity.

While their physical courtship is constantly being frustrated by Om and his father (L. Shastri), the lovers use the radio for their private communication, albeit broadcasting it throughout the country. For instance, when Jagdish pretends to teach Gayatri to ride a bicycle, Om abruptly throws it off a cliff, presumably embarrassed by their silly courtship rituals. As proof that Gayatri took the hint, the next time the song request is read out, Om's name is left out. This conveys to Jagdish that Gayatri is finally comfortable being alone together with him. Although this means of communicating their love is seemingly ludicrous, the conservative norms of Indian society forces lovers to find circuitous ways of being together. In the scene when they finally consummate their love, their gender roles are comically inverted, with Gayatri taking the lead and Jagdish looking distraught by the end of their physical union. When he bursts into the room, Gayatri's father finds her sleeping alone, and she curtly tells him to turn off the radio, indicating to the viewer that the charade of romance is over. The intention of this over-the-top tragic parody is to liberate the viewer from the superficial tropes and conventions of popular cinema. Swaroop clearly equates the lover's film-fuelled fantasy with the naïve faith that consumers have when they buy into the capitalist promise. Both bubbles will burst, only leading to further alienation. Jagdish is not seen again until the last few minutes of the film when the spectator discovers that Gayatri has a child who she claims is a 'paying-guest'. Jagdish feebly tries to assure her that he continued to send song requests to the radio when he was in Dubai. Simultaneously, we hear the rest of their song on the radio that plaintively bemoans the cost of progress.

As it were, the lovers must advertise their love in the same way that the film songs were aired on the radio to advertise and maintain the popularity of Hindi cinema therefore adhering to the growing consumer culture of the time. To mirror the circuitous flirtation of the couple, the film chooses to substitute the directness of dialogues with the radio *farmaishes*. While conventional cinema adheres strictly to synchrony, experimental filmmakers like Swaroop found that synchresis could take place between audio and visual elements that are not directly connected to one another. Chion argued that the illusion of synchresis between these audio-visual counterpoints challenges conventions of film sound.

[24] Vebhuti Duggal, 'Imagining Sound through the Pharmaish: Radios and Request-postcards in North India, c. 1955–1975', *BioScope: South Asian Screen Studies*, 9.1 (2018), 1-23 (pp. 16-18).

Even though a synchresis occurs, the disjunction between audio and visual elements remind the audience of the manipulation involved in combining the audio with the visual.[25] By replacing the dialogues with sound bites from the radio, the fallacy of the romantic relationship and the capitalist society that it represents is exposed. In this way, Swaroop's film disturbs the complacency of its audience and necessitates a more attentive mode of listening to the film.

Although radio is usually consumed as a form of distraction, in the film, the characters pay so much attention to it that all other sounds are drowned out. By giving the radio more prominence, the film works to decentre the emphasis on comprehending its narrative through the visuals and diegetic dialogues, as typically found in conventional cinema. Since the radio is heard but not seen, the synchresis between the radio and the mind of the characters is made possible. However, the outlandishness of the song reminds the viewer of the inherent disparateness between the sound and the image. The song itself is not romantic and the lyrics are seemingly nonsensical at first but soon we realise that it epitomises the futility of their relationship as reiterated in the refrain, 'Hero, zero, pass or fail'. The prominence given to English words is not only reminiscent of the British colonisation but also points to the rise of American capitalism that once again made English the language of commerce.[26] While it is obvious to the spectator that their favourite song is a parody of Hindi film songs, it is charged with tremendous personal significance for the lovers. Yet the absurd lyrics of the song disrupts the viewer's expectations of a romantic duet. This moment of disorientation is crucial since it thwarts the process of synchresis, encouraging reduced listening instead. The reputation of the film for being impenetrable may be justified if one focused only on the visual aspects of the film (by doing so the narrative becomes highly confusing), but the audio track provided by the radio announcements, jingles and the songs clearly conveys the film's thematic focus. When we put all the pieces of the song together, we realise it encapsulates the tragedy of the character's trapped existence. Through such audio-visual counterpoints the film employs the excess that mass media produces to simultaneously critique it.

Examining the nature of different media in India and tracing their trajectories over the last century – their birth, evolution and eventual decline – is also a constant theme in Vipin Vijay's film essays. *Hawa Mahal (2004)* focuses on the radio, *Videogame (2006)* examines the shift from celluloid to digital filmmaking while *Chitrasurtam (2010)* explores the internet's virtual realms. The films investigate what is particular to a medium while also making universal connections between different media. In doing so, they force viewers to put aside their conventional expectations of a documentary, and instead allow them to participate in its carefully curated sensory experience actively. Far from tracing

---

[25] Chion, p. 63.
[26] Harish Trivedi, 'From Bollywood to Hollywood: The Globalization of Hindi Cinema', *The Postcolonial and the Global*, ed. by Revathi Krishnaswamy and John C Hawley (Bristol-Minneapolis: University of Minnesota Press, 2008), 200-210 (p. 201).

a linear history of the radio in India, Vijay's *Hawa Mahal* (named after a popular AIR program) plays with the fluidity that the acousmatic radio offers, resulting in a film that has a stream-of-consciousness style rather than adhering to a fixed narrative. Vijay invites us to appreciate the inner workings of the radio by taking us through the process of production as well as reception while continuously interrogating our relationship with sound. From its very beginning, the film reminds us that, unlike our eyes, we cannot close our ears. Vijay addresses the imbalance of sound's secondary status in conventional cinema by syncing the visuals to the audio track. This means that if a sound is distorted in the film, so is the visual. At various times, we hear the audio track of the film trying to focus on a sound, as one would when tuning the radio to a particular channel, and simultaneously we are shown the shift from a blurry image to the object in complete focus. In this way the film becomes the means for the audience to experience the way sound is modulated tangibly.

While the popular film songs broadcast on the radio were consumed as a type of distraction, *Hawa Mahal* compels its audience to be attentive to every aspect of its aural composition. Like Chion's Musique Concrète, it highlights ambient sounds rather than verbal or musical cues, manipulates the visuals as per the aural distortions, and incorporates 'unusable' or unpleasant sounds such that the audience's attention is continuously drawn to the soundtrack. By focusing on the sound design, the film upends the visual bias of cinema to produce an aesthetics of sound as an evanescent material. Vijay further breaks down the illusion of synchresis by distorting the film's dialogues / narration, making it seem like the voices are coming from a distance or by choosing not to show the source of the sound. This distortion and disembodiment of the voice and sounds is also an obvious allusion to the experience of listening to the radio. At one point, we witness the recording of a Bengali radio play where the actors manipulate their voice, filling it with the required emotion but without their facial expressions changing. The radio audience would hear their melodramatic dialogue delivery and automatically imagine it visually but by observing the actual process of recording this play, the film's audience is made to see through their theatrics. Similarly, the film pays homage to the famous radio prank in which Orson Welles's narration of H. G. Wells' novel *The War of the Worlds* caused panic amongst listeners who believed that a real alien invasion was taking place. In this way, we are made to acknowledge that sound can be as powerful and persuasive as the visual.

Hawa Mahal also makes us acutely aware of the hierarchy of sounds in cinema. While dialogues and songs are given prominence in conventional cinema, Vijay includes several 'unusable' sounds that often erroneously occur during recording and playback. Unpleasant sounds such as shifting from one radio frequency to the next, ambient noise, echoes, delays, and feedback would normally be cleaned and edited out of film soundtracks. By incorporating them into the sound design, the film also plays the role of an audio archive.

In the same way, Vijay saved the pieces of celluloid that were thrown away at the editing table from his 1999 short film shot and reused them in his next film *Videogame* (2004). Shots that were considered NG (not good) takes for one film became the means of interrogating media obsolescence in another film. Although both audio and images have the capacity to record and preserve the past, there is clearly a bias in what is allowed to survive. The fact that most of early silent cinema is lost while the few fragments that have survived are not being adequately preserved is evidence of such hierarchy. The film cautions us against deleting things that are not useful to us at a specific moment as there may be no trace or memory of that moment in the future. Accordingly, in his films, Vijay seeks to create a palimpsest of sounds and visuals that encapsulate the experience of media that have become outdated even before their possibilities have been fully explored. When something new comes about, it pushes the old out. The film uses the metaphor of a football field turned into a mall. As a man walks through the aisles of the mall, he recollects the victories that he shared with teammates on the erstwhile field, while his son watches a football match on the screens of TV waiting to be sold. All media eventually become outdated and all that remains is fragments of their existence.

The film is not merely an archive of memories associated with the radio in India, it also is a critique of its limitations. The film recounts the story of Janaki, one of the first singers to have her songs recorded by the Gramophone Company. She was brutally stabbed 56 times by her jealous lover and, from then on women were discouraged from singing on the radio. To compensate for the loss of female vocalists, recording companies employed young boys like Master Madan who became immensely popular but also tragically died at the age of 14. Although several of his records exist, no photograph of him has survived. Just as human life is transient, the evolution of technology will at some point make the radio obsolete. In investigating the nature of these recording devices, Vijay finds that like our memories, any kind of recording will always be incomplete. Many people share the common memories of distractedly listening to the radio while doing household chores. There are many shots of the radio providing company for women of different ages, alone inside their homes. This is one of the few moments in the film that includes popular film songs, but the feeling is of stifling claustrophobia rather than of nostalgia. The scene goes on to draw a direct connection between the loneliness of these women and the alienation that the one may feel in modern day discotheques where party-goers might be dancing alone in a room full of strangers. Vijay seems to suggest that while mass media like radio, film and television cater to a large group of people, they cannot offer them a sense of community.

Conclusion

In Swaroop's *Om Dar B Dar*, the radio becomes a metonym for mass media that promote endless consumption. The tragedy of the lovers' dependence on mediocre *farmaishes*, nonsensical film songs and advertisement jingles becomes the cautionary tale against the buying into the capitalistic promise. By revealing the mechanics behind its illusion, Swaroop hopes to disabuse his audience of the persuasiveness of the consumer culture. The film demonstrates how everything has been turned into an advertisement – the lovers advertise their love for each other on the radio which in turn promotes songs for the film industry that commodifies culture. Keskar's failed attempt to restrict the airing of film songs on the radio proved that any attempt to subdue the industry will be met with equal resistance and will eventually backfire. Not only is the film industry responsible for curbing the potential of cinema by encouraging the constant production of formulaic narratives, it has also limited the role of the radio to broadcasting popular film songs. The powerful nexus between the radio and film industry makes it almost impossible for independent and community owned radios to sustain themselves. Although media activists have worked hard to democratise the airwaves, the dominance of public and commercial radio drowns out any alternative.[27] Therefore, by staging the parody of both radio and cinema, Swaroop exposes the hegemony of the industry just as his experimental film liberates the viewer from the conventional mode of filmmaking.

With the rise of music television channels like MTV (and of personal, cd and mp3 players and more recently music streaming apps), the radio was gradually displaced as the primary source for the consumption of freshly released music. Before the potential of the radio was fully understood, newer technology had taken over. Vipin Vijay's *Hawa Mahal*, investigates this phenomenon of media obsolescence caused the rapid change in technology using the specific instance of the radio. Instead of transforming the medium, the newer digital technologies are limited to mimicking the structures and processes of the previous technology. No media exists in isolation, as media scholars like Jay David Bolter and Richard Grusin have observed, and during the remediation process the new media borrows conventions of the 'old' while at the same time the old media incorporates aspects of the 'new'.[28] Unlike the narratives of popular cinema that often pay homage to the ubiquitous presence of the radio, Vijay's film essay does not indulge in the nostalgic yearning for the past. Tracing the evolution of the radio in India and examining the nature of recorded sound allows Vijay to expose the structures of hierarchy within film and radio production.

While various Western cultures have tended to emphasise the primacy of the written word as the vehicle for communication following the democratization of printing technology, in India the oral tradition of chanting and singing has always held greater sway over the public. This crucial difference between cultures is perhaps one of the keys to understanding why it was inevitable for films in India to include songs. Furthermore, William O. Beeman observes that since cinema

[27] Vinod Pavarala and Kanchan K. Malik, *Other Voices: The Struggle for Community Radio in India*, (New Delhi: SAGE Publications India, 2007), p. 106.
[28] Jay David Bolter and Richard Grusin, *Remediation: Understanding New Media*, (Cambridge, MA: MIT Press, 1999), p. 48.

Gauri Nori

was a western import, the songs used in Indian films were freed "from the bonds of both the classical and folk tradition".[29] Although the broadcast media made classical music more accessible to the general public, the nexus between the music, film and radio industries limited the scope of the aural dimension. Instead of exploring new possibilities, each broadcast media simply carries forward the conventions of the older medium. To counter this hegemony, Swaroop and Vijay use the trope of the radio to expose the prevalence of the visual over the audio and the verbal over the musical in commercial cinemas. Their cinematic experiments challenged the illusion of synchresis and freed the aural track from its confines to the visual as theorised by Schaeffer and Chion. Hence, their films require multiple attempts of reduced listening to recognise the various formal experiments at work. Each time one watches these films, a new aspect of the auralscape is revealed and yet another preconception of sound design in cinema is dismantled.

---

[29] William O. Beeman, 'The Use of Music in Popular Film: East and West', *Society for Visual Anthropology Newsletter*, 4.2 (1988), 8-13 (p. 11).

106

Visions of China: Avant-Orientalism, Art Rock, and Conflicted Otherness

Runchao Liu, University of Minnesota, Twin Cities

Abstract

The essay reexamines the countercultural positionality of art rock musical works by considering the often-dismissed correlations between Western rock and the Oriental. Introducing the concept of Orientalism to Lawrence Grossberg's five-hypothesis proposal for studying rock affects, I will focus on the case study of the *Tin Drum* album (1981) by the British band Japan. Through a contextual analysis of the album and a symbolic analysis of the *Visions of China* music video, I will examine some intricate relations between rock's "affective Otherness" and the construct of the Oriental Otherness. Juxtaposing postmodern aesthetics with popular music and Orientalism, I will discuss the implications of reducing Orientalist cooptation to a progressive technique of music making. I will then propose the concept of 'Avant-Orientalism' to describe this series of musical practices and their representational problematics. Finally, I will argue that although the post-war context constructed the Oriental Otherness, this subjectivity was furthered by the avant-Orientalist cooptation to secure the affective positionality against the hegemonic. However, while the cooptation of Oriental Otherness reflects rock's survival strategy and anti-hegemonic agenda, it inevitably re-inscribed an Orientalist ideology under its fragmented progressiveness, making the Otherness of avant-Orientalism an always-conflicted one.

With cultural roots in African-American music, but having been disproportionately popularised by many white musicians,[1] rock music has been an important terrain for scholars and critics to investigate issues of racialisation, cultural hybridity, identity and cultural citizenship, and countercultural politics. Music and cultural studies scholars have long been interested in how the transcontinental and cross-cultural flows from urban Black America, Jamaica,

---

[1] For rock music's significant Black roots and how rock and roll became 'white', see Jack Hamilton, *Just around Midnight: Rock and Roll and the Racial Imagination* (Cambridge, MA: Harvard University Press, 2017). For another look into African/African-American musical influence on popular musical forms, see Samuel A. Floyd, *The Power of Black Music: Interpreting its History from Africa to the United States* (New York: Oxford University Press, 1995).

and Europe have influenced rock music, such as the late-1960s progressive rock and the 1980s post-punk.[2] However, academic debates surrounding these issues usually significantly overlook how Asian cultures have had a constitutive, and not just symbolic, role in complicating the trajectory of Western rock music.[3] We can see endeavors to fuse Asian musical traditions with rock as early as The Beatles' *Revolver* (1966), which is influenced by Indian traditional music. The new wave and post-punk era of the late-1970s and 1980s - coinciding with the introduction of the marketing category of 'world music' to the West, the globalization of popular music, and the general spirit of musical experimentation at the time,[4] - produced many musical works that incorporated non-Western elements. While some scholars have seen this as a postmodern 'technique' to break stylistic boundaries and create new meanings,[5] this article calls attention to musical works that exemplify a musical phenomenon that I call 'Avant-Orientalism'. These works, often created by white musicians, incorporate or experiment with the rhetoric, sounds, and images of Asian cultures in ways that misrepresent, mystify, monetise, and fetishise them at the same time.[6]

Examples of 'Avant-Orientalism' in rock music abound: Siouxsie and the Banshees have dabbled with Asian tunes and themes in *Hong Kong Garden* (1978) and *Arabian Knights* (1981); Brian Eno and David Byrne have heavily integrated sampled and recorded Middle Eastern sounds with electronica in *My Life in the Bush of Ghosts* (1981); and David Bowie has spiced up a love song with an exotic intro in the controversial single *China Girl* (1983).[7] These works, admittedly, demonstrate different composing rationales for coopting Asian cultures. This article takes special interest in the authorial intent and social meanings of a self-Othering strategy that operates through a unique practice of

[2] See Simon Reynolds, *Rip it Up and Start Again: Postpunk 1978-1984* (London: Faber & Faber, 2009).
[3] For a wholistic view on this issue, I recommend Rehan Hyder's book on British-Asian popular musicians: *Brimful of Asia: Negotiating Ethnicity on the UK Music Scene* (Aldershot: Ashgate, 2004).
[4] For more discussion of these coinciding factors, see Simon Frith, 'The Discourse of World Music', in *Western Music and Its Others: Difference, Representation, and Appropriation in Music*, eds. by Georgina Born and David Hesmondhalgh (Berkeley: University of California Press, 2000), 305-22; Timothy D. Taylor, *Global Pop: World Music, World Markets* (New York and London: Routledge, 1997); and Andy Bennett, 'The Forgotten Decade: Rethinking the Popular Music of the 1970s', *Popular Music History*, 2.1 (2007), 5-24.
[5] For an example of postmodern analysis of music videos, see Will Straw, 'Music video in its Contexts: Popular Music and Post-modernism in the 1980s', *Popular Music*, 7.3 (1988), 247-66.
[6] It is beyond the scope of this article to does not provide extensive sonic analysis of Avant-Orientalism. For examples of analyses of s Oriental/Asian riffs in Western popular music, see Martin Nilsson, 'The Musical Cliché Figure Signifying The Far East: Whence, Wherefore, Whither?', <http://chinoiserie.atspace.com/> [accessed 29 March 2019] and Charles Hiroshi Garrett, 'Chinatown, Whose Chinatown? Defining America's Borders with Musical Orientalism', *Journal of the American Musicological Society*, 57 (2004), 119–74.
[7] For current examples of Avant-Orientalism, readers can refer to examples like Katy Perry's 'Dark Horse' (2013), Blur's *The Magic Whip* (2015), Muse's *Simulation Theory* (2018), or even Nicki Minaj's 'Chun-Li' (2018).

self-Orientalisation: namely, white musicians coopting Asian elements in order to produce a countercultural stance and self-alienate from the racial and political hegemony in the post-war and cold-war conjuncture. I use the case of *Tin Drum* (1981), the last but most commercially successful album by the British band Japan, to examine these complications.

It is both important and difficult to examine this self-Othering strategy. First, besides intersectional concerns surrounding racism, sexism, imperialism, and postcolonialism when it comes to cultural appropriation, we must also examine how the intention of creating an affective and political alliance against the dominant societal structure complicates those intersectional concerns. In other words, we cannot simply generalise the band Japan's musical interventions as acts of yellow- or black-face.[8] Second, the political conjuncture of the late 1970s and 1980s – i.e. (xenophobic Thatcherism and Cold War anti-Communist ethos – complicated the social meanings of processes of musical experimentation like Avant-Orientalism. Lastly, this musical phenomenon has coincided with the 'postmodern turn' in academia, but examples of the turn in popular music studies have tended to focus on theorising postmodern patterns in stylistic and genre innovations, thus providing limited critical insights on its racial and ethnic matters.[9]

Informed by the afore-mentioned political and musical conjuncture, this article asks: How should we understand the superficial yet popular fusion of art rock and the Orient? What is at stake when these 'creative' yet purposefully anti-hegemonic fusions are constructed and delivered through reenacting and coopting a political and cultural Other? Particularly, I consider how the ideology and criticism of Orientalism provide us with alternative insights into the cultural logic behind first, the experimental and countercultural politics of rock music and second, the postmodern logic behind the crafted superficiality of art rock musical works. To explore these questions, this article combines a contextual analysis of the album *Tin Drum* (1981), a critical discourse analysis of various texts, and a semiotic analysis of the music video for the song *Visions of China*, in which we see the band members taking on the personae of 'Communist Chinese soldiers' and performing an abstract collage of their frugal yet orderly everyday life, in which they practice Chinese martial arts and marching band.

I use Lawrence Grossberg's concept of affective alliances and a five hypotheses proposal to study rock's affective power,[10] based on which I

---

[8] And, in the case of such interventions inBlack and Asian musics like Asian American jazz or Afro-Asian hip-hop, appropriate analysis of this phenomenon would require different frameworks.

[9] Some scholars have dissected the postmodernity of rock through its intertextuality and interracial identities, such as Angela McRobbie in *Postmodernism and Popular Culture* (New York: Routledge, 1994) and E. Ann Kaplan in *Rocking Around The Clock: Music Television, Postmodernism and Consumer Culture* (New York: Methuen, 1987). However, focusing on postmodern patterns may cost concrete readings of the texts. For a critique of postmodern reading of rock music, see Andrew Goodwin's s 'Popular Music and Postmodern Theory', *Cultural Studies*, 5 (1991), 174-190.

[10] Lawrence Grossberg, 'Another Boring Day in Paradise: Rock and Roll and the Empowerment of Everyday Life', *Popular Music,* 4 (1984), 225-258.

highlight three perspectives: the post-war context (after the Second World War), affective Otherness, and cooptation strategy. Broadly put, I examine a rarely-articulated connection between the countercultural politics of art rock, the postmodernisation of popular music, and Orientalism. More specifically, I examine the racial and affective complications that come along with art rock's anti-hegemonic praxis. I argue that while the post-war conjuncture produced the postcolonial and Communist Otherness of the Orientalised subjects at the time, this marginality was appropriated to construct an imagined and crafted Orient in *Tin Drum* (1981). I further contend that this manufactured Oriental Otherness was reinforced through the countercultural politics of art rock and its cooptation strategy for securing the affective possibilities to stay outside of the hegemonic. At the same time, I show how a postmodern analysis of the fragmentary contents and filming strategies of the 'Visions of China' music video accounts for the construct and reinforcement of Oriental Otherness. Finally, I argue that Orientalism is not just a symptom of the 'eccentric' taste of art rock gone wrong, but a postmodern discourse *constitutive* of art rock's survivalist creativity that often gets praised by music critics. The article concludes by calling for a careful re-examination of the scholarship dealing with the postmodernisation of popular music and critically reflecting on potential alliances with Orientalism.

Conflicted Otherness and Affective Alliances

This section explains why I call out the discourses of 'Otherness' of rock music, especially those found in experimental, avant-garde and art-school traditions, as 'conflicted' and why it needs critical attention. Following this, I explain why it is important to approach the topic with the politics of rock affects in mind. I also explain how these complications inform the proposed concept of Avant-Orientalism.

I use Otherness to describe the intentionally constructed and maintained, anti-hegemonic, countercultural positionality put forth by many rock musicians. Like many subcultures, rock has long been grappling with the hegemonic incorporation and absorption of style.[11] In a sense, self-Othering could be an apt characterisation of the kinds of strategies entailed in those struggles. When discussing the ambivalent resistance of avant rock to mainstream culture, Bill Martin differentiates between the antagonism toward becoming mainstream artists and the antagonism toward the commodification associated with becoming mainstream. He argues that the resistance of avant rock lies more in resisting commodification than going mainstream, and that this elastic relationship with

---

[11] Many subculture studies scholars have investigated this complicated process. Dick Hebdige's *Subculture: The Meaning of Style* (n.p.: Methuen, 1979) and Jodie Taylor's *Playing it Queer: Popular Music, Identity and Queer World-Making* (Switzerland: Peter Lang, 2012) are landmark studies dealing with this issue.

the mainstream is a unique dynamic of the avant-garde in rock. He explains that '[a]vant rock resists and plays off the mainstream of rock music [...], but it may not have the sort of *antagonism* [emphasis in the original] toward the mainstream that one often sees in jazz and classical avant-gardes' and that 'the antagonism is perhaps not with the mainstream artists per se, but with the market and commodification'.[12] This complicated attitude toward the mainstream is the first way in which art rock displays a conflicted relationship to the notion of Otherness.

Another layer of art rock's conflict is enacted through white avant-garde rockers actively aligning themselves with a minority identity and culture to express their own anti-hegemonic resistance. Besides the band Japan, Pink Floyd in songs such as 'Chapter 24' (1967) and 'Set The Controls For The Heart Of The Sun' (1968) exemplifies a trend of using elements of Oriental mysticism to ex-corporate themselves from hegemonic patterns of music-making. Examples are also abundant in Rock Against Racism (RAR) where many white rockers, such as The Clash and Billy Bragg, allied with Black and South Asian rockers to express a collective stance against the dominant anti-immigrant hostility of the time. As Grossberg remarks, creating affective alliances affords 'modes of survival' for rock to self-produce and survive as a resistant culture in a postmodern world where rockers experience conflicted affects 'between despair and pleasure' and 'between the desire to celebrate the new and the desire to escape it'.[13] Grossberg defines an affective alliance as 'a network of empowerment' and 'an organisation of concrete material practices and events, cultural forms and social experience which both opens up and structures the space of our affective investments in the world'.[14] Following this idea, I investigate the creation and complications of affective alliances between art rock and Oriental Otherness in *Tin Drum* (1981).

Grossberg proposes five hypotheses for analysing the intricate system of rock affects: first, rock originated within the context of the post-war era; second, meanings in rock function affectively, not just ideologically, to produce and organise affective alliances that disrupt the hegemony over pleasure and desire; third, rock locates and produces sites where pleasure is possible and important for audiences by piecing together and organizing fragments of everyday life; fourth, rock is diverse in its inscription of structural and affective differences compared to other cultures and its structures of affective alliances; and five, the cooptation of new sounds, styles and stances is a significant strategy of rock to self-produce its history and reproduce its affective power.[15] This framework captures some of the intricate, multilayered power dynamics of rock music in a time that the fine boundaries between the hegemonic and the countercultural were being

---

[12] Bill Martin, *Avant Rock: Experimental Music from the Beatles to Bjork* (Chicago and La Salle, IL: Open Court, 2002), pp. 188, 213.
[13] Grossberg, p. 235.
[14] Ivi, p. 227.
[15] Ivi, pp. 225-58. Note this proposal was originally for studying rock in the US.

tested and (re)negotiated. Like Grossberg, I am interested in investigating rock's strategic empowerment through the production of affective alliances, but I seek to enrich his original proposal by introducing Orientalism into the conversation.

I show that an affective alliance articulated around a series of vaguely imagined concepts of the Orient – such as a poorly conceived representations of Communist China, Japan, or East Asia more broadly – complicates the 'modes of survival' of rock. This affective alliance inevitably fetishises Asian cultures as something 'new' to celebrate while somehow also offering a magical solution balancing those conflicted desires. I propose the concept of 'Avant-Orientalism' to describe the conflicted affective and ideological issues of the musical phenomenon discussed above. An avant-Orientalist musical work actively incorporates musical and non-musical symbols of the imagined Orient in order to produce a quasi-sensibility of the avant-garde and experimental that does not perfectly fit the mainstream market.

Post-war Context and Affective Otherness: Constructing Oriental Others

This section considers how the conservative and activist post-war ethos in the U.K. stimulated an affect that informed the making and using of the Oriental Otherness in general, and the Otherness of the album *Tin Drum* (1981) by the band Japan specifically. I propose the musical movement Rock Against Racism (RAR) (1976-1982) and the rise of Thatcherism (1975-1990) as two particular contextual matters to better understand how and why the band constructed, mobilised, and performed a series of Oriental subjectivities through their creative agency.[16]

While music scholars and critics have referred to *Tin Drum's* (1981) musical aesthetics in terms as diverse as ethno-funk, art pop, and new romantic,[17] its *conceptual* inspiration – early days communist China – is prominently consistent throughout the album. Many track titles instantly evoke communist China, such as *The Art of Parties, Canton, Visions of China, Sons of Pioneers,* and *Cantonese Boy*. Besides the visuals of the album cover and 'Visions of China' music video, the band members also impersonate Chinese Communist soldier in the lyrics. For instance, 'Cantonese Boy' describes how an assiduous and obedient young man in Canton is hailed by the Red Army to join the mission of changing "the lives [they've] led for years".[18] In the lyrics, the band vocalist, David Sylvian,

---

[16] My use of 'Oriental' subjectivity is an intentional rhetorical decision to emphasise the fictionality and imperialism behind the Asianness invented in *Tin Drum* (1981). One can think that the Oriental subjectivity is about the quality of being Asian in an Orientalist's mind. The point is that the white avant-garde, not the Oriental, created the Oriental subjectivity; the Oriental doesn't have actual subjective agency and, honestly, doesn't exist among us.

[17] Mark Fisher, *Ghosts of My Life: Writings on Depression, Hauntology and Lost Futures* (London: John Hunt Publishing, 2014) and Reynolds, *Rip it Up and Start Again*.

[18] Canton refers to the Guangzhou Province in modern China. 'The Red Army': a direct reference of the army of the Chinese Communist Party in the 1930s; simplified Chinese: 红军; pinyin: hóng jūn.

adopts the first-person plural pronoun 'we' and expresses the hailing from the putative perspective of the Red Army: "We're singing / Marching through the fields / We're changing / The lives we've led for years / Red army calls you / Red army needs you". The lyrics conjure up a sense of unity, collectivity, and positivity toward the communist future. Specifically, a series of imagined Oriental subjectivity is performed through the Cantonese boy being framed as a "civilian soldier" who can follow orders and "bang [the] tin drum" because "only young men broke the wall".

The lyrics do not express clearly why the army calls the boy, but the positive tone towards the communist future and the Cantonese boy being needed in the army is an affective link that requires further discussion.[19] Stereotypes about Asians being polite, obedient, and lacking creativity are not new, but a positive affective link between an obedient Cantonese young adult and the army's interpellation is rather rare and, more importantly, anti-hegemonic in the 1980s UK. In *Orientalism* (1978), Edward Said writes how the Orientalist (referring to "area experts" in the original passage) sees the relationship between communist Soviets and other communist nations:

> After all, the 'West' since World War II had faced a clever totalitarian enemy who collected allies for itself among *gullible* Oriental (African, Asian, undeveloped) nations. […] The legendary Arabists in the State Department warn of Arab plans to take over the world. The perfidious Chinese, half-naked Indians, and passive Muslims are described as vultures for 'our' largesse and are *damned* when 'we lose them' to communism, or to their unregenerate Oriental instincts: the difference is scarcely significant.[20] [emphasis added]

Tellingly, the Oriental in *Cantonese Boy* that Japan created shows nonconventional Oriental subjects and traits found in Said's depiction of the Orientalist tropes of Asian peoples. The Cantonese boy might be 'gullible' but certainly is not being 'damned'. After all, as Sylvian explained to *NME* journalist Paul Morley in 1982, *Tin Drum* (1981) was not meant to concretely signify anything more than an absolute abstraction to free one's mind from subjective and objective limitations:

> *Tin Drum* wasn't 'a record about China', […] It was a state of mind being presented, thoughts and moods pushed forward *as bare as possible* [emphasis added] to not even reach the place where confusion enters into it. I want to achieve that state of mind where what I write doesn't refer particularly to time or place, but goes beyond that.[21]

[19] While I do analyse musical texts, I do to the extent that it serves to unfold bigger pictures. I kindly ask readers not to read this article as a textual analysis or a traditional musical analysis.
[20] Edward W. Said, *Orientalism: Western Conceptions of the Orient* (London: Penguin Group, 2003), pp. 107-8 [first publ. in (1961)].
[21] As cited in Martin Power, David Sylvian: The Last Romantic (London: Omnibus Press, 2004).

In retrospect, it is safe to say *Tin Drum*'s (1981) abundant tropes of Communist China and other pan-Asian symbols are not 'bare' enough to make this mission possible. Art has that potential, but the band was not there yet. Regardless, to understand the making and embodiments of postcolonial and Communist Oriental Otherness, even though they look quite different from Said's classic depiction, we need to take a closer look at the post-war context.

One rather important backdrop on cultural, political, and musical levels against which *Tin Drum* (1981) was produced is Rock Against Racism (RAR). It is possible to refer to the sentiments and issues that RAR addressed to interpret the rationale and sociocultural effects of the album, even though Japan was not an active RAR participant. RAR is a musical and political movement in the U.K. led by many punk and post-punk musicians to address racism and white-nationalism in the general public as well as among musicians. RAR aimed to break the racial boundaries of the time and brought about concerts and collaborations by Black, South Asian, and white musicians. Many participant bands were influential punk personalities at the time, such as The Special, The Clash, and X-Ray Spex. Although RAR was active only between 1976 to 1982, it has become a quintessential example of how popular music can mix politics and education, with pleasure.[22] As Simon Frith observed, to some degree, the popularity of RAR reflects a collective oppositional sentiment against Thatcherite UK: "the pop record is about the only public account of Thatcher's Britain that makes any emotional sense of what it means to be young or unemployed or black."[23] Within this affective and political context, Japan and *Tin Drum* (1981), an ostensibly anti-racist and anti-hegemonic record, could easily borrow the resistant aura from RAR while remaining 'different' from major RAR activities, which had relatively fewer engagements with Asian communities than their Jamaican counterparts.[24] In other words, singing about/for/by Asians, especially East Asian communities, remained rare.

Meanwhile, to better understand how the artistic decision of appropriating communist Chinese discourses may contribute to *Tin Drum*'s (1981) anti-hegemonic stance, it is crucial to consider cold war tensions and the rise of Thatcherism in the U.K., where neither the Oriental 'flavour' nor communism was welcomed. The popular discourses produced by *Tin Drum* (1981) praising the social order and military life of communist China disrupted the ideological hegemony in the capitalist West. By creating this affective alliance,

---

[22] Simon Frith and John Street, 'Rock Against Racism and Red Wedge: From Music to Politics, From Politics to Music', in *Rockin' the Boat: Mass Music and Mass Movements*, ed. by Reebee Garofalo (Boston, MA: South End Press, 1992), 67-80.

[23] Simon Frith, 'Post-punk Blues', *Marxism Today*, March 1983, pp. 18-21.

[24] RAR had active Asian members (e.g. Alien Kulture, a quartet having three second-gen Pakistani immigrants) and organised concerts protesting against racist attacks on Asians (e.g. the concert held by RAR groups responding to "Paki-bashing" incidents), but the involvement of Asians in RAR in general was much less than their non-Asian counterparts. See Frith and Street, 'Rock Against Racism and Red Wedge', 67-80.

the countercultural positionality of the album was constructed and reinforced. Moreover, the strong xenophobic tendencies stimulated by far-right National Front and the Conservative Party under Margret Thatcher leadership afforded *Tin Drum* (1981) more oppositional capital. Simon Reynolds notes that in 1978, 'Thatcher had expressed concerns about immigration, using the metaphor of "swamping" to describe the impact of multiculturalism on the British "character" and way of life.'[25] In an interview with *NME* journalist Ian Penman in 1982, Sylvian explained how he was drastically opposed to this sentiment and how he built the purposeful vagueness of representations of the East into the album:

> My fascination with the East has always been because it's a *totally different* culture [...]. I've never actually been to China. My fascination for it is purely in terms of imagery. I'm not really dealing with Chinese problems or the society as such. A lot of the ideas come from *totally different* places [...]. I think the Japanese way of life is a *much better* way of working in terms of society [...]. The way they live their lives is based on old ideals and traditions, as well as modern technology. That's why it works, they've kept their morals and values.[26] [emphasis added]

Singing about how the 'Japanese way of life' – or the life depicted in *Tin Drum* (1981) – was 'much better' than 'the British "character" and way of life' was certainly an Othering discourse distancing itself from the dominant lifestyle. In fact, both RAR and Thatcherism had served to secure the affective Otherness of *Tin Drum* (1981), a musical work that remains at a critical distance from the dominant Thatcherite ideology as well as at an arguable distance from RAR. In the above quoted interview, we can also sense a clear flavour of techno-Orientalism in its fetishisation of the combination of the old ('old ideals and traditions') and the new ('modern technology'). Many media critics and scholars have debunked techno-Orientalism and illustrated how a seemingly positive and harmless ideology like this has done great damage to Asians in the form of Asian erasures, the objectification and dehumanisation of Asian bodies, the instrumentalisation of Asian bodies and cultures, etc.[27] While the 'communist China' theme could be an artistic preference that explains art rock's ambivalent antagonism toward the mainstream, it does not easily mitigate the problems of appropriating Oriental Otherness, an imperialist intervention which has produced concrete collateral impacts on both the diasporic Asian communities in the West (most of whom in the 1980s UK were from ex-colonies) and Asians in Asia for centuries.

---

[25] Reynolds, *Rip it Up and Start Again*, p. 65.

[26] As cited in Martin Power, *David Sylvian.*

[27] Many media productions, such as *Blade Runner* (1982) and *Neuromancer* (1984), have been scrutinized for their techno-Orientalism. For such analyses see Jane Chi Hyun Park's *Yellow Future: Oriental Style in Hollywood Cinema* (Minneapolis: University of Minnesota Press, 2010), *Techno-Orientalism: Imagining Asia in Speculative Fiction, History, and Media,* ed. by David S. Roh, Betsy Huang, and Greta A. Niu (New Brunswick, NJ: Rutgers University Press, 2015), and Timothy Yu, 'Oriental Cities, Postmodern Futures: "Naked Lunch, Blade Runner", and "Neuromancer"', *MELUS*, 33 (2008), 45–71.

Orientalist Cooptation: Fabricating Superficiality

Although the post-war context has produced Oriental Otherness and secured an anti-hegemonic affect, Japan decontextualised this marginality and then recontextualised its signs in *Tin Drum* (1981), a process particularly evident in the music video of *Visions of China*. Grossberg suggests that rock is postmodern in that it appropriates hegemonic incorporation into its own discourses: while hegemony responds to resistance through *incorporation*, the power of rock would practice *excorporation* by reproducing the boundary between dominant and youth cultures as a response to the hegemonic attempts to incorporate rock into mainstream consumer culture. He explains that rock exercises *excorporation* by removing:

> signs, objects, sounds, styles, etc. from their apparently meaningful existence within the dominant culture and relocates them within an affective alliance of differentiation and resistance. The resultant shock – of both recognition and of an undermining of meaning – produces a temporarily impassable boundary within the dominant culture, an encapsulation of the affective possibilities of the rock and roll culture.[28]

On the affective level, this holds true for *Tin Drum* (1981). Many media reviews of the album expressed the sentiment that Japan removed the signs of communist China from their originally meaningful context and relocated them in *Tin Drum* (1981). In the song, the relations between the East and the West were rearranged and reimagined to construct what Sylvian deemed as an ideal way of life, which, nevertheless, was inspired by Japanese culture. Since it is the complicated ways that affect works in cases of avant-Orientalism that the present analysis is interested in, I will then show that when *Tin Drum* (1981) 'produces a temporarily impassable boundary within the dominant culture', that boundary is only possible through a synergistic effort by the social ethos of the U.K., the band's Orientalist performance, and similarly reductionist media discourse.

In the music video of 'Visions of China', the band members take on the personae of young communist Chinese soldiers and sing about the hopes and hardships of the time while reenacting multiple scenes of the supposedly everyday life as Chinese communist soldiers. In this non-linear and multi-sited music video, a minimalist setting appears first: Sylvian sits on the floor, singing and playing a jigsaw puzzle, alone in an empty room where all the viewer can see is a window with blowing curtains and a TV set. All the video's scenes in this setting are monochromatic. In the last scene after Sylvian finishes the puzzle, the puzzle turns chromatic, and then so does Sylvian as if he was lit up in the process of completing the puzzle. After Sylvian finishes the last piece of the puzzle, the viewer sees a pale naked back with a colored tattoo, and when this individual puts on a piece of kimono-looking clothes and turns around to face

---

[28] Grossberg, p. 232.

the camera, the viewer sees an East Asian woman who appears ultra-pale. She wears straight long black hair and makeup that evoke the look of a geisha, with pale complexion, largely blended red eyeshadow, bright red lipstick, and heavy eyeliner. The aesthetic and visual influence from Japanese culture is also obvious in the androgynous appearance and kabuki-style makeup taken on by the band members.[29] Under a superficial reshuffle of Chinese and Japanese symbols that are heavily framed as visions of 'China', the music video creates a sense of depthlessness and superficiality. In a television interview, Sylvian talked about the influence of Japanese culture:

> The first visit to Japan influenced us. It took us a long time to actually bring into the music, but in 79 I think it was when we first went there. I mean we were really taken by the place. And I came back to London and read a lot about the culture and so on, and went back a few more times and then slowly got an idea about the music because I was getting interested in the culture of Japan […]. Japanese music in particular, I think it's *the space, the emptiness of it* [emphasis added]. How important the spaces are, as important as the music itself and as something we try to incorporate in *Tin Drum*.[30]

As indicated in the interview, the concept of *Tin Drum* (1981) was not just built on referencing China but also Japanese culture. The minimalist setting of the music video could then be seen as a visualisation of sonic emptiness, which is a significant feature of the song. However, the music video ironically features real footage of marching armies of China as well as the band members performing Chinese culture and the life of communist Chinese soldiers. All the original scenes take on a minimalist aesthetic when it comes to space. For example, a scene depicting a Chinese lion dance[31] is arranged in an empty space with a white background and is visually blurred. Nothing else is visible on site other than the dancers; nothing else is chromatic other than the lion dancing costumes. In another similarly delivered scene, we see two individuals practicing fighting with each other using with objects that look like traditional Chinese weapons (possibly Chinese spear and sword).

A pursuit of minimalist aesthetic of space may be most strongly demonstrated in another scene where two Caucasian individuals (presumably members of the band), dressed in costumes resembling Chinese military uniforms, sit on the ground together in front of a small table. The background is extremely minimalist and empty, with just enough signifiers for a Western audience to recognise this as an imitation of Chinese communist life: a chicken, a willow tree, and a sonic signifier: Chinese sorna.[32] An austere lifestyle is enacted but the minimalist

---

[29] Paul Simpson, *The Rough Guide to Cult Pop*, (London: Penguin Books, 2004), p. 58.
[30] Toolateforheaven, *David Sylvian Ghosts and Interview 480p Quality*, online video recording, YouTube, 26 February, 2011, <https://www.youtube.com/watch?v=ZGCB6Fyn58M> [accessed 15 December 2018].
[31] Simplified Chinese: 舞狮; pinyin: wǔ shī.
[32] Simplified Chinese: 唢呐; pinyin: suǒ nà. This instrument is credited as 'dida' in the album credits.

aesthetic largely romanticises this austere, if not primitive, lifestyle. Surely, the superficial fusion of Japanese aesthetics and a communist China imagery produces a temporal hyperreality that the dominant Western culture was not able to discern: a metaphorical kiss-and-makeup session between capitalist Japan and communist China during the cold war after the Second World War. Even if this postmodern reshuffling appears shocking and incompatible to Caucasian eyes and ears, it still stirs up a long history of Orientalism that treats Asians as homogeneous, apolitical, and ahistorical subjects, as Mark Fisher aptly comments on Japan's fabricated superficiality of the album:

> Japan had pursued art pop into a sheer superficiality, which exceeded even their inspirations in its depthless aestheticism [...]. All – social, political, cultural – meaning seems to be drained from these references. When Sylvian sings 'Red Army needs you' on the closing track, *Cantonese Boy*, it is in the same spirit of *semiotic orientalism* [emphasis added]: the Chinese and Japanese Empires of signs are reduced to images, exploited and coveted for their frission [sic] [...]. Images are decontextualised, then re-assembled to form an 'Oriental' panorama that is strangely abstract.[33]

With the exception of a few critics like Fisher's, other critics considered *Tin Drum* (1981) a musical advancement under the influence of Asian music. One review compiled in *All Music Guide to Rock* (2000) exemplifies such media discourse. It praises Japan for having 'finally dropped their Bowie/Roxy fixations and began making their own music' and notes that the album is under 'heavy Oriental influence' and 'indebted to Asian music'.[34] The review specifically references the intro of the second track 'Talking Drum' as its synthesiser textures and percussion 'point to the Orient'. However, listening to the intro, it is very hard to identify any authentic Asian musical signifiers.[35] The intro arranges synth sounds in a thin yet widely spaced, monophonic texture and the percussion, starting with a quaver, delivers a polyrhythm built on a steady one drop rhythm that is in fact a popular reggae style drum beat. The overall musical texture (created by the percussion, bass, synthesizer, and vocals) is rich but does not feel overloaded due to the song's consistent simplistic approach to mixing sounds. This minimalist aesthetic adopted for constructing soundscape might be able to 'point to the Orient' but it is certainly not due to Asian musical influence found in the intro's synthesiser textures or percussion as the review suggests. Media discourses like this inevitably exoticise Eastern cultures by arbitrarily labelling unusual sounds and textures as foreign and therefore 'naturally' Oriental and Othered.

Similarly, *Alternative Rock* (2000) describes the album as '[j]ourneying deep

---

[33] Fisher, *Ghosts of My Life.*
[34] *Alternative Rock* and *All Music Guide to Rock* are compiled books of rock music reviews. See p. 579.
[35] By authentic Asian musical signifiers, I mean to emphasise that the intro doesn't demonstrate any traditional Asian/Chinese musical features (e.g., texture, instrumentation, rhythm, melody).

into the vagaries of musical structure, texture, and rhythm, weaving atmosphere as fine as gossamer' and as 'dominated by the exotic Eastern themes'.[36] Without a critical listening to the actual tracks and coopted cultures, these unusual arrangements, such as offbeat drums, rare synth sounds, and unstructured fretless bassline, were often seen as innovative, progressive, and unprecedented, signifying the Oriental. Paul Morley, in his *NME* review of the album, emphasizes how learning from Eastern aesthetics is important for breaking through the restrictions of Western pop: 'Western (pop) techniques surrender to an appreciation of greater Eastern techniques, a meditative serenity and ascetic impressionism wither the restrictive formality of the pop song [...]'.[37] Morley further suggests that 'a sense of helplessness and hopelessness' would inform the 'elusive design' to advance Western pop, which exemplifies a type of media discourse allowing us to capture the fetishisation and romanticisation of Eastern austerity and tranquility. These two types of media discourse both run the risk of Orientalism through their careless appreciation of the (problematic) musical content and Orientalist cooptation strategy.

Conclusion: Under the Progressive Superficiality

Fredric Jameson observes that some postmodern works have 'a more positive conception of relationship, which restores its proper tension to the notion of difference itself' through radical, random, discontinuous, and collagist differences from the 'old aesthetic'.[38] However, what is seen as 'differences' and 'radical' usually comes with political baggage. When a postmodern work operates around 'radical differences' through reenacting Oriental Otherness, it is crucial for us to critically and carefully re-examine the postmodern progressiveness that is usually associated with such practices.

Sue Thornham describes a postmodern panorama of popular music where 'signs are the reality and the imaginary and the real have become confused', 'time and place are hard to identify', and 'a blend of styles and references mix together'.[39] On the surface, *Tin Drum* (1981) seems to fit in this postmodern panorama. However, as noted by Grossberg, postmodern music such as new wave and post-punk is explicitly surreal, with emphasis on fragmentation and reflexivity, which acknowledges and celebrates superficiality without foregrounding interpretation.[40] There tends to be an assumed antagonism between

---

[36] Dave Thompson, *Alternative Rock* (San Francisco, CA: Hal Leonard Corporation, 2000).

[37] Paul Morley, 'Japan: Tin Drum (Virgin)'. *New Musical Express*, 21 November 1981, http://www.rocksbackpages.com/Library/Article/japan-tin-drum-virgin. [accessed 25 March 2019].

[38] Fredric Jameson, *Postmodernism, or the Cultural Logic of Late Capitalism* (Durham, NC: Duke University Press, 1991), p. 31.

[39] Sue Thornham, 'Postmodernism and Feminism', in *The Routledge Companion to Postmodernism*, ed. by Stuart Sim (New York: Routledge, 2013), 41-52.

[40] Grossberg, pp. 248-9.

postmodern patterns (such as superficiality, fragmentation, and nonlinearity) and the readability and communicativeness of messages. Under such theoretical tendency, I argue that it is imperative to reconsider this antagonism for two main reasons: first, it inevitably forecloses or invalidates critical readings of nuanced power dynamics in postmodern works like *Tin Drum* (1981), and second, it risks becoming an ally of Orientalism in representing the East as intrinsically mysterious and unreadable to Western audiences.

For *Tin Drum* (1981), it is often the identified authenticity of 'Oriental flavour' that enables its musical creativity. Even to the trained ears of many music critics, the peculiar sounds and arrangements of the album 'naturally' signify the Oriental as if they were discovered by the progressive band members for delivering musical innovations. Turning to the East to satiate an avant-garde agenda inevitably alienates the East as something both *different* from and *new* to the West, consequently reproducing and perpetuating a system of Orientalist knowledge through a white avant-garde epistemology. In this process, the East becomes *naturally* associated with *uncommon* cultural discourses and its cultural capital and history become trivialized for 'new' artistic praxis. Finally, Orientalism, I contend, has taken on the role of a postmodernising discourse that works to ex-corporate the imperialism and racism in art rock, and repackage the musical cooptation strategy with Asian elements as a postmodern intervention. Therefore, Orientalism is not just a tool or symptom of art rock's avant-garde agenda; instead, it is a constitutive discourse in the postmodernisation of popular music. Overlooking the dangerous Orientalist side of postmodern 'creative' works or assuming that postmodern theories of popular music transcend racial politics would only indicate that a renewed political reading of countercultural affects of rock music and their affective alliances is crucial.

Beyond Cinema

Vertov et la perception-caméra

Ana Ramos, Concordia University

Abstract

This article approaches cinema through a transdisciplinary perspective joining philosophy with moving-image practice to think time, subjectivity, objectivity – and relationality. Working from the example of Dziga Vertov's *Man With a Movie Camera* film, it explores the idea of the *perception-camera* as a relational point of view through which the film, as an event, evolves. It understands the film as an autonomous entity evolving through this relational point of view. In so doing, it fosters a complex approach beyond the subjective-objective perspective, and discusses what Gilles Deleuze calls the "free indirect image." This is the point of view of an unfolding *subjective form* that does not pertain to human perspective, but to the event perceiving itself as it evolves into its own accomplishment.

Se pourrait-il que la façon vertovienne de pratiquer le septième art nous apprenne davantage sur ce que pourrait être le cinéma aujourd'hui, alors que les techniques cinématographiques et la technologie sont passées au-delà de l'attendu ? Dziga Vertov (1896–1954), cinéaste soviétique du mouvement constructiviste, a filmé le quotidien de son époque avec créativité et innovation. Sa technique cinématographique (et ce qu'il exprime à travers celle-ci) atteint son zénith dans *L'Homme à la caméra* (*Chelovek s Kinoapparatom*, 1929), film qui a laissé sa marque dans l'histoire du cinéma. Le résultat est une œuvre inclassable qui dépasse la logique des genres avec une structure narrative disperse et une pratique de l'auto-référentialité[1] à travers laquelle la caméra occupe un rôle de premier plan. Le début du film annonce : *L'Homme à la caméra* est une expérimentation de communication cinématographique sans l'aide d'intertitres, scénario ou acteurs…[2]. L'élan d'une narrative singulière qui s'exprime à travers

---

[1] Vlada Petrić, *Constructivism in Film: The Man with the Movie Camera: A Cinematic Analysis*. Cambridge, Cambridge University Press, 1987, pp. 81–84.
[2] Dziga Vertov, *Kino-Eye: The Writings of Dziga Vertov*, Berkeley, University of California, 1984, p. 83.

la perspective de la caméra est ainsi déclenché. Les conséquences esthétiques d'une telle attitude sont remarquables.

Vertov s'est dédié au genre documentaire pour filmer « la réalité » et chercher à raffiner l'art cinématographique. Il voulait développer un langage universel du cinéma. Son objectif était de faire émerger un nouveau modèle de cinéma qui engagerait le spectateur en une activité active pendant et après le visionnement. Il a ainsi déclaré la mort aux films romancés pour que l'art cinématographique puisse s'élever au-dessus de ce qu'elle avait été. À travers le refus de la fiction cinématographique, « la réalité » qu'il voulait enregistrer a engendré un genre de documentaire unique qui touche le cœur du processus social. *Kinopravda*[3], la mise en pratique de sa théorie du cinéma-vérité, a donné naissance à des films dans lesquels des fragments d'actualité s'agencent en direction d'un sens propre à la singularité de cet agencement même. La « réalité » est formée, dans ses films, par la présentation d'une simultanéité d'expériences de la vie quotidienne. Montrer cette simultanéité a comme effet de capter la variation même d'un champ relationnel déterminé par la caméra. Selon sa vision du ciné-œil, *Kino-Eye*, le montage est l'âme du film[4]. Il agence un point quelconque de l'univers à un autre point – et ce dans n'importe quel ordre de temps.

L'originalité de la vision vertovienne est l'émancipation de la caméra en tant que *perception-caméra* et l'institution d'une forme de faire du cinéma qui se plaît à nous faire sentir la présence de la caméra. Ce mode de faire du cinéma s'appuie sur une esthétique qui mise tous ses efforts dans une caractéristique assumée de la caméra : celle de percevoir plus et mieux que l'œil humain. Il ne s'agit pas d'une perception « des » choses. Au contraire, elle est « dans » les choses – Gilles Deleuze appelle cette approche le matérialisme vertovien[5]. Selon lui, « l'image-mouvement a deux faces, l'une par rapport à des objets dont elle fait varier la position relative, l'autre par rapport à un tout dont elle exprime un changement absolu. Les positions sont dans l'espace, mais le tout qui change est dans le temps. »[6]. Dans la façon vertovienne de pratiquer le cinéma, la position relative des objets se transforme constamment à travers des micro-intervalles de façon à porter, par la simultanéité même d'actions, l'emphase ailleurs. Ce qui en découle est un déplacement du point focal de la perspective de l'espace vers le temps : « les positions sont dans l'espace, mais le tout qui change est dans le temps »[7]. En transposant la perception dans la matière elle-même, ce qui est manifesté comme produit final du montage est une image du temps. Ainsi, l'originalité d'une perception-caméra est la proposition d'une pratique de la perception qui

---

[3] Ivi, p. 42.
[4] Ivi, p. 40.
[5] Gilles Deleuze, *Cinéma 1. L'Image-mouvement*, Paris, Les Éditions de Minuit, 1983, p. 60.
[6] Gilles Deleuze, *Cinéma 2. L'Image-temps*, Paris, Les Éditions de Minuit, 1985, p. 50.
[7] Ibidem.

est « dans » les choses. En proposant une vision de la réalité qui émerge de ce point de vue non-anthropocentrique, le temps lui-même devient l'exprimé du film.

Temps et virtualité

> Du début à la fin d'un film, quelque chose change, quelque chose a changé. Seulement, ce tout qui change, ce temps ou cette durée, semble ne pouvoir être saisi qu'indirectement, par rapport aux images-mouvement qui l'expriment. Le montage est cette opération qui porte sur les images-mouvement pour en dégager le tout, l'idée, c'est-à-dire l'image *du* temps[8].

Dans le langage de Deleuze, le temps pur se réfère à une dimension temporelle dans laquelle les éléments ne sont pas organisés de forme logique, juxtaposés en une ligne du temps qui suit un avant-pendant-après. Ce temps pur est une forme de profondeur qualitative du temps qui est appelée virtuelle. Virtuelle car rien n'est encore développé (sorti de son enveloppe). De ce point de vue, lorsque *la caméra* enregistre des moments de la vie quotidienne en images, c'est une tranche de temps pur qui nous est présentée. Une femme se lève. L'Homme à la caméra part au travail. Un train passe. Un visage se fait laver. Une fenêtre : des stores qui s'ouvrent et se referment; des lentilles de caméra qui s'ouvrent et se referment. Ce ne sont que des potentialités enroulées dans un seul temps car elles se donnent toutes en même temps. Elles ne se déploient pas en histoires individuelles, mais s'impriment (comme les images sur la pellicule photographique) sur un temps fait de multiplicité: la simultanéité. Bien qu'il s'agisse d'éléments de potentiel plein, suggestifs de ramifications infinies, aucune de ces lignes de devenir n'est suivie, aucune ne se déroule dans l'espace. Il s'agit d'éclairs d'existence agencés par la perception-caméra. La femme qui se lève du lit, la pancarte « le réveil d'une femme » et toutes les autres personnes qui simultanément se lèvent forment un réseau d'éléments qui communiquent entre eux selon un schéma rhizomatique[9].

Le système rhizomatique n'a pas de point d'origine, mais des dimensions qui communiquent entre elles de façon transversale. Par exemple, entre 25 et 28 minutes, des scènes variées esquissent, comme le reste du film, le quotidien russe de l'époque. La différence se situant, par contre, dans le fait que, entre ces trois minutes, la juxtaposition effectue une émergence de centre de gravité. Ponctuées par de gros plans sur la ville avec ses divers piétons habitant les rues, ces scènes traitent des thèmes du mariage, du divorce, de la mort et de la naissance de façon entremêlée. Ce centre de gravité émerge en tant qu'intensité. Contrairement

[8] Gilles Deleuze, *Cinéma 1. L'Image-mouvement*, op. cit., p. 46.
[9] Gilles Deleuze et Félix Guattari, *Mille plateaux. Capitalisme et schizophrénie*, Paris, Les Éditions de Minuit, 1980.

au système arborescent qui fonctionne par principe de cause nécessaire, de progression et de conséquence, selon Gilles Deleuze et Félix Guattari, le système rhizomatique consiste à « soustraire l'unique de la multiplicité à constituer »[10]. En d'autres mots, le centre de gravité affecte et est affecté par l'ensemble du film ne s'offrant pas en tant que clé d'interprétation ou comme représentation de la réalité. Le système rhizomatique ne se réfère ni au film comme un tout, ni à la réalité comme généralité. Ce centre de gravité ainsi effectué est lui-même affecté autant par la singularité du film comme un Tout qu'elle affecte que par la multiplicité qui compose ce Tout. Ainsi, le point de gravité n'est pas un principe premier commandant le sens du film. Néanmoins, il est cette rencontre imprévisible qui permet de réévaluer le tout par la création d'un point de vue inédit[11]. Ce qui est singulier avec *L'Homme à la caméra* est que ces points de gravité se multiplient. Tout éclot ici et là, à tout instant, il n'existe pas *une* racine responsable de toutes les branches, mais le centre est partout et aussi nulle part car il se déplace constamment. D'autres schémas de sens comme celui-ci sont construits, plusieurs éléments se connectent sans que l'un ne dépasse l'autre en importance. Ils sont, pour ainsi dire, sur un même plan — et ce plan de temps enroulé forme un système ouvert qui n'a pas d'axe, ni centre, droite ou gauche, haut ou bas : que des dimensions.

Chaque image de ce système ouvert est mouvement qui se meut : Henri Bergson appelle la singularité de chaque mouvement, le *mouvant*. Selon lui, « il y a des mouvements, mais il n'y a pas d'objet inerte, invariable, qui se meuve : le mouvement n'implique pas un mobile »[12]. C'est-à-dire que chaque mouvement est lui-même une singularité. Il s'exprime à travers les objets qu'il traverse. Par conséquent, chaque dimension de ce système rhizomatique composé par le film exprime la qualité de temps propre à ce qui veut s'exprimer. C'est cette dimension qualitative de temps qui prend le devant de la scène dans *L'Homme à la caméra* laissant en deuxième plan la position relative des objets. En fait, le seul objet qui prend vraiment le premier plan est la caméra et ce avec l'objectif de faire émerger une vision qui est « dans » les choses. Ainsi, chaque image porte le mouvant à l'intérieur même de sa configuration, en même temps que celui-ci s'étend dans le mouvement du montage comme durée. L'articulation d'éléments cinématographiques à l'intérieur de cette durée résulte en une *image indirecte du temps*. L'image *du* temps ainsi articulée est l'image d'un temps virtuel, originaire, enroulé. Normalement, le temps virtuel ne se dévoile pas aussi clairement. Il nous enveloppe, plutôt, de son manteau d'immanence. Nous ne le remarquons pas car nous sommes *dans* le temps. Au contraire des cinéastes qui moulaient le regard de la caméra sur notre propre regard sur le monde, Vertov a fait éloge de son pouvoir de voir davantage afin qu'elle puisse nous montrer ce qu'elle voit et

---

[10] Ivi, p. 13.

[11] François Zourabichvili, *Le Vocabulaire de Deleuze*, Paris, Ellipses, 2003, p. 72.

[12] Henri Bergson, *Henri Bergson. Œuvres*, Paris, Presses universitaires de France, 1963, p. 1382.

non pas ce que nous sommes habitués de voir[13]. En appliquant le point de vue subjectif-indirect libre dans *L'Homme à la caméra*, Vertov libère le discours *sur* le temps pour illustrer *le* temps à partir de centres germinaux de relation.

Dans la singularité que le film exprime, nous ne trouverons aucune histoire précise. Cette singularité s'exprime à travers des thèmes. Vlada Petrić[14] répertorie cinq types d'images : construction industrielle, trafic de véhicules, machinerie, récréation et visages de citoyens travailleurs. Le traitement de thèmes comme l'urbanité, la mort et la naissance, le travail et, par conséquent, le travail en commun (par extension, la constitution de la société en commun) se fait par l'entremise de la perception-caméra qui n'est pas effectivement engagée dans ces événements. C'est pour cette raison qu'elle est au-dessus d'eux, même si elle est une présence dans l'acte de filmer. Son point de vue ne se confond pas avec le point de vue d'un personnage quelconque et n'est pas non plus extérieur à l'univers qu'elle filme. Au contraire, la caméra est littéralement *dans* le film. Selon Deleuze, tandis qu'une branche de l'école soviétique (incluant Eisenstein et Dovjenko, par exemple) propose une dialectique entre l'Homme et la Nature, au contraire, Vertov propose une dialectique de la Nature en elle-même, soit de la matière avec la propre matière[15]. C'est pour cette raison que le cinéma de Vertov est aussi appelé matérialiste. Dans ses films, des machines, des paysages, des édifices et des hommes se présentent en tant que « systèmes matériels en perpétuelle interaction »[16], c'est-à-dire que nous avons la rencontre entre l'œil surhumain et la matière. La caméra se présente en tant qu'élément catalyseur des relations qui constituent le film, permettant ainsi la perception d'un intervalle de monde[17].

La plus petite unité de mouvement est l'intervalle, en opposition au Tout que le film constitue. Il s'agit ici de deux aspects du temps : le Tout comporte un ensemble de mouvements, tandis que l'intervalle traduit une action dans cet ensemble. Dû au fait qu'il n'a pas de point de vue fixe, le ciné-œil s'étend du point où s'initie l'action jusqu'au point où s'ensuit la réaction : « l'intervalle de mouvement, c'est la perception, le coup d'œil »[18]. Sa vision est globale. La différence entre l'intervalle de temps que l'œil humain peut percevoir et celle que le ciné-œil perçoit est notable. La perception de la matière, le ciné-œil, contient une simultanéité qui permet la perception de plusieurs « systèmes matériels » en même temps, tandis que l'œil humain se restreint au système auquel il appartient. C'est cette simultanéité qui fait le *non-temps* : si tout nous était donné d'un seul coup, la

[13] Dziga Vertov, *Kino-Eye: The Writings of Dziga Vertov*, op. cit., p. 15.
[14] Vlada Petrić, *Constructivism in Film*, op. cit.
[15] Gilles Deleuze, *Cinéma 1. L'Image-mouvement*, op. cit., p. 59.
[16] Ibidem.
[17] Ivi, p. 60.
[18] Ibidem.

perception temporelle délaisserait la logique linéaire. Le cinéma vertovien réussit toutefois à incorporer ce non-temps à une certaine forme de linéarité en traitant la simultanéité par le moyen de l'intervalle car, au moins en ce qui a trait à l'image-mouvement, l'image *du* temps ne peut nous être donnée qu'indirectement. La façon comment Vertov traite la simultanéité consiste à présenter certains éléments d'expérience de manière entrecoupée. Au début du film, par exemple, lors de la séquence de la femme qui se lève du lit, nous ne voyons pas toutes les scènes qui se rapportent à elle juxtaposées les unes aux autres. Ce que nous voyons est une séquence d'actions qui ont lieu en même temps : plusieurs personnes qui se réveillent, qui se préparent pour la journée. Ces images, même étant juxtaposées, n'ont pas pour fonction de proposer une expérience linéaire. Nous comprenons que tout cela se passe simultanément : la ville se réveille.

Éventuellement, nous verrons à nouveau la femme en question affairée à se laver, la rue un peu plus remplie, la ville qui se met en marche et c'est ce qui donne la sensation du temps qui passe. Un sens émerge des images. Mais la négation de la narration déconcerte et surprend car l'idée du film se construit aux dépends d'une trame dramatique. Ce qui est proposé est avant tout un point de vue différent. Le mouvement que Vertov présente à travers ces images et cette expérience de non-temps est la relation du spectateur avec un Tout, soit avec le monde : un monde que l'univers du film retient fragmentairement. Le premier aspect du temps, le Tout, se présente comme une spirale ouverte en ses extrémités qui enlace le passé et le futur. Le deuxième, l'intervalle, comporte le présent. Il existe une corrélation entre les deux aspects du temps qui fait en sorte que, infiniment contracté, le Tout passerait à l'intérieur de l'intervalle. Ainsi, chaque image du film contient la même empreinte de singularité mouvante, la même qualité esthétique, qui anime tout le film. Le contraire est aussi vrai : infiniment dilaté, le présent s'élargirait en passé et en futur. C'est ce que la mise sur un même piédestal des thèmes universels de la naissance et de la mort, du mariage et du divorce opère. Dans le Tout du temps existe cet intervalle de temps, le film. Celui-ci propose une expérience de vision élargie, pour un instant, pleine : la compréhension d'une partie du tout. De la sorte, ce que l'expérience de non-temps propose est la compréhension de la partie dans le tout et du tout dans la partie.

La Perception-caméra

Sera subjective une perception où les images varient par rapport à une image centrale et privilégiée;
sera objective une perception, telle qu'elle est dans les choses, où toutes les images varient les unes par rapport aux autres, sur toutes leurs faces et dans toutes leurs parties[19]

[19] Gilles Deleuze, *Cinéma 1. L'Image-mouvement*, op. cit., p. 111.

La décision de faire un film sans scénario a comme effet la dissolution d'un centre autour duquel est développée l'idée du film. Où trouver alors l'intrigue du film *L'Homme à la caméra* ? Il n'est pas possible d'affirmer que le film ne contienne pas de personnages, mais aucun d'eux ne se détache des autres en importance, chacun représentant un bourgeon d'expérience dispersé dans l'univers changeant. À l'exception d'un personnage : la caméra. Déjà au début du film, à la première image, apparaît le sujet principal du film : une caméra géante avec un minuscule caméraman sur elle en train de manier une deuxième caméra plus appropriée à sa taille. Tout au long du film, aucun élément n'est aussi présent que la caméra : qu'elle soit maniée par le caméraman, qu'elle se fasse présente à travers les lentilles qui nous observent, ou encore dans les bandes de film qui sont maniées par l'éditrice dans la salle de montage. Le titre *L'Homme à la caméra* pourrait indiquer que le cameraman n'est qu'un individu parmi tant d'autres citoyens travailleurs et que c'est lui le personnage principal[20]. Toutefois, la caméra possède une certaine autonomie. En effet, celle-ci atteint des capacités humaines après la première heure de film. Elle opère toute seule, marche sur ses trois « jambes »[21] tout en filmant indépendamment du caméraman (tel que l'indique la manivelle qui tourne par elle-même). Ainsi, c'est justement elle, la caméra, le personnage principal du film. Cet « anthropomorphisme »[22] ne diminue pas la difficulté de faire un film où la négation de la narration annule tout développement de personnages dramatiques.

Mais si anthropomorphisme il y a, qu'en est-il de la nature du point de vue adopté par la caméra ? Selon la définition de perception de Bergson, nous soustrayons des éléments de la réalité pour entrer en relation avec une portion d'éléments[23]. C'est dans le cadre de cette opération que nous pouvons agir sur cette portion de réalité. Il s'agit d'une perception dite éliminatoire car nous ne pouvons être en relation avec la totalité de la réalité :

> La chose, c'est l'image telle qu'elle est en soi, telle qu'elle se rapporte à toutes les images dont elle subit intégralement l'action et sur lesquelles elle réagit immédiatement. Mais, la perception de la chose, c'est la même image rapportée à une autre image spéciale qui la cadre, et qui n'en retient qu'une action partielle et n'y réagit que médiatement. Dans la perception ainsi définie, il n'y a jamais autre ou plus que dans la chose : au contraire, il y a « moins »[24].

C'est le cas d'un acte de *perception* dite *subjective*. Quant à l'acte de *perception objective*, les relations ne sont pas formées à partir d'un seul centre relationnel, mais à partir d'une pluralité de centres qui varient simultanément les uns par

---

[20] Vlada Petrić, *Constructivism in Film*, op. cit., p. 80.
[21] Ivi, p. 83.
[22] Ibidem.
[23] Gilles Deleuze, *Cinéma 1. L'Image-mouvement*, op. cit., p. 93.
[24] Ibidem.

rapport aux autres. Dans cet univers dépourvu de centre unique à l'intérieur duquel tout réagit à tout le reste, la courbature ne se fait pas en fonction d'un seul élément, mais en tous les sens, en tous lieux. En ce qui concerne la perception cinématographique, Deleuze mentionne: « la difficulté, c'est de savoir comment se présentent au cinéma une image-perception objective et une image-perception subjective. Qu'est-ce qui les distinguent? »[25]. Selon lui, la première est composée par la perception d'un personnage participant qui la « qualifie », tandis que la deuxième est composée par une perception extérieure à l'action en question. Toutefois, comment savoir si cette perception ne finirait éventuellement par appartenir à l'action? Le propre de l'image-perception cinématographique serait justement ce va-et-vient entre les deux pôles[26]. C'est cette ambivalence que le concept « discours indirect libre »[27] tend à résoudre en constituant un point de vue qui va au-delà de la dichotomie objectif-subjectif.

La « réalité » que Vertov a enregistrée dans le film *L'Homme à la caméra* ne révèle pas une journée dans une ville russe, mais une perception de la ville en elle-même et la caméra en tant que moyen pour cela : une perception-caméra. Les thèmes du film ne se courbent pas autour de son centre et la plupart du temps n'entrent pas délibérément en relation avec elle, même si nous pouvons témoigner de quelques inévitables réactions à la présence de la caméra[28]. La caméra s'établit en tant que *centre de perception*. Mais, même si la perception-caméra est réductive, il ne s'agit pas pour autant d'une perception purement subjective. Essentiellement par le fait que la caméra ne se confond pas avec un personnage qui agit dans l'intrigue, et qu'elle ne souffre aucune transformation à travers les relations qu'elle établi. Ainsi, son positionnement libère les événements cinématographiques d'une relation avec la caméra. Il ne s'agit pas d'une perception fixe sur laquelle se précipitent les événements et auxquels celle-ci répond à travers l'action. Elle ne devient pas pour autant point de vue objectif. Elle ne se situe pas complètement à l'extérieur de l'univers qu'elle fait paraître, mais ce qu'elle montre se présente comme une vision autonome du contenu. La perception-caméra se confond avec les choses, elle est ciné-œil qui enregistre les transformations autour de soi. Ce que le ciné-œil produit, par l'entremise de sa capacité de voir plus que ce que l'œil humain en est capable, est un « discours indirect libre », une perception telle qu'elle se donne sous le point de vue de la matière, pouvant s'étendre du point où commence l'action jusqu'où s'étend sa réaction[29]. Ce qui est exprimé est le mouvement en soi, des « intervalles de mouvement ». Elle est *point de vue mobile* et c'est ce qui fait l'essence du film,

---

[25] Ivi, p. 104.
[26] Ivi, p. 105.
[27] Ivi, p. 106.
[28] Vlada Petrić, *Constructivism in Film*, op. cit., pp. 81–82.
[29] Gilles Deleuze, *Cinéma 1. L'Image-mouvement*, op. cit., p. 60.

ce qui construit l'idée directrice et la cohérence du récit, rendant le montage le point crucial de son succès.

La Perception pure

> The instant field of the present is always experience in its "pure state", plain unqualified actuality, a simple *that*, as yet unqualified into thing and thought, and only virtually classifiable as objective fact or as some one's opinion about fact. This is as true when the field is conceptual as when it is perceptual[30].

Dans la vision de monde développée par William James, l'empirisme radical, la différence entre sujet et objet n'est pas une différence ontologique, mais seulement de point de vue. Le sujet est défini comme « celui qui cherche la connaissance » et l'objet en tant que « ce qui se fait connaître ». Le différentiel de l'empirisme radical est que le sujet et l'objet forment une triade : il tient compte d'un troisième terme à part entière, « la relation ». Cette dernière n'est pas simplement le point commun entre le sujet et l'objet. La relation mobilise qualitativement l'expérience : c'est l'événement. Alors que le documentaire traditionnel positionne l'observateur complètement à l'extérieur de la situation qu'il décrit, Vertov positionne la perception-caméra au centre de l'action. Toutefois, puisqu'il s'agit d'un positionnement « subjectif-indirect libre », la perception-caméra est aussi potentiellement en-deçà de la dichotomie sujet-objet. Le point de vue de la perception-caméra n'est pas purement objectif car elle n'atteint pas un pouvoir omniscient. Même si tel pouvoir demeure une tendance, celle-ci ne peut pleinement se réaliser. La caméra *peut* tout voir, mais il existe une sélection de la réalité qui est faite est c'est cette sélection qui définit la relation qui s'établit entre la perception-caméra et le monde. Ce positionnement n'est pas subjectif non plus car ce qu'elle voit et, par conséquent, enregistre, n'est pas guidé pas des « déformations psychologiques »[31]. Le découpage de la réalité est guidé par la « forme subjective »[32] qui émerge sous la forme du film qui deviendra *L'Homme à la caméra*. La qualité de cette émergence est moulée par l'élan subjectif qui se forme comme événement. C'est la forme subjective qui soutient le film tel qu'il se déploie comme événement à travers la prise de vue et le montage qui, par conséquent, oriente la « relation » de la caméra avec ce qui l'entoure. La perception-caméra constitue ce que James appelle le « noyau objectif d'expérience »[33]: un continuum perceptif qui change à mesure que ce corps bouge dans l'espace. Les regards qu'il recueille, les sourires qu'il

---

[30] William James, *Essays in Radical Empiricism*, Mineola, New York, Dover Publications, 2003, p. 39.

[31] Ismail Xavier, *A experiência do cinema: antologia*, Rio de Janeiro, Graal, 2008, p. 178 (ma traduction).

[32] Alfred North Whitehead, *Process and Reality*, New York, Free Press, 1978.

[33] William James, *Essays in Radical Empiricism*, op. cit., p. 34.

alimente et les mouvements mécaniques auxquels il témoigne se croisent en un système de connaissance, le film. Ce que la perception-caméra exprime est la présence au monde, une présence qui n'est qu'un témoin. Le point de vue de cette perception-caméra se situe entre le sujet et l'objet, précisément au point de la relation. Il est événement.

Puisque la perception-caméra occupe un point de vue impossible à adopter d'une perspective humaine, cette relation prend un caractère abstrait qui, dans un premier abordage, fuit à notre entendement. Il s'agit d'une « perception pure », concept que Bergson défini comme un fil continu de visions instantanées qui font partie des choses et non de nous-mêmes[34]. La raison pour laquelle nous l'appelons « pure » est due au fait qu'elle se situe à un point où aucun adjectif n'a encore été affecté à la relation par une des entités qui la composent : sujet-objet. L'adjectif, au contraire, émerge de la relation comme affect et lui empreint sa singularité. Ce niveau d'expérience se défini comme un *futur antérieur* car il ne s'est pas encore concrétisé totalement ; il s'agit de la racine de l'expérience, où le sujet connaît l'objet, avant qu'il réalise ce qu'il a connu. Cet état germinal passe inaperçu dans le cas d'une perception subjective où l'expérience s'est déjà enracinée dans un présent presque passé. N'est-il pas, justement, l'essence du « présent » de passer et de laisser ainsi la place au *futur du présent*? Dans cette étroite fenêtre de temps où les expériences font encore partie des *choses*, soit, de la relation, où objet et sujet font un, a lieu ce que James appelle « l'expérience pure »[35]. C'est dans cet intervalle de temps suspendu qui se constitue un temps appelé virtuel, ou le *non-temps*.

La perception subjective des choses ne se rapporte pas à des moments réels des choses, mais à l'expérience de ces choses. La *perception pure*, au contraire, étant une « perception virtuelle des choses »[36], serait directement reliée à la simultanéité intrinsèque à la durée des choses, se situant dès lors dans un non-temps où tout point de l'univers peut rejoindre n'importe quel autre, selon une logique « rhizomatique »[37]. C'est-à-dire que, dans notre expérience du monde, les choses durent dans le cadre d'une durée individuelle, propre à l'agglomération d'expériences reliées par un facteur d'immanence au corps et à la temporalité de ce corps. La perception-caméra, au contraire, rassemble les choses qu'elle perçoit sous la forme d'un « être de sensation »[38]: l'organisation et l'incorporation des « qualités sensibles de la matière »[39] dans des figures esthétiques. L'*être de sensation* n'est pas composé des matériaux qui font l'œuvre. Il est un composé

[34] Henri Bergson, *Henri Bergson. Œuvres*, op. cit., p. 212.
[35] William James, *Essays in Radical Empiricism*, op. cit.
[36] Henri Bergson, *Henri Bergson. Œuvres*, op. cit., p. 189.
[37] Gilles Deleuze et Félix Guattari, *Mille plateaux*, op. cit.
[38] Gilles Deleuze et Félix Guattari, *Qu'est-ce que la philosophie?* Paris, Éditions de Minuit, 2005.
[39] Henri Bergson, *Henri Bergson. Œuvres*, op. cit., p. 216.

de forces, de devenirs non-humains (affects) dans lesquels l'artiste s'engage pour faire émerger une matière d'expression. C'est pour cette raison que cette perception n'est pure qu'en droit. La caméra, comme foyer d'expression de forces qu'elle organise, découpe dans le paysage potentiel ce sur quoi elle est en position d'assembler comme forces créatives. Dans le cas de la subjectivité humaine, c'est le « souvenir »[40] qui travaille conjointement avec le corps pour que l'individu puisse agir dans le monde. Ce faisant, le souvenir teinte la perception en faisant émerger non pas des expériences pures, mais mixtes : des expériences des choses perçues. Parce que la caméra est d'abord véhicule d'expression d'un être de sensation, sa perception est moulée par l'élan subjectif qui se supporte. Ainsi, c'est la forme subjective qui soutient le film, tel qu'il se déploie comme événement à travers la prise de vue et le montage, qui oriente la « relation » de la caméra avec ce qui l'entoure. La perception pure se situe dans la relation. Mais au-delà d'un certain tournant de l'agencement des devenirs non-humains dans lesquels l'artiste s'engage pour faire émerger la matière d'expression du film, il y a émergence de forme subjective. La perception n'est donc pure qu'en tant qu'oscillation virtuelle entre potentiel plein de filmage et expression de forme subjective sous forme d'être de sensation. Dans cette perception mixte teintée par l'élan créatif qui soutient le « processus d'auto-accomplissement »[41] du film, ce qui perçoit est l'être de sensation en devenir.

[40] Ivi.
[41] Alfred North Whitehead, *Process and Reality*, op. cit.

Reviews / Comptes-rendus

Warren Buckland
Wes Anderson's Symbolic Storyworld. A Semiotic Analysis
New York and London: Bloomsbury Academic, 2019, pp. 224

In this volume, Warren Buckland applies a method of analysis derived from the structural anthropology by Claude Lévi-Strauss to the corpus of Wes Anderson's films. A curious and daring choice, of which it is crucial to understand both the reasons and the limits.

Chapters 1 and 2 introduce the method of analysis. Following Lévi-Strauss, myths should be interpreted by identifying certain major, underlying content categories: raw/cooked, life/death, water/fire, etc. These categories appear as binary oppositions because the cultural function of myths is that of mediating, in symbolic terms, between two irreconcilable categories. In any case, the French anthropologist indicates the opportunity to overcome a linear and syntagmatic analysis to access the achronic paradigms underlying the story. The reconstruction of the symbolic system of a single myth can then be compared to that of other myths, to obtain an 'archi-mythical' matrix of invariants belonging to a specific cultural environment (type level), of which the single myths would have many variants (token level). In applying Lévi-Strauss's paradigmatic method of analysis to Wes Anderson's films, Buckland proposes replacing the concept of archi-myth with that of the author's specific 'narrative world': this should not be seen as a single, mimetic, diegetic world, but precisely as the system of invariants in Anderson's cinema that the analyst must reconstruct. The second chapter is devoted to a review of the previous application of the structural method to the filmic text: Buckland favours those authors who, between the Sixties and Seventies, attempted the structural analysis of the content universes of specific film directors: G. Nowell-Smith, A. Lowell, Jim Kitses, R. Abel, B Houson and Marsha Kinder, but above all P. Wollen, to whom we will return. Other approaches to textual analysis, more focused on single sequences (such as those of R. Bellour) are considered less functional to the methodological structure of the volume.

Chapters from 3 through to 10 are devoted to the analysis one of Anderson's films (the director's filmography is covered in full, except for *Isle of Dogs*, released too recently). For each film, Buckland offers a plot synopsis divided in sequences, and analyses the core meanings organized in paradigmatic oppositions. Finally, chapter 11 reconstructs 'The Symbolic Storyworld of Wes Anderson' as a whole. According to Buckland, this universe is dominated by 'three types of kinship structures?' ('death/the absence of parents or spouses';

'intergenerational relationships'; 'interethnic relationships'); 'death/life (funerals and pregnancies)'; 'exchange and gifts'; 'mediation'; 'relative worlds'; 'water and drowning'; plus 'verticality, movement and water' (p. 169). In a summary table (p. 184) Buckland examines the recurrences and displacements of these categories from one Anderson film to another.

As I mentioned in the first few lines, it is useful to reflect on both the reasons and limits of such an intentionally 'outdated' methodological experiment. Let's start with the reasons. Buckland claims to refer to the 'auteur structuralism' proposed by Peter Wollen in *Signs and Meaning in the Cinema* (first edition, 1969). If we reread the fifth and definitive edition of Wollen's book, which brings together all the materials accumulated in previous editions, we can read that it is 'a book that constantly reimagines itself and gains new powers by responding to new contexts'[1]. Indeed, Wollen, after having started a modernist and structuralist theory of cinema, re-thinks it repeatedly in a post-structuralist key; in this sense, the 'auteur structuralism' is later deeply criticized by the author himself. It is therefore symptomatic that Buckland chooses to rely on the 1972 edition of Wollen's book: in this way, he explicitly states his intention to 'freeze' the development of cinema theory just before the advent of both Grand Theory and Post Theory. Starting from this point, I would argue that Buckland is proposing a peculiar way of doing film theory, *by re-enacting specific theories and methods of analysis of the past.* In other words, after carrying out a critical reconstruction/deconstruction of some film theories[2], Buckland reverses the operational direction and experiments with their 'rebooting'. In short, Buckland's theoretical gesture recalls the work of a media archaeologist, who recovers machines and appliances from the past and puts them back into use; only, Buckland moves this project from media devices history to film theory.

Finally, the limits of such an operation are profoundly linked to its premises. I will quickly highlight two. First, by dismantling the diachronic dimension, Buckland becomes unable to analyse how, in Anderson's cinema, paradigmatic core-meanings are translated into syntagmatic narrative architectures. In this respect, Buckland's analysis is more prone to an anthropological approach than a truly semiotic one: the question of the transition from basic semantic nuclei to 'surface' narrative forms, which is at the centre of Greimas' model, is not considered here. Secondly, the conscious dismantling of the film-specific and formal dimension (a critical point also in Wollen's discussion) emerges with particular emphasis in the analysis of Anderson's cinema, which finds a strong mark of authorial recognition precisely in the repetition of a group of formal stylistic patterns.

[Ruggero Eugeni, Università Cattolica del Sacro Cuore, Milano]

[1] David N. Rodovick, 'Foreword', in Peter Wollen, *Signs and Meaning in the Cinema,* 5th Edition (London – Houndmills: Palgrave Macmillan – BFI, 2013), p. xiv.
[2] Warren Buckland, *Film Theory: Rational Reconstructions* (London – New York: Routledge, 2012)

Amateur Media and Participatory Cultures: Film, Video and Digital Media
ed. by Susan Aasman and Annamaria Motrescu-Mayes
London and New York: Routledge 2019, pp. 164

In the past few decades, amateur cinema studies have overseen a significant, growing interest and a flourishing of publications devoted to various aspects of analogue amateur film practices. More recently, several scholarly contributions have also addressed the digital turn and the contemporary 'amateurized media universe' — as per Patricia Zimmermann's definition — although the study of digital amateur media raises some new and delicate issues. The already conventional and fragile distinction between 'amateurs' and 'professionals' (and indeed between amateur and professional devices, or consumption modes, and so on) have been redefined by the ubiquitousness of user-generated content; to address their somehow anarchic proliferation, their pervasiveness, the way in which they seem to elude any attempt to contain, define or classify them requires the scholar to immerse herself in the contradictions of the present.

Confronted with the difficult task of dealing with a set of ephemeral practices that present significant differences, but also unexpected commonalities, Susan Aasman and Annamaria Motrescu-Mayes — the two authors of the book *Amateur Media and Participatory Cultures: Film, Video and Digital Media* — adopt a very effective strategy. They declare at the outset that their volume does not attempt to offer a systematic study that aims to investigate amateur production exhaustively, in all its aspects, but it should rather be considered a 'work in progress, one that often combines perplexing theoretical perspectives and several open-ended analyses' (p. xii). As such, it proposes heterogeneous paths in which the forms of the past dialogue seamlessly with those of the present, bringing out some crucial and urgent aspects that concern our relationship with those amateur media that are part of our reality, that inform our imagination, that contribute to define our view of the world.

The heterogeneity of the analyses and of the approaches offered in this book is also the result of the different backgrounds and methodologies adopted by the two authors: Aasman is a media historian, while Motrescu-Mayes is a visual anthropologist. Rather than being a weakness, though, the methodological and even stylistic specificities of each of the two authors is undoubtedly one of the strengths of the book, which offers therefore two unique but effectively intermingled perspectives.

The first and second chapters, written by Aasman, consider amateur practices as the result of a complex combination of technological, social, economic, cultural and also political factors. Chapter one offers a diachronic examinations of amateur media, thus addressing at length their change of status from a marginal and somehow elitist hobby to a mass diffused practice, from a form of memory-building fostered by the temporal distance between shooting and projection to an everyday means of communication marked by immediateness and pervasiveness. In the second chapter, Aasman focuses specifically on the home movie *dispositif*, addressing in particular the shifting boundaries between its private and public dimension and the consequent complex, contradictory impulses 'since the amateur filmmaker/media maker's identity and political economies have now entered a highly public and commercialised space' (p. 7). Chapters 3, 4 and 5, instead, are written by Motrescu-Mayes as an almost continuous discourse on the ethical and political aspects of amateur images, especially those that deal with violence and trauma.

Motrescu-Mayes's analysis begins with a discussion on the concept of ephemerality as both something intrinsic to amateur images — more subject to be discarded, not preserved because of their low commercial value — but also something that is presented as a feature of many digital platforms, that therefore are mistakenly perceived by users as free environments within which they can perform their own or new identities. The very concept of ephemerality in relation to amateur media is addressed through an analysis of the practices of recycling, re-use and resemantization of private images. In chapter 4, Motrescu-Mayes investigates what happens when the right to narrate and interpret suffering, trauma and violence passes from (political, economic, cultural) institutions to individual citizens, those netizens that challenge the dominant ideological narratives and frameworks, thus 'acting as *memory agent*' (p. 99) and helping to construct not only a 'visual memory of trauma', but also those counter-histories analysed in chapter 5. In it, she argues how 'what appears at first to be brief and possibly inconsequential, ephemeral images (visual constructions) of other people's trauma, become in time an ongoing exercise in shaping and challenging visual identities of the global 'I' — an 'I' unified by the power of shared anonymity' (p. 128). The last chapter, by Aasman, addresses a crucial issue, once again related to memory: the practices of archiving and preservation of digital amateur media. Aasman acknowledges that 'the complexities and contradictions that characterize present-day amateur media cultures are mirrored by, and reproduced in, the complexities and contradictions of archiving digital memories' (p. 148). As such, it is not possible to conceive easy solutions in order to face the fragile, ephemeral nature of digital media, affected by the paradox of being sharable and easy to circulate — so as to appear eternal — but instead subject to obsolescence or, worse, erasure — for example, the removal of contents considered offensive or that infringe copyright laws implemented by YouTube. However, by listing a series of individual or collaborative archival practices, Aasman's analysis suggests some possible virtuous strategies, while pleading for both the need to preserve the memory of our digital present and our right to oblivion.

The non-systematic nature of the volume does not coincide, therefore, with the lack of a coherent general perspective. Its cohesion as a whole is guaranteed by a common purpose shared by the work of Aasman and Motrescu-Mayes: they both approach amateur media from a fresh, open, multidisciplinary angle, which combines a wide range of theoretical contributions — not only from anthropology and history, but also from sociology or psychology, to name just a few — in order to address the relationship between amateur media and memory, identity and social structures from a profoundly ethical and political perspective. This book is indeed a work in progress, in the more positive sense: through the questions it raises, it is a compelling invitation for the whole scholarly community to take a closer look at amateur practices with a renewed perspective. Although ephemeral and often mundane, they can enable, after all, an authentic dialogue with our past, and they represent the living, beating heart of our present.

[Chiara Grizzaffi, Università Iulm, Milano]

Stories. Screen Narrative in the Digital Era
Edited by Ian Christie and Annie van den Oever
Amsterdam: Amsterdam University Press, 2018, pp. 208

If there is an aspect towards which the interest of narrative scholars has consistently grown in recent years, this is represented without any doubt by the impact of digital technologies on the way stories are constructed and shaped, as well as on how they are experienced by their audience. Indeed, a number of books and journal special issues, but also conferences and seminars, has been devoted to the study of both these aspects, and more in general to the attempt at mapping the broader transformations of the very idea of narrative in the contemporary mediascape.

Stories. Screen Narrative in the Digital Era, the volume curated by Ian Christie and Annie van den Oever for the Key Debates series of Amsterdam University Press, participates in this trend in a significant way. Not only does it recapitulate some of the key issues in the debate on the relationship between narratives and the digital, but moreover it proposes new perspectives on it, especially concerning so-called 'screen narratives', i.e., the narratives that we nowadays experience through the mediation of a screen, being it that of a movie theatre, of a personal computer, or of a mobile phone.

As the editors suggest, the premise of the volume is to answer two main questions: first, whether storytelling, or 'story-following', has changed decisively 'either during the era of "cinema" or, perhaps more pertinently, in the postcinema era of digital and interactive media' (p. 12); secondly, whether the 'overuse of the term "story" devalue[s] or detract[s] meaning from what we would formerly have called a story' (Ibidem).

In order to respond, the authors of the fifteen contributions collected in the volume draw upon different methodologies, adopt different styles (besides 'classical' scholarly contributions, there are interviews, and journalistic or journalist-like pieces as well), and — perhaps more relevantly — problematize the contours of the debate, thus suggesting from the outset that easy answers cannot be given. Or, at least, this is what emerges from the first essay, in which Jan Baetens discusses the inequalities of stories, namely that, beyond the idea that Roland Barthes once famously promoted that stories are universal and ubiquitous, they are not equal at all. By looking at how comics and graphic novels have been historically overlooked — with comics for a longtime occupying 'the margins of the cultural system' before being accepted, along with his most 'serious' twin, 'in the field of culturally legitimate storytelling' (p. 40) — Baetens reflects on how the social status of stories, as well as 'the degree of acceptation of storytelling in different fields' (p. 33), can dramatically change depending on the society and the historical context in which they appear. This idea resonates even more vividly in a world such as ours, where, as Ian Christie puts it in his essay, 'stories and storytelling have been placed at the center of vast areas of human activity' (p. 87), and where we seem constantly involved in a process of 'storification', i.e., a process by which we are invited to give shape and enjoy whatever content, even the more mundane, as if it were a story.

Building on this awareness, each contributor focuses on a specific media product or set of products, pondering the extent to which the stories 'contained' within depart from traditional notions of storytelling. However, seeking a common denominator among all the essays, there are at least two main aspects that emerge distinctly.

On the one hand, they all seem to share the idea that if a change has happened in the way stories look like today, this has to do with their complexity. Many of the stories we commonly experience are characterized by intricate plots, sophisticated characters as well as by unconventional visual forms. This is, for instance, what Miklós Kiss and Steven Willemsen argue in their essay, a revised version of the last chapter of their monograph *Impossible Puzzle Films*. The authors discuss a range of popular films (most notably, David Lynch's *Mulholland Drive*, Spike Jonze's *Adaptation*, and Christopher Nolan's *Inception*) 'that evoke pervasively confusing viewing experiences, undermining narrative comprehension by means of various complicating storytelling techniques and the eliciting of dissonant cognitions' (p. 56), which, for this reason, invite viewers to speculate on the possible ways to come to terms with such complexity. Similar claims are also made by Ian Christie in his discussion of *Dickensian*, the BBC TV show which projects a storyworld where characters from different novels by Charles Dickens meet and interact, thus expanding the story in an intertextual direction; by John Ellis, who in a dialogue with Annie van den Oever acknowledges that many contemporary TV series are likely to exhaust, more than classical series and of feature-films, 'the possibilities of the characters, situations, and themes' (p. 160); and in particular by Dominique Chateau, for whom the third season of Lynch's *Twin Peaks*, due to its complexity and its dream-like qualities, erases the boundary 'between film and television series' (p. 120).

Complex formal and narrative qualities are also crucial aspects of the works of Michelangelo Antonioni and Chantal Ackerman, whose oeuvres are discussed respectively by José Moure in an essay devoted to the 'endless endings' of the films by the Italian director, and by Eric de Kuyper in a dialogue with van den Oever about Ackerman's *La captive* (2000). And also Robert Ziegler, even though he states that, from his perspective as a conductor, 'the role of music in making narratives convincing hasn't really changed all that much' (p. 193), he also agrees with Christie that nowadays music needs to be adapted to 'much less defined narrative arcs, use of "dead time" and wide variations of pace that would been unthinkable in the 1940s and 1950s, and even later' (pp. 194-95).

However, as Sandra Laugier reminds us in her essay on *Game of Thrones* and its astounding success, such complexity is not just thematic or formal. Indeed, there is a moral element involved in many of the stories we currently enjoy: fictional universes as the one projected by *Game of Thrones* are permeated by a sort of 'moral atmosphere', i.e., by 'a plurality of singular expressions, stage arguments and debates' (p. 145) which invite viewers to reflect on important moral questions.

This observation helps to highlight the second aspect that is central to the essays collected in the volume: namely, that if stories have changed and become increasingly complex, their audiences have undergone a similar transformation. Not mere passive spectators, viewers are increasingly attracted by complex films and TV series, to the point that they seem more interested in feeling challenged by them than by solving their puzzles, as Kiss and Willemsen argue. This does not come as a surprise, though. Indeed, this is the premise of transmedia storytelling, whose recipients, according to Melanie Schiller, are not satisfied solely by enjoying a story, but also by being someway involved in it, making connections among different media contents, expanding them via fan fictions, and more in general manipulating the materials of which a story is made.

Furthermore, it can be argued that this kind of involvement with stories informs also our everyday experience with the devices with which we usually interact. For instance, according to Vincent Amiel our use of mobile phones, portable computers and other devices changes significantly the way in which we look at images and interact with them. Since within such devices 'images and frames are moved, interlocked, and zoomed in or out according to the viewer's will', this familiarizes us with a range of experimentations with images that were still precluded a few years ago, at the same time opening the ground to 'a new conception of storytelling' (p. 52), one that is probably less author-driven than in the past. This is also what Roger Odin suggests in his short but very compelling contribution, focusing on the aesthetics of the single shot which dominates our use of mobile cameras. He argues that we have 'incorporated' the basic figures of filmic language, thus suggesting that 'we can no longer film naively' (p. 167). According to Odin, the way in which we approach communication devices and screens can often produce, even beyond our intention, artistic effects, thus introducing creativity in the space of everyday communication.

In a sense, this last remark is likely to synthesize in a rather provocative way the double assumption that underlies *Stories*: that the very idea of narrative is evolving in quite unexpected ways, and that we are probably becoming not just, as Jason Mittell puts it, self-trained narratologists, but also self-trained filmmakers, who learn the ways in which films, TV series and stories more generally work, not just by looking at them, but also actively exploring the possibilities and the limits of the images and the screens around us.

[Filippo Pennacchio, Università IULM, Milano]

Projects & Abstracts

Shadows of Hopes: Landmarks for a Plastic History of the Twentieth Century Experimental Film Journals

Andrea Pierron / Ph.D. Thesis Abstract[1]
Paris III Sorbonne-Nouvelle

This Ph.D. thesis analyses periodicals published during the twentieth century by visual artists and filmmakers in the realm of avant-gardes and experimental cinema. The journals are conceived as plastic, conceptual, complex, and composite objects where text and image interact, cinematic images are reproduced, and photomontages are created.

The dissertation aimed at understanding the unique ways used by visual artists and filmmakers periodicals to create, defend, document, visualize and analyse cinematic paradigms. To what extent have journals become experimental works of texts and images? This study focused on the characteristics of the history of film periodicals, how layouts exhibit aesthetical, theoretical, and poetical dimensions of the cinematic image, how they call into question the perception and the cinematic paradigms, how they offer another insight into the critical history of cinema.

The cinematic image used within journals is a reprint of a single or several frames, either consecutive or isolated. The reprographic technique dematerializes and reifies the image, shifts the photochemical elements onto paper. The layouts of journals, in extracting and staging frames and stills, could recreate filmic idioms in paradoxically relying on stillness. Following the reification process, how do processes like transposing and transforming aim to objectify the image? To what extent do reification and objection address the cinematic image as the material and plastic product of a spatiotemporal apparatus? The reprinted frame is thus observed as the plastic inscription, the second degree of the artwork and the cinematic movement.

The frame gives an introspective look on the overall film from which it is extracted. The objection constitutes a new process in which the image is sensitively and intelligibly objectified. The reification on paper then enables a material, plastic, critical and/or symbolic study. The term 'objection' would describe the actualisation of the object's paradigms, while 'symbolisation'

---

[1] Ph.D. Thesis supervised by Professor Nicole Brenez. For information: andreapierron@gmail.com

would refer to its depiction. Which proportions of objection and symbolisation compose the process?

The process of layout can be interpreted as taking the film to pieces and exhibiting it, leading to the recreation of visual interaction between exhibited frames. To what extent do the reproductions and layouts exhibit the display of spatial, plastic and meaningful interrelations between frames? The layout would compose a visual and textual display of frames taken apart and exhibited, introduced to new forms and significations. These displays are however designed to show, transcribe and comment on the film.

The study aimed at understanding what elements gave the extracted image this exemplary role, to consider the ways film journals form objects in which the artworks exist through interposed articles, frames and stills, in which the context is reflected, timeframes are intertwined between synchronicity and historicity. How do film journals create paradigms of textual and visual interplays: plastics, through material and formal processes of reification and objection, or discursive, through interrelations between texts and images? What form will these new paradigms take: exemplary, illustrative, iconic, demonstrative?

Film journals imply historical paradigms: on the one hand, the specific cultural backgrounds from which they appear, on the other hand each journal aims at documenting cinematic forms. How does an editor-in-chief design a medium, select a corpus and leave their mark upon plastic and critic histories of cinema? How are documentation and subjectivity intertwined? Will journals become archives of ideas and forms, platforms of interpretation? How do journals share a common history? What recurrences or transformations occur?

Journals are used to ensure the movement of the editors' ideas, either collective or singular. How do journals support the editor-in-chief's efforts in building an alternative cinema domain? Details from avant-garde film journals shed a different light on the links between avant-gardes and commercial or institutional cinematographic domains. Studying journals allow an understanding of the various influences of these domains through artworks, artistic careers and frequentations, to reconsider the original secession, autonomy if not separatism of a cinematographic avant-garde domain.

The dissertation focused on a corpus of journals that share similar editorial boards: strictly created by filmmakers and plasticians within the avant-garde realm. The thesis details the paradigms created by each journal and depicts a progressive specialisation. It opens on *Dada I* (1916) by poet Tristan Tzara and visual artist Hans Arp as well as *Dada Sinn der Welt* (1920) printed by artists George Grosz and John Heartfield as to distinguish two original interpretations of the plastic and critic interrelations of texts and images. The comparative approach of journals will reveal the specificities, as well as the shared aspects and differences of these two models.

The second part of the thesis opens on the second issue of *Promenoir* (1922) funded by filmmaker and poet Jean Epstein, which introduces the problem of the cinematic form and apparatus. Without reproducing cinematic images, the problems are discussed only through the articles.

Then the study turns to the issue 5-6 *Film* of *G. Material für elementare Gestaltung* (1926), created by painter and filmmaker Hans Richter in which cinema becomes for the first time the epicentre of a single issue. *Close Up*, created by filmmaker and poet Kenneth Macpherson, poet H.D. and writer Bryher, lands solid aesthetical and theoretical basis for avant-garde filmmaking within a collection solely devoted to film. The study of the fifth issue of the second volume (1928) will uncover the characteristic editorial lines of the publication.

Finally, the last part of the study revolves around two journals specialized on experimental cinema: issue 31 of *Film Culture* (1963–1964) published by Jonas Mekas and issue 51–52 of *Cantrill's Filmnotes* (1986) created by filmmakers Arthur and Corinne Cantrill.

Each issue was chosen either for its exemplary and synthetic elements in dealing with the plastic and discursive questions, or the introduction of specific changes that crystallize undergoing transformations. The analysis of each issue follows a similar and systematic scientific method in which the object is at first observed according to the plastic and problematic specificities of the reproduced images and the designed layouts, then according to the problems unveiled by the corpus and the textual and visual interrelations. The analysis details the precise characteristics to replace the conception of a visual and textual discourse.

The contemporary study of each issue is seized through crossed readings of the archive documents allowed by the editor-in-chief and their collaborators, contemporary journals and writings about art and human sciences. It corroborates and widens the spectrum of understanding of general or specialized artistic questions during the time studied. The confrontation with various implantations and periods, of plastic, theoretical and practical paradigms challenges the intrinsic dimensions of the magazine revealed by the analysis, and replaces it within a widened context. The studied journals will link in a chronological succession, of which incidence would seem reinforced by the progressive specialisation firstly around the cinematic image, then around the avant-garde cinematic image.

Crime, Guilt and Testimony: On Performativity and Nonfiction

Giulia Scomazzon / Ph.D. Thesis Abstract[1]
Università IULM, Milano

This thesis explores how nonfiction cinema intersects with the ethical and political problems of crime and guilt, playing a role in public debates about justice and punishment. The starting point of this thesis is a careful analysis of problems and issues associated with the performative quality of documentary described by Stella Bruzzi in her influential book *New Documentary*.[2] Bruzzi's notion of performance draws upon J.L. Austin's speech act theory and Judith Butler's ideas on the performance of gender. By examining differences and analogies between the concept of performativity described in Austin's work on ordinary language and the idea of performance developed by Butler's critical theory, the research investigates the complexity and the usefulness of these reflections in the field of nonfiction studies.

The writings of Stanley Cavell and Shoshana Felman are discussed in order to focus on questions that are crucial in understanding the ethics and the aesthetics of the performative. Specifically, Cavell and Felman have stressed the constitutional possibility of failure of speech acts in Austin's theory, and have described the responsibility of the enunciator in terms of a non-sovereign self.[3] The purpose of Chapter 1 is to recognize the quest of knowledge as inherent within the performative documentary. The epistemic sense of nonfiction film could be interpreted in terms of keeping an authentic promise. As Felman has argued reading Nietzsche, a promise constitutes a paradox which is founded upon the relationship between language and body.

This indissoluble and problematic bond is relevant to central issues of testimony and guilt which is explored in Chapter 2. The vision of human being as a 'speaking

---

[1] Ph.D dissertation supervised by Professor Luisella Farinotti and Professor Marina Sbisà. For information: giulia.scmzn@gmail.com
[2] Stella Bruzzi, *New Documentary: A critical introduction* (London and New York: Routledge, 2000).
[3] See Stanley Cavell, *Philosophical Passages: Wittgenstein, Emerson, Austin, Derrida* (Oxford: Blackwell, 1995); Shoshana Felman, *The Juridical Unconscious: Trials and Traumas in the Twentieth Century* (Cambridge: Harvard University Press, 2002); Shoshana Felman, *The Scandal of the Speaking Body: Don Juan with J. L. Austin, or Seduction in Two Languages* (Stanford: Stanford University Press, 2003).

body' and as a field of vulnerability brought to light by both Felman and Butler plays a significant role in this transition from the analysis of performativity to the question of testimony. As it has been pointed out by John Durham Peters, 'to bear witness is to put one's body on the line'.[4] Witnesses in a courtroom make a commitment to tell the truth about something they acknowledge as a result of their corporeal presence at an event. Furthermore, in trials witnesses testify at risk of punishment if they fail to keep their promise of truthfulness. Chapter 2 offers a brief comparison of Adversarial and Inquisitorial Theory in order to discuss the ways in which democratic regimes structure the legal notion of testimony. This analysis addresses Foucault's genealogy of punishment and discipline in the modern state and the positive aspects of legal proceedings guaranteed by the establishment of Fundamental Rights in the European Union and by the criminal justice reform in Italy.

In a pragmatic perspective, I seek to compare the conventional procedure displayed by fair trials to Austinian conditions of felicity of the speech act and to conversational maxims and cooperative principle described by Paul Grice. Reading Arendt's work, we focus on the idea of witnessing as a practice for securing a relevant truth, namely a truth that we, as a society, need to know and judge.

The structure developed in Chapters 1 and 2 provides a theoretical framework for the case studies analyzed in Chapters 3 and 4, from *Aileen: Life and Death of a Serial Killer* (Nick Broomfield, 2003) to *Wormwood* (Errol Morris, 2017). The aim of my research is not to establish a methodology, but to define an interdisciplinary approach to the most important moral issues raised by many filmmakers in the past two decades.

Chapter 3 traces different 'strategies of authentication'[5] adopted by filmmakers in order to represent criminals and to deal with the pursuit of justice within a democratic society. Throughout a selection of films between the years 2000 and 2020, we shall investigate the ways in which documentary practices encounter the social and moral drama of guilt and the political issue of responsibility. We argue that Broomfield, Herzog, Morris, Jarecki and other filmmakers have actively contributed to the public debate about criminals and punishment. Their works show how nonfiction discourse is capable of accessing reality and bearing witness through narration and argumentation. As Linda Williams has pointed out, truth is not guaranteed by any nonfiction techniques.[6] Nonetheless, documentary discourse, as we show through case studies, may be used to expose lies and to reveal their circulation in our media-saturated world.

---

[4] John Durham Peters, 'Witnessing', in *Media Witnessing: Testimony in the Age of Mass Communication*, ed. by Paul Frosh and Amit Pinchevski (London and New York: Palgrave Macmillan, 2009). p. 308.
[5] See Carl Plantinga, 'Rhetoric of Nonfiction Films', in *Post-Theory. Reconstructing Film Studies*, ed. by David Bordwell and Noël Carroll (Madison:The University of Wisconsin Press, 1996).
[6] Linda Williams, 'Mirrors without Memories: Truth, History and the New Documentary', *Film Quarterly*, 46.3 (1993).

Chapter 4 introduces the nonfiction genre of 'true crime' and discusses its popularity in the age of streaming TV. It is necessary to recognize the popular fascination with crime stories that affects western mass culture and to problematize the discursive construction of criminal subjects that informs a large part of true crime entertainment. In particular, Chapter 4 addresses the concerns about media obsession with criminals and criminality pointed out by Philip Jenkins and Frank Furedi.[7] Despite the recognition of these valuable concerns, the case studies investigated here share a critical approach to the question of guilt and punishment. The rise of true crime documentary, especially on streaming platforms, is founded upon the huge public success and the impact of the podcast *Serial* (2014–), HBO's miniseries *The Jinx* (HBO, 2015) and Netflix series such as *Making a Murderer* (2015–2018) and *The Keepers* (2017). Many of these works cannot be reduced to 'leisure interest products'.[8] On the contrary, they involve the viewers in a critical search of the truth that intersects with the social experience of crime and justice. The chapters conclude with three case studies — *The Jinx, The Keepers* and *Wormwood* — that explore miscarriage of justice engaging the spectator in a discussion about the criminal justice system, the right to a fair trial and the victim's desire to seek justice.

---

[7] Philip Jenkins, *Using Murder. The Social Construction of Serial Homicide* (New York: Aldine de Gruyter, 1994); Frank Furedi, *Therapy Culture. Cultivating Vulnerability in an Uncertain Age* (London-New York: Routledge, 2004).
[8] Anita Biressi, *Crime, Fear and the Law in True Crime Stories* (London: Palgrave Macmillan, 2001).

Contributors / Collaborateurs

Marie Sophie Beckmann is a PhD candidate in the Graduiertenkolleg 'Configurations of Film' at the Goethe University, Frankfurt. She received her B.A. in Media and Cultural Studies at the University of Düsseldorf and completed the M.A. program Curatorial Studies – Theory – History – Criticism at the Goethe University and the Städelschule, Staatliche Hochschule für Bildende Künste, Frankfurt (Academy of Fine Arts). As a writer and independent curator, she focuses on contemporary film, video art and feminist art practices.

Simone Dotto is a post-doctoral fellow and a lecturer in History and Techniques of Television and New Media at the University of Udine. His research deals with sound studies, media history and archaeology, sponsored and non-theatrical cinema. He is a member of the *Cinema&Cie* editorial boards and one of the scientific coordinators of the FilmForum International Film and Media Studies conference. His essays has been published on several national and international journals and collections, and he recently authored his first monography "Voci d'Archivio" on the history and theory of phonography as an archival medium in interwar Italy (Meltemi, Milan 2019).

Donal Fullam is a PhD researcher in University College Dublin analyzing algorithmic composition and the rationalization of music within algorithmic culture. He is primarily concerned with video game music as it is procedurally constructed, but also with the material and historical conditions in which this musical approach has developed. As an aspect of contemporary algorithmic culture, video game music can be understood in terms of a historical impulse towards the transformation of human expression into the logic of data and computation. Donal makes games in UE4, plays with the National Concert Hall Gamelan Orchestra, and various underground punk bands..

Matias Guerra (Santiago - Chile 1973) is a painter, multimedia artist and musician focusing mainly on video and sound experimentation, his work often reflects this diverse expertise highlighting the relationship between man, machine and chance. He collaborates with artists, musicians and composers and with associations as an organizer or cultural promoter, prioritizing collective and self-sustained projects. Has held workshops and lectures at *IED* and *Standards*, in Milan, at University of Pisa, at Venice Biennale. His work has been shown in galleries and contemporary art museums (most recently at *MACRO* in Rome). Since 2008 he collaborates with *La Camera Verde* in Rome.

Sandra Lischi is full professor in "Cinema, Photography and Television", University of Pisa. Her research focuses on the language and aesthetics of video-art, experimental and independent cinema, innovative television, the relationship between cinema, video and the arts in media history, themes which she has dealt with in monographs, essays in volumes, contributions in journals, articles, books and catalogues. She has taught and held lectures in universities, cultural centers and museums in several european and non-european countries. She is co-curator of the "Invideo Festival" in Milano and curator of the "Ondavideo" activities and screenings in Pisa.

Runchao Liu is a Ph.D. candidate and graduate instructor in the department of Communication Studies at University of Minnesota Twin Cities. Her research intersects with critical media studies, cultural studies, feminist and queer theory, and sound studies. She is currently working on her dissertation project examining the musical perspective of Asian American diasporas and the postcolonial politics of experimental popular music. She also writes about rock music politics, performative feminist activism, transnational musical communication, women in music, and youth culture and identity.

François Mouillot holds a joint Research Assistant Professor position in the Department of Music and in the Department of Humanities and Creative Writing at Hong Kong Baptist University. His research is at the intersection of Music and Cultural/Media Studies and focuses on the mediation of popular and experimental music practices through their infrastructural and technological dimensions, and on contemporary identity politics in relations to these practices and other forms of popular culture. He has particular interest in music scenes of various industrialized minority cultures. His work analyses historic and current developments in the recording and live music industries, digitization, the evolution of contemporary urban cultures, the construction of contemporary minority identities, as well as improvisation and Do-It-Yourself practices in music.

Gauri Nori is a PhD researcher at the English and Foreign Languages University, Hyderabadand has a Masters in Film and Literature from The University of York,U.K. Her research explores spaces for radical and alternative thought and seeks to delineate experimental film practices in India. She has taught various Liberal Arts courses with an emphasis on Film and Gender Studies at the graduate and undergraduate level.

Ana Ramos holds a Ph.D. from the department of communication, University of Montreal. Her current postdoctoral research at the SenseLab, Concordia University, is devoted to process philosophy inquiry in the field of aesthetics and affect theory as related to art experience and techniques of the body. Her research work spans questions concerning technology, perception, and collective subjectivity applied to media studies. In her publication "On Consciousness-with and Virtual Lines of Affection" (*Evental Eesthetics*) she acknowledges an affective dimension of the body.

Francesco Spampinato is a contemporary art and visual culture historian and writer and senior assistant professor at the University of Bologna. He holds two degrees from the University of Bologna, in *Preservation* (2003) and *Art History* (2004), an MA in *Modern Art* (2006) from Columbia University, New York, and a Ph.D. in *Arts et Média: Études Cinematographiques et Audiovisuelles* from Sorbonne Nouvelle, Paris. From 2011 to 2015 he was Adjunct Professor at Rhode Island School of Design, Providence, US, teaching courses on contemporary art history, and performance art's relations to media. His articles have been published on academic journals such as *NECSUS, PAJ, Senses of Cinema*, and *Stedelijk Studies*, as well as magazines such as *Abitare, Blueprint, DIS, Flash Art, Kaleidoscope* and *Mousse*. In 2015 he authored the books *Come Together: The Rise of Cooperative Art and Design*, Princeton Architectural Press, New York, and *Can You Hear Me? Music Labels by Visual Artists*, Onomatopee, Eindhoven, and in 2017 *Art Record Covers*, TASCHEN, Cologne.

Maria Teresa Soldani holds a Ph.D. in *History of Art and Performing Arts* (Pegaso Program – Universities of Florence, Pisa and Siena, Italy). She is webTV author/editor and video archivist at the "Luigi Pecci" Center for Contemporary Art in Prato. Her research focuses on American independent cinema, film music, underground cultures, experimental cinema, and video art. She published the monograph *Naked City. Features of Identity, Independence, and Research in the Filmography on New York City* (Quaderni di CinemaSud, 2013), essays and video-essays in books and journals, such as *Imaginations, Cinéma&Cie, Cinergie, L'Avventura, SegnoCinema*, and *Duellanti*. She is also composer and musician, in particular for many film scores of Daniele Segre's documentary films.

PRINTED BY DIGITAL TEAM
FANO (PU) IN JUNE 2020